BEHIND CLOSED DOORS

THE RISE AND FALL OF CANADA'S EDPER BRONFMAN AND REICHMANN EMPIRES

BEHIND CLOSED DOORS

THE RISE AND FALL OF CANADA'S EDPER BRONFMAN AND REICHMANN EMPIRES

Susan Gittins

Prentice Hall Canada Inc.
Scarborough, Ontario

Canadian Cataloguing in Publication Data

Gittins, Susan
   Behind closed doors: The rise and fall of Canada's
Edper Bronfman and Reichmann empires

Includes index.
ISBN 0-13-182189-X

1. Bronfman family. 2. Reichmann family.
3. Edper Investments - History. 4. Olympia &
York Developments - History. 5. Edper Investments -
Reorganization. 6. Consolidation and merger of
corporations - Canada - History. 7. Corporate
reorganizations - Canada. I. Title.

HD2810.12.E47G58 1995 338.8'6'0971 C95-930719-2

Prentice-Hall, Inc., Englewood Cliffs, New Jersey
Prentice-Hall International (UK) Limited, London
Prentice-Hall of Australia, Pty. Limited, Sydney
Prentice-Hall Hispanoamericana, S.A., Mexico City
Prentice-Hall of India Private Limited, New Delhi
Prentice-Hall of Japan, Inc., Tokyo
Simon & Schuster Asia Private Limited, Singapore
Editora Prentice-Hall do Brasil, Ltda., Rio de Janeiro

ISBN 0-13-182189-X

Production Editor: Kelly Dickson
Copy Editor: Kate Forster
Production Coordinator: Anita Boyle-Evans
Interior Design: Monica Kompter
Cover Design: David Schembri Design Associates
Cover Photo: Templeton Studios
Page Layout: Steve Lewis
Author Photo: Lynn Farrell/Financial Post

1 2 3 4 5 RRD 99 98 97 96 95

Printed and bound in the USA.

For my parents,
Roy William and Christina Galbraith Gittins.

CONTENTS

PREFACE

"Dynasties, economies, empires come and go in cycles long or short."

— Christopher Ondaatje

This book is about unprecedented corporate power and how it was lost. It tells the story of the collapse of the interlocking Edper Bronfman and Reichmann empires, as the Finance Age ended and the Information Age began. Although the great recession of the 1990s traumatized all businesses, big and small, no two corporate empires had farther to fall.

Less than a year after the stunning 1992 collapse of the Reichmanns' Olympia & York, the greatest property empire on earth, Canada braced itself for another corporate disaster. In early 1993, the public learned of meetings between governments and financial regulators to discuss ways of shoring up the Canadian dollar and the financial system in the event of a failure by the Edper Group, the country's largest conglomerate. There was widespread fear that Edper was headed for a fall as precipitous as Olympia & York's.

In less than three decades, Edward and Peter Bronfman, led by dealmakers Trevor Eyton and Jack Cockwell, had acquired control over $100 billion of assets in the resources, real-estate and financial-services sectors. It had been an extraordinary orgy of corporate empire-building.

In 1979, Edper's Eyton and Cockwell had collided with Paul and Albert Reichmann in a battle for control of Trizec Corp., then the largest publicly owned real-estate company in North America.

A chance encounter led to an agreement to establish links between the Edper Bronfman and Reichmann empires, beginning with Trizec and then Royal Trustco and climaxing ten years later with a secret deal: The Reichmann family swapped its partnership interests in New York's World Financial Center for cash from the Edper Group.

By then, Jack Cockwell and his partners had taken Edward Bronfman's place at the top of the reorganized Edper empire, in partnership with Peter Bronfman.

But when the recession hit in 1990, the fallout from the collapse of another Canadian developer, Campeau Corp., had a domino effect on the Edper Bronfman and Reichmann empires. With Edper shares in a freefall, the group told the Reichmanns it wanted to sell its partnership interests in the World Financial Center. At the end of October, the Reichmanns bought back half of those interests, financed with a loan from Edper's merchant bank, Hees. And the Edper Group implemented a capital-recovery program to recession-proof its companies.

Then, in early 1992, Olympia & York imploded, buckling under $14.3 billion of debt and making headlines around the globe. The resulting credit crunch cast a shadow over the Edper Group, although its financial foundation was common equity, not debt. "The public are our partners," Peter Bronfman once told me.

Yet a crisis of investor confidence almost destroyed the Edper Group. There was a scandal in the autumn of 1992 when the secret deal between the Reichmanns and the Edper Group was revealed. But that was minor compared to the country's outrage over the seemingly sudden collapse of blue-chip Royal Trustco. In 1993, the Edper Group lost the trust company.

When the dust settled, Peter Bronfman agreed to hand over control of what was left of the Edper Group to Jack Cockwell and his partners. (The third generation of Bronfmans had made their investments in the communications-media-entertainment industry.)

Next to go was Trizec, the building block of the Edper empire. This time the financially distressed developer was rescued by Peter Munk's Horsham Corp., the newest corporate empire to rise in Canada.

This book is also the story of these driven financiers. Personalities matter, especially when the players are larger than life. The Bronfmans and the Reichmanns are mythic figures in the Canadian landscape. Some of the country's finest writers have populated their fiction with characters based on them. But the real-life drama is just as gripping — if not more so.

I wanted to write a book that would appeal as much to those who care nothing about finance as it would to those who regard finance as the most important thing in their lives. I hope I have done that.

ACKNOWLEDGMENTS

My shift from accounting to journalism, and from Vancouver's Howe Street to Toronto's Bay Street, officially began in January 1988, when my first byline appeared in *The Financial Post*. The story was the size of 12 small postage stamps and contained one quote by phone from an assistant vice-president, corporate finance, at Wood Gundy in Toronto, who'd had a bad day at the dentist. It turned out he was a friend of a friend of a friend of mine.

It was proof that Canada, despite its vast size, could be a village. This is particularly true of Canada's corporate elite in their clubby little world on Bay Street. As a former member of The Fitness Institute on top of one of the black-box towers, I sometimes found myself stationary-cycling next to Wood Gundy's Ted Medland in the weights room or jogging on the spot next to Royal Trustco's Michael Cornelissen in an aerobics class.

Because I have written about some powerful Bay Street players, most of my sources have requested anonymity. Without them I could not have reconstructed the drama, and I thank each and every one of them. In the text of *Behind Closed Doors*, I have tried, as much as possible, to give other journalists credit for their work in exposing the secrets of the boardrooms and backrooms.

In addition to the people named in the text, others who provided inspiration for this book, whether they realized it or not, included: Tom Burrow and his wife Helen Hanfield-Jones (Toronto); Bruce Cohen (Toronto); Maria and Brad Dallas (Vancouver); Mr. Eric Gittins, Dr. Jeremy Gittins and his wife Clare Loeffler (London); Deborah Gittins and Keith Sangster (Vancouver); Natasha and Drummond Hassan (Toronto); Grep Ip and Nancy Nantais (Toronto); Karen Kendall and her husband Scott Muncaster (London); Dr. and Mrs. Frank Loeffler, Juliet Loeffler and her husband Michael Patsalos-Fox (London); the McLean women: Catherine (Tokyo), Anne, Helen and Lorie (Toronto); Mr. and Mrs. Don McLeod, Michael McLeod and Tammy McLeod (Vancouver); Elisabeth Neinhous and Chris Tattersall (Toronto); Moira and Jackie Reid and Miss Nancy Renton (Scotland); Bing and Bonnie Thom (Vancouver); John Weston (Taipei); and Mrs. Ann Wilder (Belmont-Bretenoux, France).

Among the revolving staff of talented writers, photographers and editors at *The Financial Post*, I would like to acknowledge editorial cartoonist Phil Mallette, who often made me laugh out loud at his witty caricatures of Bay Street's high and mighty.

At Prentice Hall Canada Inc., part of the mighty Viacom empire, I would like to thank David Jolliffe, part editor and part therapist; Kelly Dickson; and their assistant Sharon Sawyer, without whom nothing would ever get to print; as well as the sales managers, who made me feel so welcome at their mid-1994 gathering on the shores of Fairy Lake, Ontario. Also my thanks to copy editor Kate Forster, who focused the narrative; to Tanya Long, who championed the book early on; and to my lawyer Marianne Hebb, who has a soft spot for struggling writers. And a special thank-you to Brian Rogers for his laughter during the final read-through.

Finally, my deepest gratitude goes to my parents, Roy and Christina Gittins, who wanted me to get a real job as a CA, but supported my dreams.

Susan Gittins
Toronto, March 1995

PROLOGUE

Late one March evening in 1979, Edper envoys Trevor Eyton, Jack Cockwell, Michael Cornelissen and Harold Milavsky headed back to the Churchill Hotel in London's Portman Square, not far from the fictional home of Sherlock Holmes at 221B Baker Street.

The four men were bone-tired. Headquartered at the Churchill, they had spent the last week or so studying financial reports supplied by the management of English Property Co. PLC and racing around Europe on a grand tour of English Property's holdings, along with their two financial advisers from the venerable British merchant bank S.G. Warburg.

The Edper team had to move quickly to counter a public offer by the Reichmann brothers for all the shares of English Property, Britain's third-largest developer and Edper's partner in Trizec Corp. It feared the Reichmanns' real target was Trizec, then the biggest publicly owned real-estate company in North America. Paul Reichmann had recently told the press that agreements between Edper and English Property would stand if his company, Olympia & York, won the bidding war. But Edper doubted that a rival developer with a $150 million stake in Trizec would confine itself to a passive role and not get involved in management. And the bidding deadline of Friday, March 23, 1979, was fast approaching.

As the Edper team entered the vestibule of the Churchill, Trizec's president, Harold Milavsky, spied a tall, stoop-shouldered man with a rabbinical beard. It was the mysterious Paul Reichmann, who apparently had checked into the wrong hotel, leaving through the revolving door just as the team was entering.

As Paul Reichmann was about to get into a cab, Harold Milavsky urged Trevor Eyton, the most affable member of their group, to go out and introduce himself. Eyton did, and Reichmann seemed charmed by the slightly rumpled, bespectacled lawyer — at Reichmann's suggestion, the men went back inside the hotel and sat down on a bench to discuss a compromise arrangement. It took ten minutes for them to reach an understanding, narrowly averting a full-scale feud between two of Canada's wealthiest families.

Talks resumed later in Olympia & York's 72-storey First Canadian Place, the tallest building in Toronto, Canada's largest city and its financial centre. "The discussions were held in Albert [Reichmann]'s office because his [was] neat and tidy, whereas Paul's office [was] piled with papers," Trevor Eyton told author Peter Newman. "Whenever we reached a difficult point, Paul and Albert would excuse themselves, step outside the door, and return after thirty seconds with a little smile, saying they'd just had a board meeting and here was their answer."

The deal was beginning to take shape. On Thursday, March 15, 1979, just minutes before the start of the nineteenth annual meeting of Trizec in Montreal, Harold Milavsky apprised his boss, Peter Bronfman, of the surprising development. Bronfman told the shareholders gathered in the downtown hotel that Edper was interested in buying English Property to protect its investment in Trizec from the Reichmann family. Edper people had put their "blood and guts on the line" to turn Trizec around, Bronfman told reporters after the fifteen-minute meeting. Then he quipped, "We should be making peace, not war."

Settlement was within sight the following Thursday, March 22, 1979, in Montreal when both sides gathered after lunch in Edper's offices on Peel Street. It was at this meeting that Trevor Eyton and Jack Cockwell began to develop their reputation as the "finest one-two punch in Canada." Cockwell was the financial strategist, who crunched the numbers, while Eyton, the facilitator, steered discussions along and brought the conflicting sides to a peaceful resolution. At nine o'clock, Peter Bronfman joined the Edper team, comprising Eyton, Cockwell, Harold Milavsky and Trizec director Sam Pollack, in their negotiations with the Reichmann brothers. Shortly before midnight the two sides signed an agreement.

Under the terms of the agreement, Edper would retain absolute management control of Trizec and be able to force a sale if

Edper and Olympia & York proved incompatible bedfellows. Edper also had an option of buying another million shares of Trizec from English Property — assuming Olympia & York was successful in its bid for English Property. Olympia & York would get two seats on Trizec's 17-member board in exchange for an assurance that there would be no conflict of interest between the two developers. It was the beginning of a beautiful friendship.

PART ONE

The
Rise

Chapter 1

A Beautiful
Friendship

Edper had evolved from a series of private trust funds set up in 1942 for the future offspring of Mona, Edward and Peter Bronfman, scions of the Bronfmans' Seagram liquor dynasty. Edward and Peter both had expected a place in the family liquor empire, but by the time they were finishing their education in the early 1950s, relations between their uncle, Samuel Bronfman, and their father, Allan, had deteriorated to the point that the tyrannical Sam was openly contemptuous of his younger, milder-mannered brother.

It hadn't started out that way. Sam was the third of the four Bronfman brothers, whose parents had fled persecution in Czarist Russia for a Jewish colony farm on the Canadian prairies. The Bronfmans, whose name meant "whisky man" in Yiddish, soon left the cruel winters of the farm to seek their fortune in booming Brandon, Manitoba, where they lived from hand to mouth with a small fuel and frozen-fish business, supplemented by the odd construction job. Their next venture was the horse trade: rounding up herds of wild mustangs on the prairies and selling them at horse fairs. The family then moved into innkeeping, buying a string of little hotels near railroad yards in three prairie provinces, which were later described in a U.S. congressional investigation of organized crime as the kind of hotels where "people sleep very fast, they rent them quite a few times during the night." This Bronfman enterprise thrived until Canadian prohibition wiped out profits from the hotel bars. Not long after the First World War, Sam took advantage of a legal loophole in Canada that allowed interprovincial trafficking in liquor, by establishing a mail-order whisky business for the family and competing coast to coast against huge enterprises like Hudson's Bay Company.

During American prohibition, the Bronfmans also supplied booze from "export houses" along the Saskatchewan border to American bootleggers in their stripped-down "Whisky Six" Studebakers. Although these activities weren't illegal, they were dangerous. American whisky-runners murdered a Bronfman brother-in-law in 1922. Two years later, Sam decided it was time for the family to move to Montreal, then the financial centre of Canada and its largest city, and become distillers. He shoved aside his older brother Harry, who had run foul of the law back on the prairies, to become president of the new enterprise. Allan, a graduate of the University of Manitoba Law School, left his Winnipeg law firm to become Sam's second-in-command.

In 1928 the Bronfmans, in partnership with the venerable Distillers Company Ltd. of Edinburgh, Scotland, took over Ontario's Joseph Seagram & Sons, and began supplying liquor to whisky-running boats on the Windsor-Detroit Funnel and the Great Lakes. By the time Prime Minister William Lyon Mackenzie King — a podgy, pro-temperance bachelor — had cracked down on the Great Lakes routes, Distillers Corporation-Seagram's Ltd. had set up an agency on French islands off the coast of Newfoundland to sell directly to U.S. customers. When U.S. Prohibition was repealed in 1933, Seagram moved into the opened market in what American competitors called an aggressive foreign takeover of an American industry.

In the early years, Sam and Allan's disparate personalities complemented one another. They had chosen to live side by side on Belvedere Road at the top of Montreal's affluent Westmount, a Scottish-Presbyterian enclave cut high into the slopes of a mountain, where the fieldstone mansions rivalled "the grandest homes of Edinburgh." The families were so close that the two brothers had the house in between torn down to create a private playground for their seven children, with a swimming pool, hockey rink and bicycle path.

Around the same time that they moved into these mansions, Sam Bronfman had offices erected on Peel Street as a miniature version of a 16th-century Scottish castle, whose architecture was once described as "the worst Tudor and Gothic with early Disneyland."

As the head of the Canadian Jewish Congress from 1939 to 1962, Sam Bronfman was the foremost Jewish leader in the country, first accompanying a delegation to Ottawa in 1938 to entreat Prime Minister Mackenzie King to sanction the admission to Canada of Jewish refugees fleeing the rise of Nazism. But with Seagram's "wet invasion" of the U.S., Sam and Allan were spending more of their time in New York, living in luxury hotel apartments during the week and commuting home by train to Montreal on weekends to see their families.

And as Seagram grew, becoming North America's top distiller, so did the Bronfmans' sibling rivalry. In 1951 Sam dismantled the original Bronfman family trust set up for Sam, his three brothers and four sisters, taking the lion's share of the $20 million in cash and the half stake in Seagram for himself and his heirs. "The business is mine," Sam told Allan. "You must understand that the words 'we' and 'us' no longer apply." As a man who lived his life at the head of the table, Sam could not appreciate a Bronfman, who seemed, by comparison to himself, to be weak and uncertain. Sam's verbal abuse of his better-educated and more presentable brother had become legendary. The office staff had become used to the sound of Sam spewing obscenities at Allan.

In 1952, the year Peter Bronfman graduated from Yale University, his uncle passed a resolution barring Allan's sons (their sister Mona had committed suicide two years earlier) from working at Seagram. They couldn't even keep an office in the Seagram headquarters in Montreal. So Edward and Peter, both in their mid-twenties, established a small office across Peel Street in the Peel Centre building, the former Mount Royal Hotel, and continued to have their calls put through the switchboard in Seagram's baronial castle.

But the interference didn't stop there. Sam's advisers wouldn't let Edward and Peter withdraw large amounts of capital from their Edper group of trusts, which owned most of their father's Seagram stake, arguing that the trusts' purpose was to look after their children, not to set up Edward and Peter in business. That limited the brothers to small real-estate ventures and minority investments in private companies, but they persevered.

Eight years later, Sam pounced again. This time he forced Edward and Peter to sell more than half of their father's Seagram stock at a price 20% below market to their cousins' group of trust funds, called CEMP after Sam's four offspring, Charles, Edgar, Minda and Phyllis. A refusal would have meant further humiliation for Allan, who desperately wanted to hold onto his vice-presidency at Seagram.

But the sale did give Sam's nephews almost a $15 million grubstake. In 1962 Edper Investments Ltd., the holding tank for Edward and Peter Bronfman's money, hired Austin Beutel, a freshly minted MBA from Harvard University, who, in turn, hired Ned Goodman, a geologist with a graduate business degree, and the part-time services of accountant Paul Lowenstein. For the next four years, any company seeking Edper financing spoke to Beutel or Goodman. That's where Goodman learned his craft. He said, "You look forward, do a little forecasting, get involved in projects before they're obvious, make sure you're right more often than you're wrong and there's good money to be made."

In 1966 Ned Goodman ran across an old venetian blind company, a Toronto-based public company called National Hees Enterprises Ltd., with an interest in a metal casting operation. Trevor Eyton, a 32-year-old partner in the Toronto law firm Tory Tory DesLauriers & Binnington, was Edper's lawyer on the Hees investment.

John "Trevor" Eyton's childhood in a small pulp-and-paper mill town near Quebec City on the St. Lawrence River was far removed from the privileged Westmount world of the Bronfmans. Eyton's Welsh father,

Jack, worked as an electrical engineer for Abitibi in Quebec until he was promoted to the company's head office and the family moved to Toronto in the summer of 1947, when Trevor turned 13.

At Jarvis Collegiate, one of the oldest public high schools in Toronto, Trevor Eyton made a name for himself as a prankster.

At the University of Toronto, Trevor Eyton was captain of the Varsity Blues football team, playing on a formidable line called "Granite," where the 230-pound Eyton gained the advantage by stomping on his opponents' toes. In his second year at Victoria College, the university's main college for the publicly educated middle class, Eyton married Jane Montgomery, the privately educated daughter of a Rosedale doctor, whom Eyton had met when she caddied for him on a local golf course. A star student, Eyton was awarded a gold medal and then top honours at the university's prestigious law school. Julian Porter, who played varsity football and attended law school with Eyton, recalled that Eyton was one of the few people he knew at university who was frank about his white-hot ambition to become a millionaire.

In 1960 the fun-loving Eyton took a step towards his goal of riches when he set up the Canyon Beauport Investment Club, named after the financial canyons of Toronto's Bay Street, with 19 friends including Julian Porter, Charles "Chuck" Loewen, Christopher Ondaatje, Fred McCutcheon, Patrick Keenan, S.B. "Bruce" McLaughlin and Allan Slaight. Two years later, law professor Bora Laskin, later chief justice of the Supreme Court of Canada, reportedly recommended that the about-to-graduate Eyton join Tory Tory DesLauriers & Binnington, founded by the father of Toronto establishmentarian twins James and John Tory (John had married Eyton's Jarvis Collegiate classmate, Liz Bacon). The law firm's major clients included Royal Bank of Canada, Wood Gundy Inc. and Eyton's father's employer, Abitibi. In 1964 the young Eyton grabbed Edper as a client when he and Loewen put together a financing package for a chemical company and sold units to Edper. A few years later, Eyton was put on retainer as Edper's Ontario lawyer.

Meanwhile, in Montreal, Edper's Austin Beutel and Ned Goodman were ready to make their investment philosophy work for themselves. In 1967 they split from Edper to form Beutel Goodman. "We didn't foresee it would become the largest investment counselling firm in the country. We did it because it would allow us to invest our own money," recalled Goodman, who admitted he wasn't sitting on a fortune. "Nevertheless, I had aspirations." The Bronfmans gave Beutel and Goodman some money to manage, and their vacancies at Edper were filled by financial analysts Neil Baker and Len Spilfogel, while accountant Paul Lowenstein was brought on full-time. Baker and Lowenstein's first deal for Edper was the spring 1968 acquisition of Toronto-based Great West Saddlery, the parent company of Hees. It marked the first time Edward and Peter Bronfman had offered their senior staff some shares in their enterprise — something Beutel and Goodman both had lobbied for — even providing small loans to finance their managers' purchases of Great West Saddlery stock, which became Bay Street's "fastest flyer" on the strength of the Bronfman name. "I can remember buying Great West Saddlery shares in the 60s and I think the going price was 60 cents," Trevor Eyton later recalled. "And it reached a high of something like $28 in about a year and a half. Those were the days." That was also the start of the Edper "pay for performance" mantra.

A few months later Edper decided to combine its hodgepodge of real-estate holdings, valued at $14 million, with the holdings of Peter Bronfman's long-time associate, Calgary developer Samuel Hashman, and move the combined assets into Great West Saddlery, in a complicated restructuring involving a non-arm's-length transfer of assets. Trevor Eyton did the legal work; chartered accountancy firm Touche Ross & Co. in Montreal was hired to do the independent valuation, assigning a 27-year-old manager named Jack Cockwell to the task.

Born and raised in the Indian Ocean port of East London, South Africa, Jack Lynn Cockwell was the son of a stern, unforgiving, English postal worker, who ruled his family with an iron fist.

Fortunately some of Jack's aggressive temperament found an outlet in the sports of boxing and rugby, and he excelled at both in national competitions. Jack, a Queen's Scout, attended a state school, not the private-school network of the South African white elite. Later, while taking a chartered accountancy course by correspondence and articling with a small, local accounting firm, he reportedly kept chickens, collected the eggs and sold them around the neighbourhood to raise extra money to pay for his accounting texts. The Cockwell family moved west to Capetown in 1960 — the same year that tens of thousands of black migrant labourers protesting apartheid marched 10 kilometres across the flats from their townships to within three blocks of Capetown's Parliament buildings. The 19-year-old Jack decided to walk the 1,000-kilometre distance from East London to Capetown, along the rugged cliffs of the south coast, in a 12-day hike. At specific intervals where he had calculated his shoes would wear out, he reportedly had arranged to have a fresh pair waiting. "Jack plans everything," his brother Peter told *The Globe and Mail* more than 30 years later. Cockwell dismissed the story as an exaggeration.

In Capetown, Jack Cockwell joined Touche Ross & Co., where he met Bryan McJannet, whom he later credited with "teaching him how to make the dullest audits come alive"; no small feat, as any articling CA knows. Cockwell worked full-time at Touche Ross during the day and attended classes at the University of Capetown at night. Strictly disciplined, he would then study until 11:00 p.m., break for a run on one of the paths around Table Mountain, and study again until 2:00 a.m. The regime proved effective when he was awarded a Bachelor of Commerce in 1964, a Master of Commerce with honours in 1966, and a CA designation with distinction.

Jack Cockwell was still a fledgling CA when he left Capetown, in 1966 to go to work for Touche Ross in wintry Montreal. He arrived at the age of 25 with his fiancée in tow and together they found a small apartment on Sherbrooke Street. But she didn't get to see much of him; he was spending the bulk of his time with four of his fellow grunts at Touche Ross: Tim Price, Tim Casgrain, David Kerr and Machiel "Michael" Cornelissen.

In addition to the mandatory 16-hour workdays during audit season, Jack Cockwell began a habit, which persists today, of arriving at the office every Sunday afternoon and working through the evening, organizing his files for the week ahead. Under the tutelage of Touche Ross partner Don Wells, Cockwell was also refining his management-consulting approach to auditing, going so far as to have some of his working papers typed, an unprecedented event at Touche Ross. Even then, Cockwell considered his work worth preservation. Thus Edper's restructuring of Great West Saddlery in September 1968 did not pose a huge challenge for Cockwell and Tim Price, a descendant of the "poor" side of the Montreal family who co-founded Abitibi-Price and Cockwell's junior on the assignment. They did the work quickly and efficiently, and over the Christmas holidays, Neil Baker hired the soon-to-be-divorced Cockwell as his junior at Edper.

The successful restructuring of Great West Saddlery in 1968 did prompt another blast from Sam Bronfman; infuriated by the publicity his nephews were receiving because they were "using the Bronfman name," he reportedly cut off the Edper phone-line at Seagram. It had little effect. Flush with success, Neil Baker already had chosen Great West Saddlery's first big takeover target, Great West Life Assurance Co. of Winnipeg, then Canada's fourth-largest insurance company.

It was an audacious move, if premature. Edward and Peter Bronfman didn't have the temperament for a public brawl, especially after their uncle, Sam, attempted to sabotage the 1969 bid by strongarming several banks into withholding financing from his nephews. Great West Saddlery was about to seize control, with about 35% of Great West Life shares in hand, when Peter Bronfman decided to withdraw and instead offered the block to French-Canadian conglomerateur Paul Desmarais, who later made a follow-up bid and rolled the company into his Power Corp. empire.

Paul Desmarais, a shy, stuttering young man afflicted with asthma attacks, was an unlikely candidate to lead the surge of francophone business power in Canada. Born and raised in Sudbury, Ontario, the son of a local lawyer-businessman, Desmarais took over his father's investment in a nearly bankrupt bus company at the age of 25, after dropping out of Osgoode Law School in Toronto. As the story goes, Desmarais did all the maintenance on the fleet of 19 buses, and even paid his drivers with bus tickets when there was no money. Once the bus line was profitable, Desmarais arranged a bond issue to raise the cash he needed to buy a larger bus company in Montreal. From a transportation base, Desmarais expanded into the media, purchasing *La Presse*, one of Montreal's biggest French-language newspapers, in 1967. In 1968, the year Pierre Elliott Trudeau became Prime Minister, Desmarais, who had known Trudeau since the early 1960s, rolled his assets into Power Corp. for a 50% stake in the company, with its investments in Canada Steamship Lines and newsprint maker Consolidated Bathurst, as well a mountain of cash from the recent sale of its utilities to the government of the Province of British Columbia. Desmarais used the cash to add Great West Life Assurance to his Power Corp. empire in 1969.

Edward and Peter Bronfman reportedly took a $25 million "greenmail" profit on their failed takeover attempt of Great West Life; they also decided to move Great West Saddlery's headquarters to Calgary, where Sam Hashman lived, and to rename the company Great West International Equities. Paul Lowenstein resigned in protest. Neil Baker was forced out six months later, moving on to co-found Gordon Eberts & Co., a predecessor firm of Gordon Capital Corp., later joined by his friend Jimmy Connacher. Over the next several years, Jack Cockwell brought over *his* friends Tim Price, Tim Casgrain and David Kerr from Touche Ross to fill the gap at Edper. Cockwell, having divorced his first wife, married Lowenstein's secretary.

In 1971 Edper and Sam Hashman sold their 72% interest in Great West International Equities to Trizec Corp., in return for $12 million cash, almost 10% of Trizec's shares and two seats on the company's board of directors, filled by Peter Bronfman and Sam Hashman. Trizec had risen from the rubble of William Zeckendorf's crumbling real-estate empire in 1960 when the reckless American developer teamed up with a large British company, Eagle Star, in a desperate effort to complete Zeckendorf's grandest Canadian project, the cruciform Place Ville Marie in Montreal, designed by

architect I.M. Pei. But their partnership was marred by bitter cul-
ture clashes, and by 1965 Eagle Star had forced out Zeckendorf.
The cautious Eagle Star then embarked on an uncharacteristic
buying spree in 1971, gobbling up Edper's Great West International
Equities and the Cummings family's Montreal real-estate company,
Cummings Properties Ltd., with $115 million in assets, for Trizec.

That same year Sam Bronfman died at home, not long after
the fourth of his "eightieth" birthday parties. It is said that Sam
considered his greatest setback to be his failure to become Canada's
first Jewish senator, despite his many years of bankrolling the
Liberal party. As Sam protested, "It should have been mine. I bought
it! I paid for it! Those treacherous bastards did me in!" But Sam
never expressed regret over the break with his brother, Allan, apparently considering it a necessary step to secure the succession of
his own sons, Edgar and Charles, and prevent dynastic squabbling
over Seagram, his life's work. Sam's death in mid-1971 was significant to Edper because it meant he could no longer hamper the
company's growth. That must have been a great relief to his
nephews, although they never said as much in public.

At the end of 1971 Edward and Peter Bronfman tiptoed back
into the limelight with their successful $13 million takeover of
Canadian Arena Co., owner of hockey's greatest dynasty, the
Montreal Canadiens, and of the Montreal Forum. The Bronfman
consortium, which originally included John Bassett of Toronto
(who dropped out a year later), picked up Canadian Arena not long
after it was listed on the Montreal Stock Exchange by three cousins
of the Molson brewing family. Outraged at the loss of their beloved
hockey team, the Molson clan broke ranks with the traitorous
cousins. The Bronfmans' Quebec lawyer, Jacques Courtois, became the visible face and public voice of Canadian Arena. Two
years later Edward and Peter, the so-called "poor" Bronfmans, cut
the last of their business ties to Seagram, when Jack Cockwell persuaded them to sell the rest of their father's Seagram stock.

Edper's attention then focused on its minority interest in Trizec,
where the financial situation had become precarious. To meet debt

payments, Trizec was liquidating assets. In late 1975 Trizec sold 16 properties, including controlling interests in two hotels, one in Yorkville (now the Four Seasons) and one in Vancouver (the Hyatt Regency) to developer Bramalea Ltd. for $100 million. Bramalea, celebrated for building the Toronto suburbs of Brampton and Unionville, also picked up controlling interests in Trizec's nine shopping malls and five office buildings in Western Canada. By the spring of 1976 Eagle Star's real-estate arm, English Property, had conceded there were big problems at Trizec and asked Edper for help. For $52 million in cash, Edper snagged a 50.1% controlling interest in Carena Properties Ltd., a new company formed in partnership with English Property, and a resulting 58.8% voting control of Trizec, with its $900 million in assets.

After Edper gained control of Trizec, Jack Cockwell, then 35, forced out its chief executive officer, James Soden, who had successfully rescued Trizec from Zeckendorf more than a decade earlier. Peter Bronfman recruited Harold Milavsky as Trizec's new president, moving the head office to Calgary from Montreal to accommodate the Westerner. Milavsky's job was to develop properties; Cockwell would oversee the financial restructuring.

Trizec was the big test case for the set of principles Jack Cockwell had developed in his years as an auditor. First, he sketched out a T-account, with Trizec's assets on the left and its liabilities on the right. On the left side, he divided the assets into three categories. At the top: cash and very liquid assets that could be realized quickly. In the middle: assets that would produce returns over the middle term, such as real-estate developments coming on stream. At the bottom: the long-term and strategic assets, whose value might not be realized for several years. On the right side, he performed the same exercise. At the top: the current liabilities, including accounts payable, bank lines and commercial paper. In the middle: term debt, debentures and other credit locked in for long periods. At the bottom: shareholders' equity. Cockwell's maxim was that assets on each level of the ladder should match the liabilities on the corresponding level opposite. In a workout situation, it was usually the top left (cash) and the bottom right (equity) that were out of kilter. So workouts, using Cockwell's formula, involved a step-by-step process that began on the bottom right corner of the balance sheet, with an injection of new equity.

To execute the Trizec turnaround, Jack Cockwell brought in a former Touche Ross colleague, Michael Cornelissen, a tall, lanky workaholic, as the company's vice-president of finance. Cornelissen, the son of Dutch immigrants to South Africa, had graduated from the University of Natal in the Indian Ocean port of Durban. When Cornelissen qualified as a CA, he transferred to the Montreal office of Touche Ross in 1967, where he worked as a junior to Cockwell. In the early 1970s Cornelissen returned to South Africa, but he kept in touch with his mentor while toiling for a large public company in Johannesburg, the country's financial centre. By the mid-1970s, Cornelissen was ready to return to Canada, so Cockwell got him a job with Edper's then-tiny merchant bank in Montreal, Mico Enterprises Ltd.

At Trizec, Michael Cornelissen, then 34, and his controller Kevin Benson, 30, a friend of Cornelissen's who had articled with Coopers & Lybrand in Durban, started to implement Jack Cockwell's financial plan. Cornelissen later described to authors Patricia Best and Ann Shortell for their 1988 book *The Brass Ring* how he had started raising Trizec out of bankruptcy by balancing its assets and liabilities: matching a long-term lease with a long-term obligation and a U.S. property with a U.S.-dollar loan. Cornelissen and Benson began their "ladder of financing" by issuing "equity," retractable floating-interest-rate senior preferred shares, which they sold to large institutions. That set the pattern for future workouts. Edper companies would borrow by issuing preferred shares, rather than taking bank loans, because the favourable tax treatment of preferred-share dividends meant they could pay a lower rate than the prevailing prime lending rate.

Trizec then issued senior debentures and some Swiss franc-denominated Eurobonds, sold mainly through Swiss financial institutions like the Union Bank of Switzerland. Finally, the company reportedly arranged a revolving-term loan with 35 banks. At the same time, the Edper team encouraged Trizec management to buy common stock in its own company and slashed Trizec's operating overhead.

"The financial restructuring at Trizec was to set new standards, certainly for the real-estate industry, but also for other [Edper] group companies," Michael Cornelissen told Best and Shortell. "The Trizec experience was also a major and successful test of group business values."

But there was little time to celebrate its success. In early 1979 trouble blew in from another direction. Edper's partner in Trizec was experiencing financial difficulties at home in Britain and indicated it was looking to sell. In early January, Canada's mysterious Reichmann brothers began accumulating shares of English Property.

Paul Reichmann is the fourth of the five Reichmann brothers, whose mystery is rooted in their turbulent family history. As descendants of Hungarian Orthodox Jews, the family spent the early years of the Second World War one step ahead of the German troops.

In 1938, shortly after the Nazis marched into Vienna, where the father, Samuel, had established a profitable egg-wholesaling business, the Reichmanns fled to Paris. Thirty-six hours before the Nazis stormed Paris in 1940, they decamped to Biarritz near the Spanish border.

Their father had driven on ahead to see if the family could enter Spain without visas and was told the border would shut at three o'clock that afternoon. He reportedly rushed back to Biarritz to pick up his wife, Renée, and their six children. The family slipped into Spain an hour before the border closed. The Reichmanns kept moving south, crossing the Strait of Gibraltar into the no-man's-land of Morocco in North Africa.

Safe in the unregulated trading mecca of Tangier, about 450 kilometres north of Casablanca, Samuel opened up a money-lending and currency-trading operation, using funds from Britain that he had managed to keep out of Nazi hands. Meanwhile, the Holocaust continued to ravage the Reichmanns' Austro-Hungarian homeland. In mid-1944 Renée Reichmann managed to persuade the Governor of Morocco to issue Spanish visas for 500 Hungarian children await-ing shipment to a Nazi death camp. Later she succeeded in placing 700 adults under the Spanish goverment's protection. All of the 1,200 names on Reichmann's List survived the war, living in safe houses in Budapest, and the Reichmann apartment in Tangier later became a halfway home for Jews who had not perished in the slaughter.

All of the Reichmann brothers, Edward, Louis, Albert, Paul and Ralph, were raised as Orthodox Jews, but Paul was the only one to prolong his Talmudic scholarship, pursuing six years of advanced study in various *yeshivas*. Almost ten years after the end of the Second World War, the Reichmann family decided it was time to find a new home. After an extensive search, the eldest son, Edward, chose Canada, opening up a trading company in Montreal. By 1959 all five brothers and their parents were living in Toronto, which Paul later described as "a quiet little English town, not unlike Birmingham." Meanwhile, their sister Eva had married a British banker and moved to London.

Beginning with a small tile company in 1955, called Olympia, the Reichmanns soon discovered they needed a new warehouse when their decorative-tile franchise outgrew its rented building. They built the warehouse themselves in Toronto and found putting up buildings was more profitable than selling tiles. After all, their fa-ther had not only established a small merchant bank out of his money-trading activities in Tangiers, he had also owned the con-struction company that built the local stock exchange. From these beginnings in tile franchising and in development projects in Toronto arose Olympia & York. Where Olympia & York's real-estate ven-tures were concerned, the brothers increasingly deferred to Paul. His philosophy was simple: buy cheap land and put up quality buildings.

Paul also handled the financial and political negotiating. He told author Diane Francis for her 1986 book, *Controlling Interest*, how the complexities of money trading had proved useful to him as a young refugee. He said he learned the business of trading, how to work the spreads between cost and price — such as the cost of financing and the return from development. After the two eldest brothers, Edward and Louis, left Canada in 1968, Albert supervised the construction details and the youngest brother, Ralph, ran the tile business.

By the early 1970s Olympia & York had built over 100 commercial buildings in boomtown Toronto and was ready to attract international attention with its first office city, First Canadian Place. Built in the heart of the financial district, the Bank of Montreal's Toronto headquarters was 72 floors high, with four floors below grade, making it the world's tallest building outside the U.S. The land was cheap — it was partly owned by the Bank of Montreal — and the quality of the building was high. The Reichmann brothers had quarried part of a mountain in Italy to get the 25 square kilometres of white marble used to clad the tower's face and interior. First Canadian Place, completed in 1975, was a major milestone for Olympia & York.

Two years later the Reichmann brothers closed the deal that made them famous. Warner Communications was looking for a buyer for nine skyscrapers in mid-town Manhattan that one of its units had acquired three years earlier, just before New York City real estate went in the tank. The CEMP Bronfmans' Cadillac Fairview had looked, but didn't buy. By contrast, Paul Reichmann bet his company on a recovery, signing the contract on September 19, 1977, which made the Reichmanns New York City's second-largest landlord, behind the Rockefellers. Olympia & York paid about US$320 million (US$50 million in cash) for the buildings, known as the Uris package, which Olympia & York later refinanced for US$1.8 billion, clearing almost US$1.5 billion on its investment. Within six years, the buildings were worth over US$3 billion. Before the Reichmann brothers made their final decision on what was later dubbed the deal of the century by the American press, it is said that Albert Reichmann personally interviewed many of the Uris buildings' tenants, including the street-floor concessionaires.

Eager to spend some of the windfall of earnings from their privately owned properties in North America, the Reichmann brothers scouted around for a publicly owned real-estate company. In early 1979 they made an offer for all the shares of English Property in a deal that would have given them control of English Property's Trizec stake. Edper was counting on a Dutch property company to win the bidding war for English Property, but the Dutch appeared to lose interest in the takeover battle on February 26 when Olympia & York countered the Dutch group's second offer in less than half an hour. Withdrawal of the Dutch company pushed Edper to the wall, and its four-man team flew to London to examine a possible bid, which had to be made before March 23, when Olympia & York's offer expired. The Edper team's chance encounter with Paul Reichmann at the London hotel resulted in its partnership in Trizec.

Why did they make peace? If Edper had won the bidding war, it would have had to send a team over to London full-time to manage the European properties of English Property. Trying to outbid the Reichmann brothers, as well as gaining control of the property portfolio, would be costly. The Reichmann brothers, who had already been bid up twice by the Dutch real-estate firm, had begun to realize the cost of the takeover too.

So the Reichmann brothers added English Property to their real-estate empire for $157.3 million. That gave them a majority interest, but not operating control, in Trizec. When the empires collided in early 1979 an Edper spokesman had warned, "The conflict of interest is obvious. A banker or tenant having a dispute with Olympia & York would be sure to view Trizec with disfavour. Furthermore, Trizec has a very open management style. If Trizec were planning a project, how would any Olympia & York directors on the board close their eyes?"

But the partnership worked. In 1980 Paul Reichmann introduced Trizec President Harold Milavsky to U.S. shopping-centre magnate Ernest Hahn, who had offered to sell control of his company, with almost $1 billion in assets, to Olympia & York. Reichmann turned the file over to Trizec, which acquired a controlling interest in Ernest W. Hahn Inc. of California for US$267 million, effective mid-November 1980, and financed the deal by offering shareholders, like Edper and Olympia & York, new Trizec shares in proportion to what they already held. Before the Hahn acquisition was fully digested, Trizec swallowed up 20% of U.S. real-estate giant The Rouse Co. for US$81 million in late 1981. There was also a slight restructuring of the partnership when Edper acquired an option from Olympia & York to up its voting interest in Trizec to 64%, completed in 1982.

By the end of 1982, the revitalized Trizec had more than doubled the value of its assets in six years, and reported a year-to-date profit of $35.8 million. Michael Cornelissen, who moved on to his next turnaround assignment at Royal Trustco in the spring of 1983, was credited with the corporate rescue. At Trizec, Cornelissen claimed to have cut costs, paid down debt and moved to lock in interest rates. When the real-estate industry was ravaged by double-digit inflation and high interest rates in the recession of 1981–1982, Cornelissen recalled that Trizec was in much better shape than its competitors, like rival developers Daon Development Corp. and Cadillac Fairview Corp., then controlled by the CEMP Bronfmans, the cousins and childhood playmates of the Edper Bronfmans.

Indeed, the revitalized Trizec was ready for another challenge. In 1984 Trizec reconnected with Bramalea, the developer that had snapped up $100 million of Trizec's office buildings, shopping malls and hotels in 1975, the year before Edper began to resuscitate the distressed company. Trizec bought $60 million of Bramalea's treasury shares and $100 million of convertible debentures, giving it a 31%, fully diluted, stake in Bramalea. When Bramalea stakeholder Richard "Dick" Shiff fell ill, Trizec also reached a private agreement to swap the Shiff family's block of Bramalea shares for Trizec preferred shares valued at $70 million, giving it a 43%, fully diluted, interest in Bramalea.

Bay Street applauded the innovative financing techniques used by Edper and pronounced the arrangement of benefit to both developers, but Bramalea's minority shareholders were outraged. Arguing that the Shiff transaction was a sneaky form of a takeover, not a partnership, they lobbied the Ontario Securities Commission to step in and force Trizec to give them the same value for their Bramalea shares. The OSC reportedly disagreed, concluding that the two parties had "the legal right to enter into this kind of agreement without triggering takeover provisions." As Dick Shiff explained at the time, "This is basically a partnership. It is not a takeover by any means."

But the so-called Trizec-Bramalea partnership soon deteriorated into a battle for operating control of Bramalea. In 1986 the two developers decided to pool their shopping centres in a new company, called Trilea Centres Inc., which would be owned by Bramalea but managed by a Trizec appointee — veteran real-estate executive Gordon Arnell, a Calgary next-door neighbour of Harold Milavsky. In a complicated transaction, Bramalea sold most of its shopping centres to Trizec for a net gain of $221 million that was used to offset an earlier loss from an investment in a junior oil and gas company. Bramalea then bought back its shopping plazas plus Trizec's own shopping malls in exchange for a note payable, assumption of debt and enough of Bramalea's common shares to give Trizec a controlling 63%, fully diluted, stake in Bramalea.

By 1987 Bramalea's other major stakeholder, a frustrated Kenny Field, had called on Olympia & York's Albert Reichmann to see if Reichmann could use his influence with Trizec to stop Trizec management from interfering with Bramalea's business. One showdown had developed already over whether Trilea Centres would use Bramalea's computer system or Trizec's. Field and his right-hand man Benjamin Swirsky argued that Bramalea owned the 30 Canadian shopping malls, so its computer system should be used. Harold Milavsky and Kevin Benson countered with the fact that Trizec now controlled Bramalea. "At the Edper level, chief strategist Jack Cockwell and the Bronfmans were thrilled with Bramalea management, and wanted us to have complete operational control," Field recalled for Gayle MacDonald in an interview for *The Financial Post*. "But Trizec — not Edper — was the investor. And Harold Milavsky and Kevin Benson didn't see it that way." Although the computer system squabble was ultimately settled by Cockwell, who reportedly decided to support Trizec management but install Bramalea's computers, the fundamental conflict over operational control was unresolved. Reichmann read the file Field had prepared for a book he planned to write about Trizec's "mismanagement" of Bramalea.

It was a difficult situation. After all, the Reichmann brothers' partnership with the Edper Group was still thriving. It was eight years since the brothers had signed their "no conflict of interest" agreement with Edper, and Olympia & York had just withdrawn a bid for the Canadian Broadcasting Corporation's new Toronto headquarters, after the Reichmanns discovered that Trizec was also planning a bid.

Trizec had become a crown jewel under Edper's management. Jack Cockwell later claimed that the corporate rescue of Trizec in the late 1970s was a turning point as important to Edper as its epic battle for Brascan Ltd. in 1979, the upset victory over the Toronto WASP establishment which catapulted Edper into the big leagues. Peter Bronfman disagreed; for him, Brascan was the seachange.

Chapter 2

Deals, Deals, Deals

The corporate warfare over Brascan officially began in late 1978 when Edper bought a 50-share toehold in the Toronto-based empire, shortly after the huge conglomerate turned into a hot takeover prospect with the sale of its Brazilian power utility to the Brazilian government for $450 million in cash.

Edward Bronfman did not involve himself in the hostile takeover; he was devoting more of his time to charity work. The brothers had agreed in 1978 that Peter Bronfman's children would inherit control of Edper.

Peter Bronfman and his hired hands had prepared for their assault on Brascan by selling assets and shifting their base of operations to Toronto from Montreal. They joined the exodus of tens of thousands of anglophones who fled from Quebec during the 1970s, a decade that began with the October Crisis, caused by the FLQ's kidnapping of a British diplomat and murder of a Quebec labour minister, and Prime Minister Pierre Trudeau's invocation of the War Measures Act against the terrorists. Trudeau lost control of the Quebec agenda as René Lévesque's separatist party, the Parti Québécois, was elected as the majority provincial government in 1976. CEMP's Charles Bronfman, co-chairman of Seagram, publicly threatened to leave Quebec after the Parti Québécois, or "those bastards" as he called them, came to power. But he remained, and it was his cousin Peter who left.

In Toronto, Edper had cash in its war chest from the recent sales of its 40% stake in developer S.B. McLaughlin; its 25% stake in Canadian Cable-Systems, then the country's second-largest cable television operator, to Ted Rogers for $35 million; and of the Montreal Canadiens back to the Molson family, who had won a bidding war with rival brewer John Labatt Ltd. Peter Bronfman had persuaded a reluctant Edward Bronfman to sell the Habs for $20 million in August 1978. After seven glorious years of hands-off ownership of the winning hockey dynasty, not to mention four Stanley Cups and the 1972 Soviet-Canada series, some of the thrill was gone. Edper kept the Forum (the Molsons got a 30-year lease), which remained the property of Carena (formerly Canadian Arena Co.), and the brothers maintained close friendships with former Canadiens general manager Sam Pollack, captain Jean Beliveau, defenceman Bob Gainie and goalie Ken Dryden, who lived in Toronto.

When Edper got serious about its Brascan bid in early 1979, it turned to Jimmy Connacher at what was then Gordon Securities, one of the predecessors of Gordon Capital. By late February, Gordon had rounded up 800,000 Brascan shares. Meanwhile, lawyer Trevor Eyton was busy lining up an ally for Edper, setting up a meeting between Peter Bronfman and one of Eyton's law clients, the wealthy Patino family, who had made their fortune in South America. Jack Cockwell suggested the formation of an Edper subsidiary, Edper Equities, with the Patino family as a 34% partner.

Edper's creeping assault on Brascan was put on hold for several weeks in early March when Trevor Eyton and Jack Cockwell flew to London to protect Edper's investment in Trizec from the Reichmann brothers. After Edper struck a partnership with Olympia & York on March 22, 1979, the dealmakers turned their attention back to Brascan.

By the end of March, Edper and the Patinos had accumulated some 1.3 million Brascan shares, making the Edper investment subsidiary the largest single shareholder of Brascan, at 5%. Trevor

Eyton and Jack Cockwell set up a secret meeting with Brascan CEO Jake Moore and his lawyer on April 5, 1979, in a suite at the Royal York Hotel. Eyton briskly outlined Edper's intention of making a 51% takeover bid, but the imperious Moore wouldn't take the upstarts seriously. Brascan was plotting to use up all the cash from the sale of its South American utility by bidding just over $1 billion for control of American retailing giant F.W. Woolworth Co.

The following Friday at Brascan's board meeting, the Woolworth bid went public. Cockwell quickly crunched some numbers to get a detailed cash-flow analysis of the proposed deal, estimating that Brascan's acquisition of Woolworth would produce a $100 million cash-flow deficiency. As a result, Edper made its 51% takeover offer for Brascan conditional on the withdrawal of the Woolworth bid. But the Ontario Securities Commission ruled against Edper; the conditional offer would not proceed.

Then Brascan shareholders Andrew Sarlos and Max Tanenbaum, who together controlled one million shares, joined the Edper camp. Sarlos, who had gone to see Jack Cockwell and secured his agreement to name Tanenbaum to the Brascan board if Edper won its battle, began to publicly attack Brascan's arrogant attitude, accusing Jake Moore of grossly misleading shareholders and questioning his motivation for the Woolworth purchase. Sarlos recalled in his 1993 memoir, *Fireworks*, that he was "particularly incensed that the board had approved the Woolworth bid, which would have forced the company to dump its existing assets at fire-sale prices, without consulting shareholders."

By Sunday, April 29, 1979, Edper was ready to make a major grab for Brascan shares. Tim Price and Gordon's Jimmy Connacher flew to New York and checked into the Waldorf-Astoria Hotel. On Monday morning Jack Cockwell telephoned to give Price his preliminary instructions. Earlier that morning, Fred McCutcheon, Trevor Eyton's Canyon Beauport Club crony and a Patino director, had made a sweep of the London Exchange but had picked up only 15,000 shares. After Price got the green light from Cockwell, Edper began buying Brascan stock on the American Exchange.

Among those who sold their shares to Edper were the CEMP Bronfmans and Power Corp.'s Paul Desmarais. By the end of a record-breaking two-day buying spree, Edper had spent $174 million to buy 6.5 million Brascan shares. And Edper had effective control of the Brascan empire, with its valuable interests in Brascan Resources, various Brazilian assets, John Labatt Ltd., Great Lakes Power and London Life Insurance — acquired in 1977 when Jake Moore's Brascan had helped the Jeffrey family thwart a creeping takeover of London Life by the CEMP Bronfmans.

On Sunday, May 27, 1979, Jake Moore and Peter Bronfman met for the first time at the offices of Trevor Eyton's law firm, Tory Tory DesLauriers & Binnington. Two days later, after a trading injunction (the byproduct of a volley of lawsuits and countersuits) was lifted, Edper bought another $140 million worth of Brascan stock, to bring its holding up to 50.1%. From the Toronto Stock Exchange president's gallery overlooking the tumult of the trading floor, Eyton called the Edper offices with the good news. "We shook hands, grinned for about eleven seconds, then got back to work. We're not gloaters," Peter Bronfman told Peter Newman. "Jack is too smart to gloat and I'm too nervous." Altogether, Edper and the Patinos had spent about $350 million in cash to get control of Brascan's $2.5 billion in assets.

That summer Trevor Eyton, at age 45, took a leave of absence from his law firm and with Jack Cockwell, 38, flew to Rio de Janeiro to check out Brascan's Brazilian interests. After three months of analysis of the Brascan empire, the pair presented their business plan to Edward and Peter Bronfman in September and, at Cockwell's suggestion, Eyton was appointed Brascan's president and CEO for a two-year term. Cockwell took the lesser title of senior vice-president of corporate planning. The new executive team quickly upped Brascan's stakes in Labatt and London Life Insurance, sold off its Brazilian Bank and fired almost half of Jake Moore's 115-member entourage in Brascan's Commerce Court West headquarters, prompting some ex-employees to rename the company "Brass Canned."

But Eyton and Cockwell still didn't know how to invest the cash in Brascan's treasury. Ultimately they picked Noranda Inc.,

Canada's legendary multinational mining conglomerate, as their takeover target, embarking on a fractious two-year battle to get control of the Canadian resources giant.

On September 28, 1979, Jack Cockwell learned that Conrad and Montegu Black were willing to sell Hollinger Inc.'s 10% stake in Noranda. Brascan bought it on Friday, October 5, and then went back into the market to buy an additional million shares of Noranda to make it the company's largest shareholder. Trevor Eyton immediately took a Commerce Court West elevator three floors down to Noranda headquarters, intending to tell Noranda CEO Alf Powis that Brascan expected at least two seats on the Noranda board, and planned to boost its stake in Noranda so that it could equity account the investment (count a proportionate share of Noranda's earnings on Brascan's income statement). Powis was out of town, but the two men met five days later for a private four-hour dinner at Toronto's Sutton Place Hotel. During the meal, Powis promised Eyton there would be no decision about Brascan until Noranda's next full board meeting on Friday, November 16. But, at a directors' dinner on November 15, Powis double-crossed the Brascan CEO by getting approval for the so-called Zinor option. On the morning of Sunday, November 18, at Eyton's country estate in the hills of Caledon, northwest of Toronto, Eyton and Powis nearly came to blows when Powis dismissed the Brascan request for board representation and laid out his Zinor deal, which effectively allowed Noranda to swallow itself by issuing treasury shares to Zinor Holdings, a company controlled by three Noranda subsidiaries. Eyton escorted Powis off his property.

Outfoxed by Alf Powis, Trevor Eyton and Jack Cockwell flew to Montreal to try to line up Noranda's second-largest shareholder, the Caisse de dépôt et placement du Québec — which administered Quebec's portion of the Canada Pension Plan and was dubbed *La Machine à milliards* — as a partner for Brascan. When Conrad Black had sold Hollinger's 10% block of Noranda shares to Brascan six weeks earlier, he had turned over the Noranda shareholder list and his own extensive correspondence with the Caisse about a possible joint takeover bid for Noranda. That November, Eyton and Cockwell met three times with Caisse chairman Jean Campeau, a Quebecker with separatist leanings, to work out an arrangement.

On Wednesday, December 5, 1979, Eyton reportedly gave Noranda's Powis an ultimatum, threatening legal action to dissolve the Zinor agreement, Edper backing of a takeover bid for 50% of Noranda and solicitation of anti-management proxies for the next annual meeting. Powis called Eyton on Friday, January 4, 1980, to tell him that the Noranda board had turned down every one of his demands. Ten days later Noranda purchased Maclaren Power and Paper Company, diluting Brascan's 20% interest in Noranda.

Almost a year and a half later, Noranda took another step to ward off Brascan by purchasing half of forestry giant MacMillan Bloedel Ltd. for $129 million in cash and $500 million in preferred shares. At that point, the CEMP Bronfmans asked to buy Brascan's diluted stake. The answer was no; after 16 months of lying low, the Edper Bronfman lieutenants were ready for a major thrust forward. On Thursday, June 4, 1981, Brascan bought more than five million Noranda shares for close to $200 million in a record-setting block trade on the Toronto Stock Exchange, handled by Gordon Capital, that brought its interest in Noranda back up to 20%.

Later that month Trevor Eyton and Jack Cockwell flew to Montreal for another meeting with Jean Campeau. Strategy was set at Brascan's regular board meeting on Wednesday, July 22, 1981. Brascan and the Caisse would grab effective control of Noranda in an undertaking codenamed Granite, after Eyton's university football team. The following day, Eyton and Campeau announced the formation of Brascade Resources, owned 70% by Brascan and 30% by the Caisse, into which they rolled their Noranda holdings.

During the next ten days, Edper's Brascan team — Trevor Eyton, Jack Cockwell, Robert Dunford, Paul Marshall and public-relations specialist Wendy Cecil-Stuart — rounded up financing while Noranda searched for another way to dilute its stock. Alf Powis even approached the Reichmann brothers, forgetting about their thriving partnership with Edper in Trizec. Meanwhile, Brascade locked up more than $1 billion in credit lines from the country's biggest banks and brokerage firms. The day before Noranda's Wednesday, August 12, 1981, board meeting, Trevor Eyton delivered a letter, composed by Eyton and Jack Cockwell, listing their demands. This time a compromise was reached, giving Brascade six seats on an expanded 18-member Noranda board, as Brascade agreed to buy 12.5 million Noranda common shares for $500 million in cash and Noranda agreed to swap 10 million common and 1.8 million preferred shares for Brascade preferred shares, giving Brascade a 42%, fully diluted, interest in Noranda. When the deal was concluded at five o'clock, Eyton and Cockwell were said to have taken the elevator down to Noranda's headquarters to have a "celebratory" cup of tea with Powis, who reportedly kidded Eyton that there wasn't enough room at the Noranda board table to accommodate both Brascan and the Caisse. Cracked Eyton, "We'll be happy to sit in the second row."

Brascade infused $500 million into Noranda at the top of the resource cycle in November 1981, much to strategist Jack Cockwell's later embarrassment. A slump in resource commodity and share prices during the recession of 1981–82 turned Noranda's fortunes, resulting in its first ever loss. In 1983 Edper's Hees acquired the Patino family's 34% interest in Brascan Holdings (the renamed Edper Equities), becoming a significant Brascan shareholder just as the conglomerate began to accumulate huge losses from Noranda. By 1984 Brascan had become a cash-flow-deficient company. For the next three years, Cockwell worked on a restructuring plan for Noranda. In 1986 the gap-toothed, clean-cut David Kerr, a Hees partner and Cockwell's former Touche Ross colleague, was parachuted into Noranda to execute a turnaround of the resources giant.

The Bay Street village had expected Michael Cornelissen to be Noranda's workout wizard, but Edper wanted Cornelissen to continue to manage its Royal Trustco investment, purchased in partnership with the Reichmann brothers after the Reichmanns helped thwart upstart developer Robert Campeau's takeover attempt.

Royal Trustco was a sleeping giant on Wednesday, August 27, 1980, when a frenetic Robert Campeau suddenly appeared at CEO Lt. Col. Ken White's summer compound in the Eastern Townships of Quebec to announce he was taking over Royal Trustco that very afternoon. White, who had been eating his breakfast, is said to have gripped Campeau by the arm and brusquely ushered him off the estate, back to the rented limousine waiting outside the gate, shouting, "Pull that bid! Pull that damn bid!" But the French-Canadian public-school dropout was undeterred, launching a $453 million takeover bid for Royal Trustco later that day.

A self-taught carpenter, born in Sudbury like his business hero Paul Desmarais, Robert Campeau had started out building his own houses in Ottawa, then moved on to develop subdivisions, apartment buildings and office towers, which he leased to the federal government through high-powered connections like his frequent skiing companion, then-Prime Minister Pierre Elliott Trudeau. Out of nowhere, Campeau became the Canadian government's largest landlord. Then, in 1970, Desmarais's Power Corp. took temporary control of the financially troubled developer as Campeau went through a period of severe depression before regaining control of his company three years later.

Emotionally unstable, Robert Campeau had a secret history of a mistress, a double family and a nervous breakdown. After nineteen years of marriage to Clauda, his teenage bride, and three children (one daughter and two adopted sons), Campeau had embarked on an affair in 1961 with a 21-year-old German blonde named Ilse Luebbert, whom he had hired as a stenographer. After Ilse got pregnant with their first son, Campeau set her up on a farm outside Montreal, and for the next three years he shuttled back and forth between the two women, until Clauda found out about his clandestine family. Campeau then went to live with his mistress and saw his wife on the sly, until Clauda filed for a divorce in 1969. The emotional distress triggered Campeau's first nervous breakdown, which was prolonged by the loss of control of his company to Paul Desmarais. Back and forth Campeau went until 1971, when he returned from a retreat in Florida to marry Ilse. The newlyweds moved to Ottawa, building a lavish home within a mile or two of Clauda, who died of breast cancer at the end of 1979. Campeau's eldest son never forgave his father for not visiting his ex-wife in her dying months.

The Bay Street establishment had other reasons to link arms against this upstart developer. In the mid-1970s, on the much-disparaged Toronto waterfront, Campeau had put up the Harbour Castle, along with some adjoining condominiums. Campeau's 1976 opening party for the hotel, held in honour of himself, had appalled the stuffy Torontonians who attended largely out of curiosity. His bid for Royal Trustco was another who-does-he-think-he-is? kind of affront.

Lt. Col. Ken White had told the parvenu before he booted him off his estate, "I really don't like you, Campeau, and I don't like Paul Desmarais and I don't like Conrad Black and I don't like Edgar [Bronfman]. I don't like all these guys making bids for public corporations and I wish to hell you would stay where you are and [not] bother us...I'm going to call my friends and I am going to lock up 51% of this stock before you can turn around." White's chief strategist was Austin Taylor of investment dealer McLeod Young Weir, with legal advice from Howard Beck of Davies Ward & Beck. Ultimately, 12 white knights, led by Toronto-Dominion Bank chairman Richard Thomson and Oxford Development Group chairman Donald Love, tied up 55% of Royal Trustco's stock, at a cost of $200 million. Other "friends" of White included Bank of Montreal, Canadian Imperial Bank of Commerce, Sun Life Assurance and Alf Powis's Noranda Inc.

Robert Campeau raised his bid in mid-September to break up the club, but it was a lost cause. Within a few days, Paul Reichmann's long-time lawyer Howard Beck had approached Reichmann about making an investment in Royal Trustco. An enthusiastic Reichmann said Olympia & York would take as much as 50% of Royal Trustco, but he was persuaded to come in for a smaller stake. In early October, Campeau withdrew his offer. When the shares later dropped in price, Campeau bought 8% of Royal Trustco at $19 a share and then turned around and sold the block to the Reichmanns at $22 a share in the spring of 1981, making the Reichmanns Royal Trustco's single largest shareholder, at 23.3%.

Meanwhile, Edper's Brascan had bought 14.9% of Royal Trustco shares in two large blocks — one from the CEMP Bronfmans' Cadillac Fairview and the other from Oxford Development Group — as a favour to the Reichmann brothers. Brascan later upped its interest to almost 20%. "We bought our stake in Royal Trustco at the invitation of Paul and Albert Reichmann," Trevor Eyton told Diane Francis. "Paul came over and sat down in my office saying, 'I've got 14% of Royal Trustco and I would like you to acquire a similar stake.' There was no discussion then about the deal or our arrangements, I suppose because we had worked well together in Trizec."

Although the Reichmann brothers had turned to their partners in Trizec to help manage their new investment in Royal Trustco, they advocated a slower approach in the shakeup of the financial institution than Edper had taken with Trizec. The Reichmanns wanted Royal Trustco's new owners — Olympia & York, Edper's Brascan, and the Toronto-Dominion Bank — to move cautiously in their dealings with Lt. Col. Ken White's old-guard management. But Edper's Brascan was frustrated by this slowpoke approach, so it took steps to gain effective control of Royal Trustco.

Retired Toronto-Dominion Bank chairman Allen Lambert later recalled how he had hardly left TD's executive suite when he was asked by Trevor Eyton to oversee the setting up of a new financial services group, Trilon Financial Corp. In 1982, Trilon Financial sold $100 million worth of shares to the public and hiked up its stake in London Life Insurance to almost 100%. The following year, Brascan swapped Trilon Financial shares for the Reichmanns' stake in Royal Trustco and the Toronto-Dominion Bank's stakes in Royal Trustco and London Life. In October 1984, Trilon Financial bought half of the country's largest real-estate broker, A.E. LePage, and merged it with Royal Trustco's real-estate brokerage operations. That was followed a week later by the acquisition of 100% of a property and casualty insurance company, renamed Wellington. Two months later, Trilon Financial bought 51% of a major car-leasing company.

Once Edper had control of Royal Trustco through Trilon Financial, Michael Cornelissen made the leap in 1983 to Royal Trustco management from Royal Trustco board member. Fresh from his corporate workout of Trizec, Cornelissen stormed into Royal Trustco a zealot determined to wake up the sleeping giant with the Edper ethos. But the new president and CEO had to wait until the end of the year, when Trevor Eyton temporarily replaced Lt. Col. Ken White as Royal Trustco chairman (the following year Eyton recruited patrician Hartland Molson MacDougall from the Bank of Montreal as a ceremonial chairman, a soothing presence, connected by club affiliations and schooling to the Canadian establishment). With White gone, Cornelissen took aim at two-hour lunches and mandated unheard-of 7:00 a.m. starts for senior managers. A member of the old guard recalled for Gordon Pitts, then with *The Financial Post*, how Cornelissen was "withering in his contempt of people" who didn't adapt to the Edper way of doing things and, if a minute late, a senior manager "might find a [yellow Post-it] note stuck to his chair that said, 'Where the fuck are you?'" Cornelissen had adopted the Post-it note method of management from his mentor, Jack Cockwell.

To speed up decision making at Royal Trustco management meetings, Michael Cornelissen reportedly would call for a decision just before the 6:43 p.m. Go-Train left for Oakville, a suburb west of Toronto, where most of the senior managers lived. Knowing that the trains ran only once an hour after that, Cornelissen counted on a "Go-Train decision." Those who didn't want to play by the new rules walked into the sunset. "He would beat up on people publicly, berate them in front of their colleagues," one manager told *The Financial Post*. "It made us all very unproductive." Another said Cornelissen was more single-minded and less tactful than even his mentor, Jack Cockwell. "Compared with Mike, Jack is a people person."

The churlish Cornelissen, a pitiless competitor, often referred to the old guard as "turkeys," so it wasn't surprising that the first senior person he hired was Courtney Pratt, a human resources expert from Touche Ross Management Consultants in Calgary, whom Cornelissen had used to introduce Edper values to Trizec. Pratt hired new senior executives from rival financial institutions like the Bank of Montreal, as well as some prominent recruits from unrelated fields, such as Xerox regional sales manager Paul Bates. The 34-year-old Bates was hired, along with seven others, as a regional sales manager at Royal Trustco, to help build a sales culture. "We were all in the same age group," Bates later recalled in an interview. "We felt we were on a mission. We started our days at 7:00 a.m. and ended [them] at 8:00 p.m." Cornelissen, who became known as the Clint Eastwood of the Edper Group, killed as many as five of the 12 layers of Royal Trustco management in some areas. He also offered management incentives in the form of loans to buy common stock instead of high salaries or stock options. Half the staff participated in the share-owning program for employees.

Even though Royal Trustco had been profitable for more than 80 years and did not need to be raised out of bankruptcy like Trizec, Michael Cornelissen did a financial as well as a management restructuring of the company. Using Jack Cockwell's formula, Royal Trustco matched assets and liabilities by issuing new equity by the truckload.

In 1985 Michael Cornelissen unveiled a business plan for Royal Trustco called "Vision 1990," which set aggressive internal targets of 15% annual after-tax profit growth and a consistent 15% to 20% return on common-share equity. Even his mentor, Jack Cockwell, reportedly told Cornelissen that these targets were "too stretched" and suggested he ease up. But the driven Cornelissen couldn't do it. Even in Britain, where Royal Trustco had been a small-time player for 50 years or more, Cornelissen had pushed expansion: opening up four branches outside London, acquiring a loan portfolio from the British banking subsidiary of Toronto's Household Finance Corp. and doubling Royal Trustco's portfolio of loans and mortgages in Britain to £500 million between 1984 and 1986. To meet his new targets at Royal Trustco, Cornelissen embarked on a global shopping spree.

Since the House of Commons Finance Committee had targeted the Edper Group in its 1986 investigation into complaints about commercial concentration in the financial services industry, Royal

Trustco faced restrictions on acquisitions in Canada. As Cornelissen later explained to shareholders, the "howls of protest" drove Royal Trustco, then the country's largest trust company, into other markets. "We'd rather look to greener pastures where capitalism can flourish." Canada was dominated by two handfuls of large financial institutions. The United States had 3,000 thrifts (savings and loans) and 14,000 banks vying for business. "That means there is a far greater opportunity for financial institutions to build size to achieve economies of scale. We see it as a very large, exciting market place."

In June 1986 Royal Trustco bought Dow Financial Services Corp., with asset-management operations in Europe and Asia, for $235 million, then sold off Dow's British stock brokerage firm in 1987 because it didn't fit the global private banking network. That was also the year that Royal Trustco expanded south, spending about $150 million to acquire a portfolio of investments in five U.S. thrifts. The largest single holding was a 9.9% stake in Los Angeles-based GlenFed Inc., parent of the fifth-largest U.S. thrift, which Royal Trustco hoped would become the base of its American operations.

Meanwhile, the Reichmann brothers had been busy transforming the skyline of America's financial capital. Nobody built bigger or better than Olympia & York.

Chapter 3

Bright Lights, Big City

At the beginning of the 1980s, the Reichmann brothers had won a contract, over 11 competitors, to develop the $2 billion office centrepiece of Battery Park City, a 92-acre landfill on the Hudson River at the foot of New York's financial district.

The land was cheap — Olympia & York had guaranteed several hundred million dollars of bond repayments in return for the right to develop the 15-acre site — and, in keeping with Paul's principle, the quality of the project would no doubt be high, in spite of his failure to present a design concept when he made his submission to the city authority. He would come up with a concept after the contract was won — something along the lines of First Canadian Place, Olympia & York's first office city, would do. Indeed, Olympia & York executive Ron Soskolne, the former City of Toronto architect who had grappled with the Reichmann brothers over First Canadian Place, successfully backed architect Cesar Pelli's eight-million-square-foot master plan, featuring four squat towers, 39 to 53 storeys high, each with a different geometric shape as its copper "hat."

In 1980 Olympia & York also won the contract to redevelop 25 acres in San Francisco's financial district, defeating such other Canadian bidders as Robert Campeau and the CEMP Bronfmans' Cadillac Fairview.

At the end of 1981, Olympia & York had broken ground at its Battery Park development and the Reichmann brothers began appearing regularly at the construction site in a stretch limousine, wearing their trademark double-breasted dark suits, white shirts, thin black ties and homburgs. Back in Canada, the Bay Street village had dubbed them the "Hats," because the brothers always wore fedoras or *yarmulkehs*. As ultra-Orthodox Jews, the Reichmann brothers by this time were comfortably settled in a tightly knit community of schools, synagogues and kosher butcher shops around their homes in north Toronto. In their mother Renée's enormous house, nicknamed Third Canadian Place, they had reportedly installed a Sabbath elevator that ran automatically to each floor every ten minutes from sundown on Friday until after sundown on Saturday. The Reichmann brothers also enforced the Jewish Sabbath on their construction sites. But in order to meet the strict construction deadlines on the Battery Park project, Olympia & York had to find a way for its crews to work on the Sabbath, so it reportedly sold the company that owned the project to a non-Jewish company before sundown on Fridays and bought it back after sundown on Saturdays. In all the Reichmann offices, worked stopped at 2:00 p.m. on Fridays, and no one was allowed into the offices on Saturdays, under threat of dismissal.

Despite their religious insularity, the Reichmann brothers had cracked Toronto's WASP establishment by the early 1980s. Too big to ignore, they were invited in the spring of 1981 to a black-tie dinner at the Toronto Club — the supreme seat of the establishment — to watch the hockey playoffs. But they didn't show. That summer Toronto society buzzed with reports of a private wedding reception sponsored by the brothers for a niece at the Inn on the Park (Four Seasons), with more than 1,000 people in attendance, including distant Reichmann family members from around the world. When Paul Reichmann's daughter married a man from Mexico four years later, the entire hotel was rented again for an even grander, $1 million celebration.

Away from his cloistered world in Toronto, Paul Reichmann spent most of his time in New York holed up in a suite in one of the apartment towers of the Waldorf-Astoria Hotel, as Olympia & York minions rustled up tenants for the Battery Park project.

In the spring of 1983, American Express signed a 35-year lease on the biggest building, the one with a pyramid-shaped hat, but only after Olympia & York agreed to pay US$240 million for Amex's existing headquarters at 125 Broad Street. In order to fill the buildings, the Reichmann brothers were forced to take over old leases "like second-hand cars," Peter Foster later argued. To back up the deal, the Reichmanns offered Amex the guarantee of the Canadian parent company, but refused to provide Amex with detailed financial information. The mighty Amex accepted Olympia & York's financial strength on blind faith. With Amex signed up, Olympia & York could attract other tenants at higher rents.

The development that some analysts had dubbed the "white elephant" was named the World Financial Center. In the summer of 1984 Olympia & York announced that investment powerhouse Merrill Lynch & Co. had signed a complex deal to occupy two of the World Financial Center's four towers, which it would partly own in a joint venture with Olympia & York, but only after Olympia & York had bought Merrill Lynch's existing headquarters, One Liberty Plaza.

By the time the World Financial Center was officially opened by then-New York Mayor Ed Koch on Thursday, October, 17, 1985, in the site's 120-foot-high glass-domed Winter Garden, where 16 California desert palm trees rose 45 feet out of the patterned marble floor, the Reichmanns had outstripped the Rockefellers as the largest private owners of office space in New York City. They had 11 buildings, including several skyscrapers purchased in a joint venture with JMB Realty Corp. of Chicago. The Reichmanns' 24 million square feet of New York office space represented "almost exactly one square foot per Canadian," declared *Spy*, the satirical Manhattan monthly.

In a single generation, Paul, Albert and Ralph Reichmann had amassed the greatest property empire on earth, but as many pointed out, real estate was an unstable foundation on which to build a lasting empire. The three brothers wanted to have some professionally managed, dividend-rich assets to pass on to their 14 children, so Paul Reichmann decided in the late 1970s to assemble a Canadian resource-based conglomerate like Canadian Pacific, without the railroad. This strategy was also tax-efficient, since Olympia & York reportedly had to spend at least $500 million annually in Canada to avoid being taxed as a U.S. real-estate company.

To begin their diversification out of real estate, the Reichmann brothers extracted equity gains from their real-estate portfolio through refinancings, which they used to snap up minority stakes in about a dozen, mostly resource, companies, including MacMillan Bloedel. They tendered their interest to Noranda in 1981, ending up with 10% of MacMillan Bloedel and a smaller stake in Noranda — soon to be taken over by their friends at the Edper group of companies.

By then the Reichmann brothers were ready for something big: the world's largest newsprint maker, Abitibi-Price Inc. After a long bidding war, Olympia & York ended up paying $560 million in cash to buy almost all of Abitibi-Price in 1981. Paul Reichmann was so nervous at the first board meeting, his hands shook.

In 1984, Olympia & York made a staggering bid of $2.8 billion for 60% of Gulf Canada, one of the four American-owned multinationals that had long dominated the Canadian oil patch in Alberta. But the Reichmann brothers later backed off the bid, leaving behind a $25 million deposit. In 1985 they got another shot at Gulf Canada when the company was put on the block "for sale to Canadian bidders." Olympia & York offered $2.6 billion, $200 million less than its original bid, in one of the most complicated takeovers Canada had ever seen.

First, Paul Reichmann rounded up three partners — Conrad Black's Norcen Energy, Petro-Canada and Ultramar Canada — which agreed to buy Gulf's refineries and gas stations, leaving Olympia & York with the oil fields in western Canada. Then Reichmann sought Revenue Canada's approval of a presale adjustment to Gulf's balance sheet that would restate the firm's assets at a much higher value, a tax loophole nicknamed the "Little Egypt

Bump" after a famous Chicago stripper. That resulted in a half-billion-dollar tax break when those assets were depreciated after the takeover. Finally, Reichmann got Gulf Canada's independent committee of directors, led by Noranda's Alf Powis, to agree to buy Olympia & York's 93% interest in Abitibi for a stunning $1.2 billion, twice what the Reichmanns had paid for it. The Reichmann brothers were left controlling both companies through a new holding company called Gulf Canada Resources.

In early March 1986, just six months after finalizing the deal on Gulf, Olympia & York forced its new acquisition into a spectacular deal: a takeover of liquor and resources conglomerate Hiram Walker Resources Ltd., which had been formed when Consumers Gas Co. swallowed up Home Oil Co. and then became part of Hiram Walker-Gooderham & Worts Ltd. in a 1979 reverse takeover. The 1986 takeover battle captivated corporate Canada for eight months, as the Hiram Walker management spent $35 million of the company's money trying to fend off the Reichmanns.

Unwittingly, Paul Reichmann had set Hiram Walker on a self-destructive course. Word got out that Reichmann had entertained proposals from at least six prospective buyers of Hiram Walker's distillery, including Hiram Walker's bitter enemy, Seagram Co. (Apparently the Edper Bronfmans had considered a takeover of Hiram Walker in 1979, but their CEMP cousins protested, arguing that it would be controversial if separate branches of the Bronfman dynasty together controlled Canada's entire booze business.) Hiram Walker directors voted in favour of breaking up the conglomerate they had created, rather than have the distillery taken over by Seagram. They agreed to sell the distillery to British food conglomerate Allied-Lyons PLC for $2.6 billion. The plan was to use the proceeds of the sale to bid against the Reichmanns for their own company.

Paul Reichmann claimed at a press conference in Windsor, Ontario, on Tuesday, May 27, 1986, that Hiram Walker's agreement to sell the distillery "was prompted by a mistaken belief that if Gulf Canada acquired control, it would sell the distilled spirits and wines business to The Seagram Company. The notion that we intended to sell the liquor business to Seagram has plagued this entire matter and is patently untrue." What had started off as a friendly $1.2 billion offer for 49% of Hiram Walker ended up as a $3.3 billion hostile takeover of the entire company, less its prized distillery.

Allied Lyons pressed its claim on the distillery by filing a $9 billion lawsuit when the Reichmanns threatened to renege on the sale, after the courts ruled against Olympia & York's attempted injunctions against the sale. After several months of haggling, the Reichmanns and Allied-Lyons finally reached a compromise in their custody suit. Allied-Lyons got 51% of Hiram Walker; Olympia & York's Gulf got 49%. Olympia & York ended up with mere observer status on the board and a lot of bad press.

The Gulf and Hiram Walker deals had been so clumsily executed that the Reichmann brothers had managed to get almost everybody mad at them. "The negative reaction has disturbed me greatly," Paul Reichmann said. "If I'd known all this would happen, I would rather not have gone ahead with it."

But soon they were back at it, buying shares of U.S. railroad Santa Fe Southern Pacific in May 1987, the same month they reached an agreement to sell their interest in property developer Cadillac Fairview, purchased three years earlier.

On Tuesday, June 5, 1984, rumours that the Reichmann brothers were buying up the CEMP Bronfmans' Cadillac Fairview had gone unconfirmed as Olympia & York offices closed early for a two-day Jewish holiday.

That day, millions of Cadillac Fairview shares traded on both the Toronto and Montreal Exchanges in huge blocks, just before the closing bell. The CEMP Bronfmans had to wait for press reports to find out who was buying. That Friday there was a short trading halt in Cadillac Fairview shares as the Reichmann brothers announced that they planned to spend about $179 million for a 19.9% stake in Cadillac Fairview, and had no intention at the moment of a launching a takeover bid. CEMP Holdings controlled 35% of the large public developer.

The Reichmann brothers were now linked with both branches of the Bronfman dynasty, through their new joint ownership of Cadillac Fairview with the CEMP Bronfmans and their five-year joint ownership of Trizec with the Edper Bronfmans. This did not create a conflict between the Reichmanns and the Edper Group, as many supposed, because there was no animosity between the Bronfman cousins. Indeed, if Cadillac Fairview had not averted a cash crunch during the recession of 1981–82, Edward and Peter Bronfman might have become partners with their cousins in Cadillac Fairview. The rival developer was said to have been so desperate for cash in early 1982 that it had almost approached Edper to buy $400 million of convertible debentures in Cadillac Fairview. Two years later, Cadillac Fairview had outstripped Trizec to become Canada's largest publicly owned developer.

But the Reichmann purchases of Cadillac Fairview stock in 1984 were considered unfriendly by the CEMP Bronfmans, just as the Reichmann purchases of English Property stock in 1979 had been considered "unfriendly" by the Edper Bronfmans. The purchases had come at an awkward time, because Cadillac Fairview had been attempting to buy back up to 15 million of its own shares through a formal bid that closed that afternoon. Olympia & York, Canada's largest privately owned developer, had paid $13.75 a share for its position, slightly more than the buyback offer of $13.50. And the buyback would reduce the number of Cadillac's issued shares, so it was impossible to determine the final ownership percentages until the results were in. Senator Leo Kolber, watchdog of CEMP Holdings, made arrangements to meet with the Reichmanns. By June 15, 1984, Charles Bronfman had bought enough additional Cadillac Fairview shares and warrants, through a private company, to bring the total Bronfman holdings in Cadillac Fairview up to a control position of 51.4%.

Charles Bronfman had met Leo Kolber at Montreal's McGill University in the 1950s, a WASP bastion that gladly accepted Sam Bronfman's money for two Bronfman professorships endowed to the business school, but put off naming him a governor of the university or ending its anti-Jewish student quotas. Apparently Sam approved of his son's friendship with Kolber. "A touch of poverty around the place [won't] do the children any harm at all," he told a biographer. When Charles later suggested that Kolber, a struggling lawyer, take over management of CEMP Holdings in 1957, Sam agreed, noting that Kolber was a "little Jewish boy on the make. That's the best kind to have handle our money." Kolber moved CEMP Holdings into commercial real estate. On a base of a few million dollars plus $10 million borrowed from the banks, CEMP built up a portfolio of shopping malls and office buildings, and launched construction of the Ville d'Anjou in Montreal, the Toronto-Dominion Centre in Toronto and the Pacific Centre in Vancouver. Through Cadillac Fairview, formed with the merger of CEMP's Fairview Corp. with Cadillac Development Corp. and the Canadian Equity and Development Corp., by 1974, CEMP controlled Canada's biggest publicly owned developer.

Meanwhile, Edgar Bronfman was the heir apparent at Seagram. Both Edgar and his brother Charles had been educated at Trinity College School in Port Hope, Ontario, where they were the first Jewish students to be admitted to the boarding school. (Their cousins Edward and Peter were educated at American prep schools.) Edgar, a wild youth, went on to Williams College in Massachusetts, where he was almost kicked out for public drunkenness when he flew off his motorcycle, landing head first in a chicken coop. Both Edgar and Charles apprenticed in the Seagram distilleries, but Edgar was the one who had a desk in his father's office. In 1952, the year their cousins Edward and Peter were squeezed out of Seagram, Edgar went to New York City to run the American branch, which by then accounted for 90% of Seagram's business. A year later he married Ann Loeb of the prestigious Wall Street investment banking family. She was an elegant descendant of the old-line German Jewish aristocracy and as snobbish as the ruling WASPs. Edgar and Ann had four children: three sons and one daughter.

By the mid-1950s, Edgar's sister Phyllis, a graduate of Vassar College who later studied architectural history at the Institute of Fine Arts of New York University, had convinced their father to commission Modernist architect Ludwig Mies van der Rohe to design the company's New York headquarters on Park Avenue. After the Seagram Building, a 38-storey bronze-sheathed glass and steel sky-scraper, opened at the end of 1957, it "came to symbolize cool elegance, even indifference."

In the 1960s, Edgar bought 15% of Metro-Goldwyn-Mayer for Seagram, reportedly with an eye to gaining control of the famous Hollywood movie studio, responsible for such film classics as *Casablanca, Citizen Kane, Gone with the Wind, It's a Wonderful Life, The Wizard of Oz* and *Miracle on 34th Street*, and merging it with Time Inc. His father Sam was skeptical about the investment, reportedly walking into his son's office and asking, "I want to know if we're buying all this stock so that you can meet some women." Edgar is said to have replied, "Father, nobody has to spend $56 million to get laid." Edgar lost his bid for control and later sold the MGM interest to financier Kirk Kerkorian, who, in turn, sold the film library to budding media mogul Ted Turner. Edgar then went on to form a Broadway production company.

Meanwhile, Charles stayed on in Montreal, where he brought major league baseball to the city in late 1969. As the principal owner of the Montreal Expos, Charles later entertained Prime Minister Pierre Elliott Trudeau, whose father had owned a share in the Montreal Royals baseball club, in Charles's multi-tiered corporate box in the Olympic stadium. Divorced and remarried, Charles had two children: a son and a daughter.

After Sam's death in 1971, Edgar moved Seagram's world headquarters to New York, where he became notorious for his personal troubles. After his bitter divorce from Ann when their two eldest sons, Sam and Edgar Jr., were teenagers, Edgar got involved with a dazzling English beauty named Lady Carolyn Townshend. They married in 1973, but Lady Townshend reportedly refused to sleep with Edgar on their wedding night, instead spending the night at her pychiatrist's house. In order to get an annulment on the grounds of sexual rejection, Edgar was forced to reveal intimate details of his sex life, or lack of it, in court. But he won back the jewellery, the baronial estate and the US$1 million in cash that he had signed away in a prenuptial agreement. In 1975, a few days before Edgar's third marriage, to a former British barmaid, his eldest son Sam was kidnapped and held for US$2.3 million in ransom. The wedding was postponed until Edgar paid the money, and Sam was released unharmed nine days later. But at the subsequent trial, his kidnappers accused Sam of being an accomplice in order to extort money from his father. Sam's captors were eventually jailed for extortion, but acquitted of kidnapping.

At the end of the 1970s, with Edgar Bronfman's personal life out of the headlines for once, he refocused on Seagram, launching a takeover of Conoco Inc., the ninth-largest oil producer in the U.S. E.I. du Pont de Nemours & Co. came to Conoco's rescue, triggering a bloody bidding war. When Du Pont won, Edgar tendered Seagram's Conoco stake in exchange for a 20% stake in Du Pont, the world's biggest chemical firm.

By then, Edgar and Charles were embroiled in private battles over succession at Seagram. There was an unwritten tradition that only two of any Bronfman generation would work at Seagram. By 1985, the two brothers' trusts held four-fifths of CEMP's 38% stake in Seagram; their sisters, Phyllis (who had just opened the Canadian Centre for Architecture, with its Desmarais theatre, in Montreal) and Minda (who had married a baron and lived in high style in Paris and New York until her death from cancer in 1985) had sold most of their Seagram shares.

In the spring of 1985, Edgar broke the news to his eldest son Sam that he would anoint his second son, Edgar Jr., 29, as his heir at Seagram. The choice was a surprise because in addition to being young, Edgar Jr., had dropped out of his Manhattan prep school and opted out of college for the movie business. When he was 14, his father had invested half a million dollars in a David Puttnam film called *Melody*, and the teenager got a job as a runner on the London movie set. Edgar Jr. went on to produce two films himself; one was *The Border*, starring Jack Nicholson. Meantime, the young producer had eloped at the age of 24 with a beautiful black actress named

Sherry Brewer, whom he had spotted four years earlier in singer Dionne Warwick's dressing room, when he was executive producer of CBS's *All Star Jazz Show*. Edgar Jr. later wrote the lyrics to "Whisper in the Dark" as a thank-you to Warwick. His father had tried to stop him from marrying Brewer, but perhaps Edgar Sr. saw something of himself in the headstrong young man. Not long after, in early 1992, he brought Edgar Jr. into Seagram as an assistant to the president. That didn't interest his son, who asked to run the European operations instead.

After a successful turnaround in Europe, Edgar Jr. returned to New York in 1984 to restructure the House of Seagram. Edgar Jr. was a good marketer like his grandfather Sam, who had sold the British aristrocratic lifestyle to Americans in ads for the Crown brands of whisky, decades before Jewish fashion designer Ralph Lauren did it with clothes. Edgar Jr. was selling a different product, but he also knew what would appeal to his market. When Seagram jumped into the wine cooler business, Edgar Jr. signed up actor Bruce Willis as pitchman — taking the Seagram brand to No. 1 from No. 5.

Thus Edgar Jr. had been at Seagram only three years when his father made up his mind. "The Second Son is Heir at Seagram," read the *Fortune* headline on March 17, 1986. Charles was reportedly upset when he saw his brother and nephew on the cover of the magazine. He thought the issue of succession should have been decided by the Seagram board of directors, and he objected to the disclosure of Edgar's choice.

That summer the CEMP Bronfmans initiated the sale of their stake in Cadillac Fairview for $1 billion-plus and the sale of other non-Seagram assets to help pay for the splitting up of their CEMP group of trust funds so that the siblings and their heirs could make separate lives. The Reichmann brothers could choose to sell their Cadillac Fairview shares, a 22% interest purchased for $232 million, along with the CEMP Bronfmans, or use their sizeable head start to buy control of Cadillac Fairview. They chose to sell on Friday, May 8, 1987, when JMB Realty of Chicago and a syndicate of 39 pension funds reached an agreement in principle to pay $2.9 billion for all the shares of Cadillac Fairview, which then boasted $7 billion in assets. The deal closed six months later.

Throughout their three-year association with the CEMP Bronfmans in Cadillac Fairview, the Reichmann brothers had stayed in close touch with the Edper branch of the family. Indeed, the Reichmanns had helped back a 1985 workout of Union Gas Ltd., one of Edper's minority investments.

Chapter 4

The Bay Street Village

With Edper Group backing, a rival merchant bank pulled off an upset victory over the Toronto establishment with its takeover of Union Enterprises Ltd., the newly formed parent of Union Gas, in March 1985.

Seven weeks earlier, Unicorp Canada Corp., 68% of which was owned by real-estate mogul George Mann, had offered preferred shares of its own company, retractable after seven years, with a 12% after-tax return, in exchange for Union Enterprises stock. Edper's GLN Investments, a subsidiary of the Great Lakes Group, was the first to swap its 17% block of Union Enterprises for Unicorp preferred shares in late January. A week later Union Enterprises asked the Ontario Securities Commission to stop the takeover bid, but the commission ruled in favour of Unicorp. The bid would proceed.

Outraged, Union Enterprises CEO and former Tory Ontario cabinet minister Darcy McKeough called in his political markers, and in mid-February the Cabinet ordered the Ontario Energy Board to investigate the takeover. A few weeks later, McKeough blackened his name, and lost some key supporters, when he persuaded the Union Enterprises board (director Trevor Eyton absented himself from takeover-related meetings because of his conflict of interest) to authorize a $125 million share swap with meat-packers Burns Foods Ltd., in order to make the utility unpalatable to Mann, who was Jewish.

The Toronto establishment in upper-crust Forest Hill had once sent their clothes to Granite Cleaners on Yonge Street at St. Clair Avenue, owned by George Mann's father. Young George, who lived with his parents in the apartment above the cleaning business, attended North Toronto Collegiate. After graduation he opted not to go to university, instead joining his father's new real-estate brokerage, Mann & Martel Co. By 1968, after running a pool hall in his spare time and making a killing investing in publicly traded REITs (U.S. investment trusts that held real estate instead of stocks or bonds), George Mann was CEO of Mann & Martel. Not long after, he merged Mann & Martel with United Trust Co., where he starred with bikini-clad women in trust ads and hired Kenny Field, a recent graduate of Osgoode Hall Law School. In 1972 Mann acquired control of Unicorp. Four years later, Mann sold United Trust to Royal Trust for Royal Trust shares, which he later sold to Robert Campeau, sparking Campeau's failed 1980 takeover bid. By 1985, George had come full circle, living with his wife Sandra and their two grown children in their stone mansion in Forest Hill, down the street from Dylex co-founder Jimmy Kay, and vacationing in their 10,000-square-foot stone mansion in Palm Beach.

On Thursday, March 14, 1985, the eve of the bid's expiry, Unicorp had 40% of Union Enterprises stock. Unicorp's financial adviser, Gordon Capital's Jimmy Connacher, suggested that George Mann go see Paul Reichmann the following morning at First Canadian Place and explain that Unicorp needed about two million more Union Enterprises shares for a controlling stake. Mann reportedly asked Reichmann to consider buying Union Enterprises shares and tendering them to the Unicorp offer. Two years earlier, Olympia & York had targeted Unicorp as a potential investment, so Reichmann was familiar with the company. "The shares traded before [Mann's] elevator hit the ground floor," Unicorp president James Leech said. Unicorp had won, but its acrimonious takeover of Union Enterprises, codenamed Strike, would not have happened without Edper.

At the subsequent two-month-long Ontario Energy Board hearings, GLN Investments made an 11-page statement, principally authored by Jack Cockwell, revealing that four Edper affiliates, GLN Investments, Brascan, Royal Trustco and Continental Bank, as well as two related companies, Hatleigh and North Canadian Oils, registered in the name of Jimmy Kay (a man who had turned over the keys of his private restaurant, real-estate and oil-and-gas empire to Edper's Hees), together had purchased about $135 million, or 70%, of the $190 million of preferred shares that Unicorp had issued to finance the Union Enterprises takeover. The purchases were "based on the investment merits afforded by the Unicorp securities," the statement said, not a reaction to Darcy McKeough's management of Union Enterprises. The Bay Street village exploded into chatter.

In his testimony, Trevor Eyton stuck to the group line: The Edper Group was a major player in the preferred share market, and the Unicorp preferred shares were a good investment; there was no conspiracy.

In an affidavit, Paul Reichmann also testified that the Unicorp preferred shares were "a good investment." He then revealed that Union Enterprises had approached Olympia & York early on as a possible white knight, but "one fact that may have made [him] more sympathetic to Mr. Mann was that [he] did not think that the purchase of Burns Foods by Union Enterprises was an appropriate transaction to have taken place during the course of a takeover bid."

The last witness, a testy Jack Cockwell, acknowledged that the group had squabbled with McKeough on several occasions over his management of Union Gas and over the "substantial cost" of his outside advisers, which included Cockwell's sparring partner, McLeod Young Weir's Tom Kierans.

In early June, the Ontario Energy Board's lawyer recommended approval of Unicorp's takeover of Union Enterprises, stating that the Edper Group ownership of Unicorp's preferred shares would have "led one to conclude that the Edper-Brascan purchases were a concerted effort by that group to make the bid successful for some undisclosed reason, except for the evidence."

After a nine-month inquiry into the takeover, the Ontario Securities Commission made Gordon pay $7.1 million into a fund for

Union Enterprises' minority shareholders, ruling that Daly Gordon Securities, another predecessor of Gordon Capital, had favoured large shareholders like the Edper Group. It was a precedent-setting settlement, but less than the OSC had hoped for. A frustrated OSC director explained how difficult it was to regulate takeover transactions where friends "acted in concert." Like any secret arrangement it was "very difficult to prove."

The Edper Group's ever-widening cabal of friends in the business, political and sports worlds was dubbed "the orbit" by the media. At the centre of the orbit was Trevor Eyton, the visible face and public voice of the Edper fortune, by then a Toronto power broker with hundreds, if not thousands, of connections. Jack Cockwell preferred to operate behind the scenes as the backroom strategist. During Edper's "orgy of corporate empire building," Eyton and Cockwell were a symbiotic team, reportedly communicating in a form of shorthand speech before a meeting and sometimes finishing each other's sentences during a meeting.

But their relationship degenerated into quasi-sibling rivalry in 1985 when Jack Cockwell — separated from his second wife — got involved with Wendy Cecil-Stuart, a 37-year-old public-relations specialist at Brascan who worked closely with Trevor Eyton.

On weekends Eyton lived the life of a country gentleman in Caledon with his wife, Jane, and three of their five grown children. He had added acreage and built a new home called Tudorcroft South, with a swimming pool, a satellite dish and a huge media room that seated 20. For Eyton's 50th birthday in 1984, Jane had organized a gala party at the Caledon Mountain Trout Club, which resembled an old-fashioned summer hotel, with grand views of the Caledon hills from its verandas. But during the week Eyton was on the social fast track, jetting around the country, lobbying, fundraising and pressing the flesh at big social events, often spending the night in his Rosedale townhouse. It was Cecil-Stuart who organized the Brascan-sponsored performances of the opera, symphony or ballet, frequently filling in for Jane as Eyton's corporate spouse, and sparking rumours of an affair which were denied by both.

Cecil-Stuart's involvement with Jack Cockwell was the new soap opera for the Bay Street village, where three topics predominated among the traders, brokers and white-collar professionals: deals, sports and sex. On Wednesday, July 30, 1986, Cockwell became a first-time father at the age of 45, when Cecil-Stuart gave birth to their daughter, Daphne Tessa (asset spelled backwards). Worried about the reaction from the puritanical WASP establishment, Eyton insisted that Cecil-Stuart leave Brascan and go to work at Edper temporarily. Cockwell later married Cecil-Stuart in a common-law ceremony in South Africa and she changed her name to Cecil-Cockwell. By the summer of 1987, Cecil-Cockwell, who had used her contacts in the media to raise Cockwell's profile, had resigned from her role at Edper and was running her own consulting business out of the couple's $1 million-plus home in Toronto's affluent WASP enclave of Rosedale. Said Cecil-Cockwell in early 1988 of Cockwell and Eyton's relationship, "Two or three years ago, they were more of a package."

In early 1986, for example, Cockwell and Eyton had come to the aid of Conrad Black.

In the last week of January 1986, Trevor Eyton and Jack Cockwell twice visited Conrad Black, then 41, at Toronto's Wellesley Hospital, where he was immobilized by acute back pains from a ruptured disc. He was also facing a desperate financial crisis.

Conrad's father, George Montegu Black, had run the brewing division of the Argus empire, co-founded in 1945 by the WASP quadrumvirate of E.P. Taylor, Eric Phillips, M.W. "Wally" McCutcheon and John "Bud" McDougald. As a male scion of the Canadian Establishment, Conrad was educated at Upper Canada College in Toronto, where, at the age of 14, he was at the centre of the biggest scandal in the school's history. In his own polysyllabic, Conradian words, Black — the runner-up for the lower school's "zebra" award for the most-frequently whacked boy — had become "completely and perniciously insubordinate and undermined the entire school in various ways, culminating in stealing the [final] examinations and selling them" to his classmates. Black had even established a sliding price scale, using a stolen copy of the academic records to determine who would be willing to pay the most. His contemporary John Fraser later recalled how Black was constantly hatching schemes to take over the college and shut it down.

After Upper Canada College, Conrad Black was thrown out of Trinity College School in Port Hope, failed his first year at Carleton University in Ottawa after spending his afternoons at the House of Commons and his evenings playing cards with Senators, and was kicked out of Osgoode Hall Law School in Toronto. In his 1993 memoirs, Black recalled how he eventually realized he had been a "rather silly and undiscriminating rebel" and decided it would be better to make a show of joining the Toronto WASP establishment, for "tactical reasons at least." At the age of 21, Black became the youngest member of the Toronto Club, at Bud McDougald's invitation. A year later he fled somnolent Toronto for historic Quebec City, where he immersed himself in the drama of Quebec politics, flirted with Catholicism, dabbled in the part ownership of small-town newspapers and resumed his academic career. He graduated with a law degree in French from Laval University in 1970 and with a master of arts degree from Montreal's McGill University in 1973. He also turned his master's thesis into a biography of controversial former Quebec premier Maurice Duplessis, published in 1976.

Meanwhile, in 1975, French-Canadian conglomerateur Paul Desmarais had attempted to wrest control of the Argus empire from the ruling founder Bud McDougald. Through Ravelston Corp., McDougald, the Black family and several other Establishment names held 60% of Argus's voting stock. Desmarais bought up a significant number of shares, but Ottawa set up the Royal Commission on Corporate Concentration to stop him. "I'm waiting at the door," Desmarais reportedly told the commission. After Desmarais's aborted takeover attempt, a vindictive McDougald blackballed him from the Everglades Club in Palm Beach.

Two years after their father's death in 1976, Conrad Black, then 33, and his older brother Montegu took their $18 million inheritance and stepped into the Argus power vacuum created by the death of McDougald. They brashly seized control of what was then Canada's biggest conglomerate, bought out Desmarais's Power Corp. interest at cost and began to sell off Argus's interests in $4 billion of assets.

Over the next six years in a "campaign of manoeuvre," the Argus Group was restructured: peddling its minority interest in Domtar; pulling out of the Massey-Ferguson mess by donating its stake to the Massey pension fund and taking a tax loss; selling 75% of struggling Dominion Stores, in a blaze of controversy over the use of employees' pension funds and store closures, with Conrad publicly accusing the employees of theft at the very moment of massive layoffs; and hiving off Standard Broadcasting Corp. to Allan Slaight, an investment club crony of Trevor Eyton's.

The reorganization also elevated Hollinger Inc., Argus's fifth investment, to a senior position above its former parent. Investment professionals grumbled about the "Black factor" — a discount applied to the stock prices because it was "impossible to predict how the group would develop or what complex related party transactions it might pursue."

Almost halfway through the reorganization, Conrad Black secretly initiated discussions with Paul Reichmann about selling Ravelston's Hollinger shares to him, but they couldn't agree on a price. Black said the proposal would have given him about $75 million of profit for two and a half years' work and a net worth of more than $100 million. But Reichmann wouldn't raise his offer the "few million dollars" required to meet Black's price.

In 1985, Conrad Black bought out his brother, as well as almost all of their Ravelston minority partners, a gaggle of Eatons, Bassetts and Websters. Hollinger, with its royalties from Iron Ore Co. of Canada, was left as the primary investment vehicle. Late that year Black transformed Hollinger into a fledgling international newspaper empire with an audacious $68 million takeover of London's *Daily Telegraph*, or the "Daily Torygraph" as it was known — later dubbed the deal of the century by the British press.

At the same time, Black initiated talks with Trevor Eyton and Jack Cockwell about selling Hollinger's 41% stake in Norcen Energy, the oil-and-gas exploration company which had played a pivotal role in the Reichmanns' takeover of Gulf Canada. In the last week of January 1986, Eyton and Cockwell brought books on backaches to Black in Wellesley Hospital, where they continued their negotiations. The three renowned asset shufflers reached an agreement in early February. Hollinger would exchange its Norcen Energy shares for about $130 million in cash and $170 million worth of Hees treasury shares, or a 16% stake. Under the Tax Act, Canadian companies could roll over assets into another corporation for treasury shares without paying tax, as opposed to selling those assets outright and incurring capital gains tax. As part of the deal, Black got three seats on the Hees board of directors for himself and two appointed representatives. Peter Bronfman would become the Edper representative on the Hollinger board.

Meanwhile, Conrad Black was going through "one of the most nerve-racking periods" in his life. Within a week of Hollinger's agreement to sell Norcen Energy to Hees, the Supreme Court of Ontario ordered Dominion Stores to repay into court $60 million in surplus that the company had claimed was "legally withdrawn" from the Dominion Stores employees' pension plan. At the same time, the Canadian Imperial Bank of Commerce called a $40 million loan to Dominion Stores. Junior officials of the CIBC harrassed the bedridden Black, now laid up in his Park Lane Circle mansion off the Bridle Path with bronchitis *and* back problems, as well as the added responsibility of a newborn son, his third child with his first wife, Shirley. The CIBC executives agitated for a fire sale of Hollinger to cover the Dominion debts. So severe was the pressure that Black even discussed with Toronto Sun Publishing chairman Doug Creighton a possible sale to the tabloid newspaper chain of part of Hollinger's *Daily Telegraph* interest. But Creighton was unable to persuade the Toronto Sun board of directors to go ahead with the plan. Black then "croakingly" called CIBC chairman Donald

Fullerton, who agreed to call off the hounds after Black "wheez-ingly" outlined a debt reduction plan. To get CIBC to honour his promissory note to his brother Montegu, Black had to mortgage his Palm Beach house to the bank "for a few months."

Conrad Black was a long-time director of the Canadian Imperial Bank of Commerce, along with other CIBC banking clients in-cluding Labatt's Peter Widdrington, Noranda's Alf Powis and Olympia & York's Paul Reichmann. Black claimed he even championed Brian Mulroney to the CIBC board when Mulroney became president of Iron Ore Co. after losing the 1976 Progressive Conservative lead-ership contest to Joe Clark.

Like Trevor Eyton, Mulroney had grown up in a small, pulp-and-paper mill town on the North Shore of the St. Lawrence River in Quebec, but Mulroney's father was working-class, not middle-class. Mulroney escaped his home in Baie-Comeau to go to university in Nova Scotia. As a Maritime leader of the Youth for Diefenbaker move-ment, also known as Rogers' Raiders because of its Toronto chair-man, Ted Rogers, Mulroney attended the 1956 Progressive Conservative convention in Ottawa, where he impressed Rogers with his zeal. Sipping brandy in comfortable surroundings, the young Rogers and his friend Hal Jackman reportedly sent Mulroney out into the snow at 4:00 a.m. to erect more Diefenbaker signs. Later Mulroney would become known as a legendary political fixer, who re-warded favours owed. Mulroney bombed out of his first year at Dalhousie Law School, but eventually graduated from Laval Law School and joined a predecessor law firm of Ogilvy Renault in Place Ville-Marie in Montreal, where Paul Desmarais became his major labour-law client. As a young bachelor about town, Mulroney caroused with Standard Brands Canada president Ross Johnson and his so-called Canadian Olympic Drinking Team in the early 1970s. Desmarais sponsored both Mulroney and Johnson, later CEO of RJR Nabisco, for membership at the tony Mount Royal Club, which had twice rejected Sam Bronfman. In 1973, the year Johnson was promoted to New York City, Mulroney married the teenage Mila Pivnicki, whom he'd spotted the summer before in her bikini beside the pool at the Mount Royal Tennis Club. Mulroney went on to become a member of the three-man Cliche Royal Commission in 1974, formed to investigate corruption in the Quebec construction unions, bringing in his Laval classmate Lucien Bouchard as associate counsel. Then, depressed after losing the 1976 leadership contest, Mulroney once again partied and drank to excess. But soon the Mulroneys were living in a fairy-tale stone house on Belvedere Road in Westmount, where their next-door neighbour was Peter Bronfman. And as president of Iron Ore Co., Mulroney insisted on a corporate jet, as he shut down the Quebec town of Schefferville on November 1, 1982, on behalf of Iron Ore's American parent, Hannah Mining of Cleveland.

When Hollinger's Norcen Energy made a play for Hannah Mining in 1981, it led to racketeering charges by the U.S. Securities Exchange Commission, an investigation by the Ontario Securities Commission and a criminal investigation by the Ontario Crown. In his memoirs, Conrad Black recalled how he told the attorney general of Ontario that "the powder trail from this trumped-up charade of an investigation leads straight to Brian [Mulroney]'s door. I understand he has to please his employer, but powder trails can burn in both directions, and before the summer's over I could be his employer." Hollinger's Norcen Energy reached a compromise with Hannah Mining, and the OSC investigation of Norcen Energy was later dropped. When the Crown investigation was abandoned in 1982 because of "insufficient evidence," Black said Mulroney called to offer his congratulations.

Not long after, Mulroney visited Black in Palm Beach to ask for his help in getting the Toronto Tory establishment to support Mulroney in his second bid for the leadership of the Progressive Conservative party. Mulroney went on to win the leadership in 1983 and the federal election in 1984, with the third-biggest majority in the history of Canada. Just before his electoral victory in 1984, Mulroney, Black, Charles Bronfman, former Liberal Prime Minister Pierre Elliott Trudeau and future Liberal Prime Minister Jean Chrétien were among 350 guests at the gala wedding of Paul Desmarais's daughter Sophie. Desmarais's second son, André, had married Chretien's daughter three years earlier.

In his memoirs, Conrad Black accused Paul Desmarais, a mid-February 1986 visitor to his sickbed, of indiscretions that led a wide circle of people, including then-Prime Minister Mulroney, to conclude that Black was on the verge of bankruptcy. Because his solvency was "under severe pressure," Black was also forced to sell the Argus corporate jet.

A little more than a year later, when a disapproving Jack Cockwell — who prohibited Edper Group executives from enjoying traditional perks like corporate jets, company apartments or chauffered cars — put Norcen's Grumman Gulfstream jet on the market in 1987, a renewed Hollinger was able to buy the aircraft. Hollinger had recently racked up a 33% profit on the sale of two-thirds of its Hees investment.

At a charity roast of Trevor Eyton that year, the theatrical Conrad Black, who had flown in from London for the occasion, reportedly entered in a "veiled sedan chair", carried by six of Eyton's closest friends, including Julian Porter, Allan Slaight and Trilon Financial's Gordon Cunningham, a former partner at Tory Tory DesLauriers & Binnington. Cunningham had helped Eyton put together a private syndicate to fund the building of a new sports stadium in Toronto.

Trevor Eyton made the cover of *Toronto Life* in May 1986, unrumpled for once in a dark, double-breasted suit, buttoned-down, striped shirt and conservative, circle-patterned tie, as No. 1 in the magazine's first annual checklist of the "Fifty Most Influential People in the City." By then, Eyton had lined up 12 private-sector companies (Toronto Sun Publishing and fourteen more were added later) to chip in $5.3 million each to the Stadium Consortium Corp.

"Trevor had no visible role in the planning stages," recalled Paul Godfrey, Toronto Sun Publishing CEO, former Metro Toronto chairman and prime mover in the grand design for a domed stadium. "Trevor had a number of contacts, and he tapped a lot of people," Godfrey said in an interview. One was Michael Sanderson, then head of Merrill Lynch Canada, who told Rod McQueen for the *Toronto Life* cover story how he had received a call from Eyton in

January 1985. "We're thinking of putting up a domed stadium for the Blue Jays [major league baseball team]. Are you interested?" Eyton asked. "I've got a few of my friends together — Labatt's, Imperial Oil, and the Reichmanns are going to take a piece. Why don't you throw in $5 million?" Later that year Eyton, then 53, hosted a dinner for Merrill Lynch's international advisory council at the Toronto Club, with Edward and Peter Bronfman, Jean Campeau and Albert Reichmann as his guests. "Fate brought us together. We really feel very highly about [Trevor Eyton's] personal capabilities," Albert Reichmann told *Toronto Life*. "He is a very able, capable administrator. He can work under any conditions and come to a rational conclusion. That's a very big advantage in big business."

Getting the Reichmanns to invest in the retractable-roofed stadium was a remarkable coup for Trevor Eyton. When SkyDome opened, the brothers' kosher food-catered private box was often dark during Blue Jays games because so many were played on the Jewish Sabbath. All of the stadium investors got a decade's use of private boxes and reserved parking, and some were awarded the rights to a particular concession. For example, Toronto Sun Publishing got the rights to tours of SkyDome, as well as exclusive rights to advertise in the stadium (shutting out *The Globe and Mail* and *The Toronto Star*). The Bitove family, who golfed with Eyton in Boca Raton, Florida, where both families owned property and co-hosted an annual Christmas party on a rented yacht, were awarded a food contract, which they shared with George Cohon's McDonald's.

Questions flew over the clubbish way in which Eyton had assembled the group of corporate financiers for the stadium, but that was his style. Eyton had spent a "lifetime building contacts in the world of favours granted and owed," concluded authors Patricia Best and Ann Shortell. "I work with people I like," Eyton told *Toronto Life*. "It has become a seamless web." Turning over the sod with a ceremonial silver spade on the SkyDome site was one of Eyton's proudest personal moments.

Less enjoyable was Trevor Eyton's spring 1986 summons to testify in defence of the Edper Group at the House of Commons'

Finance Committee hearings in Ottawa. The committee was critical of Canada's large commercial empires owning financial institutions, and was thought to have targeted the Edper Group in particular. By then the Edper Group was the biggest conglomerate in Canadian history, controlling about $100 billion of assets — two-thirds of which were deposits and other financial assets under Trilon Financial's umbrella — through its effective equity stakes in more than 30 public companies, including property developers Trizec and Bramalea; conglomerate Brascan, with its diverse interests in brewer John Labatt, base-metal miner Westmin Resources, and resources giant Noranda, with its own interests in forester MacMillan Bloedel and miner Hemlo Gold; oil-and-gas explorers North Canadian Oils and Norcen Energy; North America's fourth-largest merchant bank, Hees; the merchant bank and power generator Great Lakes Group; and financial services goliath Trilon Financial, with its controlling interests in Royal Trustco, London Insurance Group and Royal LePage.

When the Liberals were still in power, Trevor Eyton, Albert Reichmann and Allen Lambert had flown to Ottawa — as part of a group organized by National Trust's Hal Jackman that included Montreal Trust's Paul Desmarais, First City's Sam Belzberg and John Craig Eaton — to protest against the government's plan that commercial empires be limited to 10% ownership of a financial institution. Then, less than a year after the Conservatives were elected in 1984, junior finance minister Barbara McDougall proposed that such empires be allowed to hike up their cross-ownership of banks, trusts, and insurance companies to 100%, but with a ban on self-dealing.

Ironically, one of the loudest voices warning about the dangers of large conglomerates owning financial institutions was Bernard "Bernie" Ghert, president and CEO of developer Cadillac Fairview, then owned 50% by the CEMP Bronfmans and 22% by the Reichmanns — partners with the Edper Group in Trizec and Trilon Financial. Ghert argued that such powerful monopolies could restrict other companies' access to public markets and undermine the financial system. "[Ghert's] remarks amused me," Eyton said in *Controlling Interest*. "CEMP tried to get into the financial assets business themselves and attempted to take over London Life and Royal Trustco, which are now owned by Trilon. We were invited to take more shares in London Life because of fears about CEMP." But Ghert claimed to know of specific abuses by the Edper Group. The Finance Committee scheduled public hearings for mid-1986 to investigate the issue.

On the last day of the hearings, Wednesday, June 11, 1986, Bernie Ghert testified, "I know of an instance where, if the witnesses were required to testify under oath, they would have to tell you of a financial institution [said to be Royal Trustco] that had instructions from senior executives of the parent nonfinancial company to refuse a loan to one of its competitors." Ghert named McLeod Young Weir chairman Austin "Firp" Taylor (a 330-pound narcoleptic known as "the Fatman" on Bay Street) and Toronto-Dominion Bank chairman Richard Thomson (whose bank had been a partner with the Edper Group and the Reichmanns in Trilon Financial) as two men who knew of examples of self-dealing by the Edper Group. But the committee had not called Taylor or Thomson to testify, because "nothing illegal or improper was provable," a member later explained.

The final two witnesses, Trevor Eyton and Jack Cockwell, making an unscheduled appearance, told the committee that they were fed up with the public insinuations of wrongdoing by Edper. "Mr. Ghert would not be employable [in the Edper Group], given the standards that we apply in hiring people," barked Cockwell. After Cockwell testified, Finance Committee Chairman Donald Blenkarn reportedly remarked, "They should keep that guy in the back, back, back room." That summer the Finance Committee recommended that commercial empires be limited to 30% ownership of a financial institution, but with no ban on self-dealing.

The issue of the "Edper factor" did not die at the hearings. Bernie Ghert told me how Trevor Eyton and Jack Cockwell came to see him after his testimony. Cockwell demanded Ghert make a public statement that he "knew nothing wrong about [the Edper] op-eration." As Eyton squirmed, Cockwell continued, "You must." Ghert replied "Why must I?"

The Edper Group began fighting back against the Finance Committee and the innuendo circulating in the financial markets in a series of exclusive interviews with *The Financial Post*'s Barry Critchley. In July 1986, four group executives — Brascan's Trevor Eyton and Jack Cockwell, Royal Trustco's Michael Cornelissen and Hees's Willard "Bill" L'Heureux — told Critchley that they planned to meet with legislators, government officials and the financial com-munity to tell their side of the story and to publish two papers, one summarizing their views on the major financing issues, including a discussion of their own business principles. The four men argued that there was nothing wrong with a nonfinancial company being a major shareholder in a financial institution and that certain types of self-dealing, or related-party transactions, were acceptable, such as saving costs through consolidating computer facilities (soon to be-come the focus of a raging battle between Trizec and Bramalea) or providing services between group companies. On the other hand, other types of related-party transactions clearly were wrong, such as moving assets between a commercial company and a financial company. Where there was a grey area, they said that Edper had set up business conduct review committees, comprising noncompany executives, who reviewed about two dozen transactions a year. Critics pointed out that the so-called business conduct review com-mittees had not examined Royal Trustco's purchase of Unicorp preferred shares during the 1985 takeover of gas utility Union Enterprises — surely this was a blatant example of the type of transaction that should fall into the grey area, they said.

Trevor Eyton was the co-ordinator of Edper's efforts to incor-porate its beliefs into government policies. Not long after the Finance Committee hearings, Eyton and Jack Cockwell began inviting its members to lunch. And that November, Eyton and his friend John Bitove Sr. co-hosted the annual Toronto fund-raising dinner for Prime Minister Brian Mulroney. It was said that both Eyton and Paul

Desmarais, whose Power Financial Corp. then controlled Montreal Trustco Ltd., personally lobbied their friend Mulroney about the financial services legislation. When a draft policy was announced, it essentially grandfathered the Edper Group arrangement: commercial empires, which already had commercial-financial links, would be limited to 65% ownership of trusts and insurance companies.

In the autumn of 1986, Trevor Eyton was summoned to appear at yet another hearing, the 78-day Parker Commission judicial inquiry into conflict of interest by federal Industry Minister Sinclair Stevens. But this time Eyton was defending his personal reputation, as well as the Edper Group's. The problem: In 1984–85, Canada Development Investment Corp. board member Eyton had played matchmaker between Stevens's financially troubled private business and the investment bankers — Burns Fry, Dominion Securities and Gordon Capital — given contracts by CDIC to oversee the sale of Crown assets. CDIC was Stevens's ministry, and Stevens had asked Eyton to lead its privatization drive. Eyton had declined and recruited Edper Group executive Paul Marshall to head up the CDIC, but Eyton and his friend Patrick Keenan became members of the CDIC board and its special Divestiture Committee. At the same time, Stevens's personal advisers, not the cabinet minister (who was required to hand over his business affairs to a blind trust), had approached Eyton for help in refinancing Stevens's private company. "If I thought that the minister was tying together the assignment of [CDIC] work to the investment bankers with some kind of favourable response or some kind of help, even at this stage for his family company, I would have [had] nothing to do with him," Eyton recalled in *The Brass Ring*. Ten months after hearing the final oral arguments in Toronto, the Parker Commission ruled in late 1987 that the "conflict was Mr. Stevens's, not Mr. Eyton's;" but Eyton had been embarrassed by public scrutiny into what he had called his "seamless web" of connections.

While Trevor Eyton was tripping over his connections, backroom strategist Jack Cockwell had been establishing the financial base of the Edper Group with common equity, not debt.

Chapter 5

Financial

Architecture

During the 1983–87 bull market, the Edper em-
pire raised an astounding $10 billion from public share issues.
Offerings from Edper-controlled companies reportedly accounted
for one-third of Canada's equity investments during the first three
years of the bull run.

The Edper empire was built on the axiom of maximum control at minimum cost, using Jack Cockwell's knowledge of the pyramid structures of South Africa's massive conglomerates, like the
Oppenheimer family's Anglo American Corp., the world's biggest
gold and diamond empire. Edper tacticians would never have bought
almost 100% of the shares of a takeover target, as the Reichmanns
had done with Abitibi-Price. They had rules. Indeed, the Edper
Group had developed a blueprint of business principles, primarily
authored by its financial architect Cockwell, which began appearing in the group companies' annual reports:

- *Ownership of the Edper Group's public companies to be limited
  to about the 50% level.* For instance, through its 50% holding of
  publicly traded Hees, which held about 50% of publicly traded
  Brascan (through a 25% direct interest and a 25% indirect interest through Brascan Holdings, a structured partnership with
  Edper), which held almost 50% of the shares of publicly traded

Trilon Financial, which held almost 50% of the shares in publicly traded Royal Trustco, private Edper maintained control of Trilon's $65 billion of financial assets with an effective equity stake of less than 20%, and of Royal Trustco's financial assets with an effective equity interest of less than 10%.

Using a technique called top-down financing, Edper could also achieve an equity multiplier effect without jeopardizing its proportionate control. For example, if Hees raised $100 million of common stock in a public offering, Edper would buy $50 million and Hees would sell $50 million to the public. Edper would then invest $50 million and Hees, $100 million, in a $200 million stock offering by Brascan, and Brascan would tap the public for the other $50 million. Brascan would then invest the $200 million in a $400 million stock offering by its subsidiary, Trilon Financial, and Trilon Financial would sell $200 million to the public. Trilon Financial would then invest the $400 million in a $800 million offering by its subsidiary, Royal Trustco, and Royal Trustco would tap the public for the other $400 million. Thus the original $100 million put up by Edper would be transformed into a war chest of $800 million just four tiers down the organizational ladder at Royal Trustco. And Edper Group companies were careful to subscribe to just enough of each issue to maintain their proportionate equity stakes.

- *Representation on the the boards of directors of Edper Group companies to be proportional to ownership, and board decisions to be reached by consensus.* Critics said Edper used proportional representation to browbeat subsidiary management through board meetings. For example, Brascan's 50% ownership of Trilon Financial entitled the conglomerate to half the seats at Trilon's board table. Thus the Edper Group had 10 representatives on the 19-member Trilon board in 1987 — including Trevor Eyton and Jack Cockwell — even though Edper's effective interest in Trilon was less than 20%. Olympia & York had three.

- *Senior management in the Edper Group to participate in their affiliate's performance through share ownership.* This credo meant there were no telephone-number salaries in the Edper Group. Senior managers were expected to take most of their gains — and lumps — in the same way shareholders did, through the market performance of their company stock. Rather than issue stock options, which had no downside risk, the Edper Group expected its senior managers to take out five-year loans — worth up to 10 times their annual salaries — in order to buy shares, at a 10% discount. For example, group CEOs carried an average $2.5 million stock-loan package on a $250,000 annual salary.

  At the height of the bull market in 1987, Edper's dealmakers, Trevor Eyton and Jack Cockwell, were said to be worth about $50 million each, so it appeared that the Edper brand of pay for performance was a sure road to riches. That's why the level of participation had expanded to include even some junior managers, who carried a $500,000 stock-loan package on a $50,000 annual salary. Interest payments on the management loans were designed to be covered by the stock dividend payments.

- *Dividends to be set at sustainable levels and considered an "integral cost" of doing business.* Edper's operating firms were overcapitalized through top-down financing to ensure a steady bottom-up flow of dividends from affiliate to affilate up to the controlling shareholders, Edward and Peter Bronfman. Under the Tax Act, related Canadian companies did not pay tax on intercorporate dividends. But unlike equity, which multiplied as it flowed down the Edper Group, dividend income shrank as it flowed upwards, because Edper affiliates had to pay dividends to public shareholders, as well as to insiders. If necessary, the Edper Group issued more equity from the top down, to keep the dividend stream flowing from the bottom up to the Bronfmans.

  To reduce cash shrinkage for Edward and Peter Bronfman, Edper affiliates issued preferred shares, as well as common shares. The preferred shares gave the Bronfman brothers a priority claim on dividend income and on assets ahead of common shareholders, in the event of a dissolution.

The Edper Group also set up what it called "structured partnerships agreements" in 1983 between Edper and its merchant banking affiliate, Hees. These agreements created two private companies, Brascan Holdings and Carena Holdings, which owned the common shares of publicly traded Brascan and Carena. In turn, Edper and Hees split ownership of the common shares of both Brascan Holdings and Carena Holdings. Edper held the junior preferred shares of both holding companies, and Hees held the senior preferred shares of both. In these structured partnerships, the junior partner (Edper) shared equally in any asset growth, even though it had contributed less capital, in exchange for guaranteeing the dividend payments on the senior partner's preferred shares. If a cash deficit occurred, the junior partner (Edper) had to subscribe for additional junior preferred shares of the holding company in order to pay the dividend obligations to the senior partner (Hees). Thus the structured partnerships were a tradeoff between reward and risk. In the event of a dissolution, the junior partner (Edper) also had a lesser claim than the senior partner (Hees) on the underlying assets of the two holding companies, because the junior preferred shares ranked behind the senior preferred shares.

In addition to the preferred shares issued by private companies such as Brascan Holdings and Carena Holdings, private preferred shares issued by Edper's public companies, and preferred shares held by Edper's parent companies in subsidiary companies, such as Royal Trustco preferred shares held by Trilon Financial, Edper affiliates also owned one-fifth of the $5 billion of preferred shares issued by the Edper Group during the bull run. In fact, Edper affiliates bought nearly one-third of all preferred shares issued in Canada between 1982 and 1985; the other big buyers of preferred shares were the Canadian banks.

Critics like McLeod Young Weir's Tom Kierans argued that Jack Cockwell's preferred shares were the Michael Milken junk debt of

Canada, but preferred shares counted as equity, not debt, on the balance sheet. Even though these fixed-income obligations had many of the characteristics of debt — they paid fixed interest in the form of regular dividends and had to be repaid if the shares were redeemable or retractable — preferred shares had no specific call on assets in the event of a default. By the late 1980s, more than half of the Edper Group's issued preferred shares were of a perpetual, or long-term, nature. "Most of the preferreds that [the group] issued throughout the 80s were perpetual preferreds, which represent permanent capital to us," the group's preferred share specialist George Myhal later recalled. "Since June of 1987 when tax reform measures came in, the value of preferreds to us as a group diminished severely. The cost of a preferred [share issue] was raised significantly versus debt, to the extent that it [was] virtually uneconomic for us as a group to be continually issuing preferred shares. And, in fact, it's really only the banks and utilities who are able to pass that higher cost on to their users, who find this market still attractive." Until tax reform, Cockwell used preferred-share financing primarily for its tax efficiency. Issuing preferred shares was cheaper than borrowing money from a bank, because the favourable tax treatment meant Edper Group companies could pay a lower dividend rate, say 7%, on the preferred shares than the prime lending rate, say 12%.

To get Edper's equity factory operating at top speed, Jack Cockwell had backed Jimmy Connacher in Gordon's bid to break up the cartel of stock "selling groups" on Bay Street — dominated by Dominion Securities and Wood Gundy — that had long fixed underwriting fees and divided up the market between themselves. Instead of acting as a mere middleman, Gordon planned to use its own capital to buy an entire share issue from a company and then place those shares with the purchasers it had lined up in advance. Gordon's signature "bought deal" was a $228 million preferred-share offering in 1984 for the Royal Bank of Canada. If prices in the market fell while Gordon was holding the Royal Bank shares, Edper's Hees had agreed to act as a sub-underwriter and buy those shares from Gordon. Shortly thereafter, Edper's Great Lakes Group took over that function.

Other Canadian stock brokerage firms were forced to embrace the bought deal for fear of losing market share to predatory Gordon. Because bought deals were a faster, cheaper way to raise capital, the Edper Group saved hundreds of millions of dollars in underwriting costs for its almost $10 billion of equity issues during the 1983–87 bull market; and Hees and Great Lakes Group made millions of dollars in profit from sub-underwriting Bay Street's bought deals. For his behind-the-scenes role, Jack Cockwell was dubbed the "the manipulator" and regarded with a mix of awe and loathing in the Bay Street village. There were rumblings of protest about the clout wielded by "Cockwell & Co.," but few public complaints apart from McLeod Young Weir's, because the Edper Group was the investment dealers' biggest single source of revenue during the bull run.

Even the Reichmanns tapped the steaming equity markets in the final months of Canada's longest bull market, with a record public share offering, worth half a billion dollars, from Gulf Canada Resources.

During the summer before the Crash of 1987, Paul Reichmann closed the deal that cost him his empire. Never before had a real estate project been undertaken that was as big as Olympia & York's Canary Wharf development in London.

Ten months earlier, a 6'6" American developer named Gooch Ware Travelstead, a former First Boston investment banker, had called on Olympia & York executive Michael Dennis in New York to begin negotiations to secure a Reichmann investment in his pet project.

Almost everyone had underestimated the scale of Travelstead's 1985 redevelopment proposal for the abandoned docklands on the Thames River in London. Travelstead had planned to build 8.8 million square feet of office space (almost one-sixth of the total existing capacity in London's financial district, known as the City or the Square Mile) to house 50,000 office workers. The $6.3 billion project consisted of 24 buildings, including three 85-storey skyscrapers and two 400-room hotels, on 71 acres in east London. Travelstead was proposing to create an instant world financial centre to rival the Square Mile. Until then, the London Docklands

Development Corp. had promoted Canary Wharf more modestly, as a site for "small high-quality industrial development."

But Travelstead, who had lined up a consortium of American and Swiss investment banks to finance the undertaking, was not allowed to begin construction until he had signed up some major tenants. With the money running short, G.W. Travelstead, nicknamed "Gee Whiz" by a skeptical London establishment, was approached by the Reichmanns.

Paul Reichmann had first heard about Canary Wharf in early 1986 in conversation with Charles "Chuck" Young, a former Citibank Canada president who was then working in London. By September, Paul Reichmann still had not managed to see the Canary Wharf site, so he sent Michael Dennis to London to size up its potential and to review the master plan with Travelstead. Dennis reportedly concluded that there was a need for modern North American-style office space in London, where only 10% of the commercial space was what he would call "Class A." With Reichmann's backing, Dennis entered into negotiations with Travelstead and his partners, Credit Suisse First Boston and Morgan Stanley International. On several occasions over the next four months, the parties thought they were close to a deal. Albert Reichmann expressed concern about the cost and size of the Canary Wharf project, but was overruled by his brother Paul, who was convinced that the Big Bang — the deregulation of finance in Britain in September 1986 — would spark new demand for office space in London and that the city would be the financial centre of the new Europe.

Meanwhile, Paul Reichmann had been approached by another mercurial developer to invest in his pet project. Shortly after Robert Campeau's October 1986 takeover of American department stores conglomerate Allied Stores for US$3.6 billion, Campeau began looking for someone to help him make a US$150 million downpayment before the December 29, 1986, closing. Campeau, then 63, met with Reichmann in Toronto in mid-November in an effort to charm him into putting up the money. Reichmann refused, saying he didn't know anything about retailing, so Campeau turned to several

American developers, eventually striking a partnership with Edward DeBartolo, one of the top three U.S. shopping-mall owners.

Years earlier, Robert Campeau had thumbed his nose at the Toronto establishment after it linked arms and prevented his 1980 attempt to take over Royal Trustco. All but the Reichmann brothers, who had assured Campeau they had purchased their shares only after it was apparent he had lost. Paul Reichmann reportedly even called Campeau to tell him that their investment was not meant as a vote against him personally.

In 1981, Campeau and his second wife, Ilse, began construction of their new home on the Bridle Path in Toronto, tearing down the original house and erecting a 25,000 square foot mansion, a cross in style between a French chateau and a hunting lodge, but with an indoor pool and a bomb shelter. Prime Minister Pierre Elliott Trudeau was the featured guest at a gala 1984 housewarming party. Within months of the party, Campeau had his second nervous breakdown and his first facelift.

By 1985, Campeau was again talking about making acquisitions, this time in the U.S. In early 1986, Campeau secretly began buying shares of Allied Stores (Brooks Brothers, Ann Taylor, Jordan Marsh). Despite an ego-deflating Wall Street walk to find financial advisers even willing to talk to the unknown Canadian, Campeau had lucked out, ending up with First Boston, which bankrolled a street sweep of Allied stock, investing its entire corporate capital to capture 51% of the target. And Campeau borrowed all the money, even his relatively tiny US$150 million downpayment, to capture the remaining 49% of Allied — largely financed by Citibank NA and through junk bonds. Allied's CEO said he had been "blindsided by a trainload of clowns."

Meanwhile, in 1984, Robert Campeau was putting up the Scotia Plaza for the Bank of Nova Scotia at King and Bay Streets in Toronto, despite opposition from his long-time foes, Toronto-Dominion Bank chairman Richard Thomson and Oxford Development Group chairman Donald Love. They had teamed up again to defeat the $380 million tower, the second-tallest in the city next to Olympia & York's

First Canadian Place, because it had taken Oxford Development Group nearly two years to get a development approved that exceeded the city's height restrictions. Thomson reportedly spent $120,000 of TD's money to lobby city councillors and place full-page newspaper ads attacking the development.

In early 1987, Paul Reichmann finally agreed to help Campeau fund his Allied takeover by buying a half-interest in Campeau's 68-storey Scotia Plaza for $50 million. Olympia & York also took over half the $440 million in mortgages against the building.

A month later talks broke off between Olympia & York and G.W. Travelstead, in a disagreement over control of the Canary Wharf project. Paul Reichmann reportedly told associates that the developer was not the kind of man who would make a good partner. The two sides parted company in February 1987 and Olympia & York heard no more about Canary Wharf until the latter half of June, when Michael Dennis learned that the British government had set an early July deadline for Travelstead and his financial backers to agree to contribute to the transportation infrastructure at Canary Wharf in return for the land and tax breaks from the government.

When the Reichmanns heard the news, they were on a walking holiday with their families at a kosher resort for Orthodox Jews in the Swiss Alps. They had to borrow Allied's Gulfstream jet, with its gold-plated toilet seat, from Robert Campeau in order to get home because their own plane was disabled in Zurich. In London, Paul Reichmann began negotiating with the government agency overseeing the project. The deadline was extended two weeks until July 17, 1987. In a handshake deal, Olympia & York agreed to help fund transportation links between Canary Wharf and the City, almost five kilometres away, promising to spend £400 million to help build the Jubilee subway extension and an additional £148 million on the Docklands Light Railway. By the Friday deadline, the master agreement had been signed and the Reichmanns officially took over the Canary Wharf project from the consortium for a reported US$112 million. But the brothers weren't at the ceremony — they'd jetted back to Toronto for the Jewish Sabbath, as they did almost every week.

The Canary Wharf project certainly fit Paul Reichmann's criteria. The land was cheap — the 71 acres had been assembled for the first of British Prime Minister Margaret Thatcher's enterprise zones, created to attract new industry to depressed areas — and the quality of the project would be high. Although the cost of the project was then estimated at £4 billion, Olympia & York would get a tax break of about one-third that total. "We will fund it ourselves," Reichmann later boasted at a breakfast meeting with selected British journalists. "We can complete it on our own strength." Olympia & York Developments then had shareholders' equity of about $6 billion, according to internal documents (its audited fair-value-basis consolidated financial statements) and an estimated total equity value, including corporate investments, which exceeded $10 billion. Even so, it would be gambling much of its balance sheet on one project.

By that time, the Reichmann family name, which derived from the German meant "man of wealth" or "man of empire," had become synonymous with riches worldwide. And the brothers' private fiefdom, Olympia & York Developments, had no obligation to disclose anything that might bring the Reichmanns' exalted reputation thudding back to earth. The family's unwillingness to disclose financial information was legendary.

Yet Olympia & York Developments had an insatiable appetite for credit. The Reichmann brothers' prized Uris properties in Manhattan were mortgaged and remortgaged to finance the construction of the World Financial Center and the takeovers of Abitibi-Price and Gulf Canada. Except for brief periods when market values caught up with its debt, Olympia & York Developments regularly operated at a very high debt level — as high as $7 billion during the 1981–82 recession. And when values rose, it chose to refinance instead of selling the properties — to avoid tax. Traditionally, real-estate loans were done on a project basis, usually with the building as security. But Olympia & York also borrowed at the holding-company level, offering a parent-company guarantee. A few bankers received annual financial statements from Olympia & York Developments, audited by

Price Waterhouse, but this information was historical and the statements did not show parent-company guarantees on loans, cross-collateralization, cross-defaults or complicated partnership agreements. Such secrets were kept in a leather binder that never left Paul Reichmann's office, available for take-no-notes inspection only by Olympia & York's most trusted lenders, like the Canadian Imperial Bank of Commerce. And some of that information was stored only inside the brain of a Talmudic scholar — Paul Reichmann.

Despite the Reichmanns' arcane practices, few large international banks refused to lend money to their empire early on. Wells Fargo & Co. was one of the few — the bank was reportedly uncomfortable with the Reichmanns' disclosure practices and the complexity of their organization. Toronto-Dominion Bank backed off from Olympia & York in 1987, claiming that it was concerned about the risk involved in the Canary Wharf project, but there may have been another motive — that was also the year that the Reichmanns linked up with Richard Thomson's arch-enemy, Robert Campeau. Otherwise, the global banks clamoured for the Reichmanns' business.

Apart from plain vanilla bank debt, Paul Reichmann also helped develop several innovative debt financings for real estate, including mortgage-backed securities, commercial paper programs and property bonds, all backed by individual buildings. In doing so, Reichmann hooked up with one of the best acts on Wall Street, Lewis Ranieri, who had become vice-chairman of Salomon Bros. in 1984 after a meteoric rise from the mail-room triggered by his creation of a new market for mortgage-backed securities. In 1984 Reichmann and Ranieri put together one of the largest securitized mortgages ever, almost US$1 billion, collateralized by three of Olympia & York's Manhattan skyscrapers, in a private placement by Salomon Brothers to more than 40 institutional investors: mainly Ranieri's polyester-suited wheeler-dealer clients in the U.S. savings & loan industry. To get the necessary financial information for the issue, four Salomon junior executives reportedly had to memorize pages of documents taped to a desk in Olympia & York's Park Avenue offices. "No note-taking was permitted and the documents could not be removed."

In his 1989 book, *Liar's Poker*, Michael Lewis, a former Salomon bond salesman in London, told the tale of how he was transformed from a geek trainee to a "Big Swinging Dick" in 1986, when he unloaded US$86 million of Olympia & York property bonds on an unsuspecting Frenchman, the dregs of a US$630.5 million issue collateralized by a Manhattan skyscraper rather than the "full faith and credit" of Olympia & York Developments. Lewis also described how the loud-mouthed, gluttonous Ranieri spent half his days at Salomon's New York headquarters playing jokes on his traders and smoking fat cigars. Since the culture in Ranieri's mortgage security department was based on food, their days reportedly began with a round of onion cheeseburgers fetched by a geek trainee at 8:00 a.m. And each Friday was "Food Frenzy" day, where Ranieri and his staff would order in several hundred dollars' worth of Mexican food.

But amid the empty food cartons on the Salomon trading floor, the market for mortgage-backed securities exploded to US$700 billion by the end of the decade. By 1987 Ranieri was out of Salomon and running his own limited partnership, Hyperion Capital Management, with a US$30 million investment from the Reichmanns.

For his behind-the-scenes role in the development of the North American debt markets, Paul Reichmann became known as "Mr. R" or simply "the man." Unlike financial architect Jack Cockwell, Reichmann had built the foundation of his empire with debt, not equity.

That's why the announcement of the Gulf Canada Resources equity offering in mid-June 1987 sparked such a feeding frenzy among Canadian and international investors, as Merrill Lynch Canada and the other investment firms handling the issue received twice as many orders as their allotment. Gulf shares had been trading at about $15 on the Toronto Stock Exchange before the reorganization, which divided Gulf Canada Resources, then 78.6% owned by Olympia & York, into three publicly traded companies: Gulf Canada Resources Ltd., a pure oil-and-gas company; Abitibi-Price Inc., a pure newsprint producer; and a new company called GW Utilities Ltd., set up to hold the hodgepodge of interests picked up in the Hiram Walker takeover.

By the end of August, the value of the Gulf, Abitibi-Price and GW Utilities shares had almost doubled. Paul Reichmann planned to raise even more money from a worshipful public by issuing shares in Olympia & York Enterprises, a holding company for the stock portfolio, but the October market crash put an end to that scheme.

PART TWO

The Alarm Bell

Chapter 6

Blood in the Street

The panic began at 9:30 in the morning on Monday, October 19, 1987. Stockbrokers had been flooded with sell orders over the weekend, following a market slump of 234 points the previous week on the blue-chip Dow Jones Industrial Average, the barometer of the New York Stock Exchange.

Not long after the opening bell, the Dow was down by 200 points. The New York Stock Exchange chairman raised the idea of a US$1 billion rescue fund, but it was quickly dropped, and he promised not to close the exchange. After two abortive rallies, the market went into a freefall, tumbling 220 points in the last hour. This was the first high-tech crash, with portfolio insurance and futures-contract arbitrage accelerating the downward spiral of prices. It was also the worst stock market crash in world history. The Dow's spectacular single-session fall of 508.32 points, or 22.6%, wiped out all the gains made by the index since April 7, 1986.

"Don't step on the blood," one patron reportedly remarked in Toronto's Sammy's Own Exchange, a traders' bar in the bowels of Olympia & York's Exchange Tower. In that day's trading, the Toronto Stock Exchange 300 Composite Index had dropped a stunning 407.20 points, or 11.3%, to the level at which it stood on January 8, 1987. Quipped another patron, "I didn't need four Jaguars anyway. I'm going to give two back."

Those licking their wounds in the world's financial districts included not only financial services firms, but also commercial-property developers. The Crash thinned the ranks of the white-collar professionals, cutting the space requirements in the downtown offices. On Wall Street, where employment had peaked in 1987, about 40,000 jobs were lost in the wake of the market meltdown. In London, the Big Bang had opened the way to the Bigger Bang — massive investments in the British securities industry by banks and brokerage houses from around the world. But the twisted alleys of London's financial district were soon littered with dropouts, eliminating about 20,000 jobs, and the City's office market was hit with its worst recession since the Second World War.

On Bay Street, the Crash wiped out public equity values in "The Greatest Show on Earth," as *Canadian Business* called the interlocking empires of the Edper Bronfmans and the Reichmanns, whose combined annual revenues of $50 billion reportedly exceeded the Gross National Product of 122 countries: Trizec A shares fell $3 1/8 on Black Monday to close at $27 (22% below their August 1987 peak of $34 5/8); Trizec B shares tumbled $2 1/8 to $30 (17% below their high of $36); Bramalea shares slipped $1/8 to $20 (30% below their high of $28 3/4); Trilon Financial A shares shed $2 to $15 1/2 (36% below their high of $24 3/8); and Royal Trustco A shares dropped $1 1/8 to $13 1/8 (31% below their high of $19).

Edward and Peter Bronfman's combined net worth was slashed by almost a third. Edper, their prime investment vehicle, had three main holdings, Hees, Carena and Brascan, which were carried on its books at a cost of slightly more than $1 billion. On Black Monday, Hees shares plunged $3 3/8 to $19 3/4 (30% below their 1987 peak of $28 1/8), Carena shares fell $2 to $27 1/2 (28% below their high of $35 1/4), and Brascan A shares tumbled $4 3/8 to $30 (30% below their peak of $42 3/4).

The timing was unfortunate for Edward and Peter Bronfman, who had struck an agreement in 1986 which required Edper — jointly owned by the Edward Bronfman Trust and the Peter Bronfman Trust — to obtain a public listing for its common shares on the Toronto Stock Exchange during 1989, so that Edward Bronfman and his three sons, Paul, David and Brian, could cash out. Would the market recover by then? Taking Edper public was a way for the third generation to take its money out without the sale of any major strategic holding.

The Edper Bronfmans had everything tied up in Edper, unlike their cousins, the CEMP Bronfmans, who had other assets separate from Seagram. When Edgar and Charles Bronfman had squabbled in the mid-1980s, they had sold CEMP's holdings in Cadillac Fairview and Bow Valley Resources, so that the siblings and their heirs could take their money out and go their separate ways. Charles and his sister, Phyllis, transferred more than $600 million from their share of the asset sales into Claridge Investments.

By contrast, Edward and Peter Bronfman had never feuded; in late 1987 a Bronfman family lawyer could not recall a single dispute between the two brothers. They were their father's sons: cultured, thoughtful men who had been taught to avoid confrontation. Edward was an accomplished public speaker in Jewish charity circles. His father, Allan, had electrified a crowd of 15,000 with a speech at a rally in the Montreal Forum during the Second World War, in support of the Canadian Aid to Russia Fund. Peter played the piano, like his father, and wrote poetry, even collaborating on a record album when he was at Yale. Later Peter collected Canadian art, particularly landscape paintings by the Group of Seven and David Milne, and dreamed of writing the great Canadian novel.

As fledgling members of the Bay Street oligarchy in the early 1980s, Edward and Peter were not invited to join the WASP bastion of the Toronto Club, which did not admit Jews, but they did keep in shape running around the rooftop track at the all-male Cambridge Club, which later became known on the Street for its annual black-tie squash night where, behind closed doors, Toronto's old boys placed $1,000 bets on the outcomes of professional squash matches, and some even carried on at a separate after-hours party to which their mistresses, not their wives, were invited.

Then, on Monday, May 23, 1983, the twice-divorced Edward's world turned upside-down, with the death of his Air Canada flight-attendant girlfriend, Delores Ann Sherkin, 37. The police reportedly woke Edward at 4:00 a.m. to tell him that his beautiful live-in girl-friend of four years had fallen through the third-storey bedroom window of their new townhouse on Hazelton Avenue in Yorkville, where they had lived for just two days, and plunged 26 feet to the lawn. She died two hours later at Wellesley Hospital of a ruptured aorta and internal injuries, according to the autopsy. Edward, who had split his life between his beloved Montreal and Toronto, lost enthusiasm for his adopted city, until years later when his son David made plans to set up a new charitable foundation, separate from the Edper foundation, with some of the windfall the Edward Bronfman family expected to receive when Edper went public.

The Crash of 1987 wreaked havoc with the men who managed the Edper fortunes. They were burdened with more than $200 mil-lion of stock-loans for shares that had suddenly lost up to a third of their market value. The Edper Group companies loaned their senior managers more money so that they could buy more shares under their management share-purchase plans at the lower prices, thus av-eraging down their investment cost. Even so, the stock-loans had be-come golden handcuffs for some of the more recent hires, who had invested in the group late in the bull market.

With so many shell-shocked investors fleeing the stock mar-kets for the relative safety of the money markets, the Edper Group equity factory had to temporarily slow production. Common-share financings in Canada dwindled to $1 billion during the eight months to the end of August 1988, according to the Investment Dealers Association of Canada, compared to $7 billion during the same pe-riod in 1987. Jack Cockwell, who had fostered a revolution in Canada's capital markets during the 1983–87 bull market, decided to shift the group's focus back to corporate workouts. Edper's mer-chant banks — Hees, Great Lakes Group and Carena — would cap-italize on a failure boom.

Great Lakes Group President Ken Clarke later recalled getting several distress calls a day in the wake of the Crash. Great Lakes Group had been reorganized as a merchant bank in 1984 with $450 million of investment capital, contributed 65% by Hees, Brascan and Trilon Financial; 10% by Canadian Imperial Bank of Commerce; 8% by Merrill Lynch Canada; and 2% by Canada Permanent Trust; while Canada Trust, the Belzbergs' First City Trust, Hal Jackman's National Trust and the Romans' Standard Trust all purchased preferred shares. But even though Great Lakes Group had equity capital four times larger than that of Canada's largest investment house, it was not expecting a distress call from Ted Medland, the white-haired patriarch of Wood Gundy Inc., the country's second-largest investment house. Medland phoned Jack Cockwell and Clarke on Thursday, October 29, 1987, the day before Wood Gundy faced a huge underwriting loss from the British government's privatization of British Petroleum PLC, the largest international share offer ever.

At 3:30 that afternoon, Jack Cockwell and Ken Clarke arrived at Wood Gundy's executive offices on the 45th floor of Royal Trust Tower, where Medland told them that the fallout from Black Monday had wiped out the capital Wood Gundy needed to pay the first instalment of its half-interest in the $770 million Canadian allotment of the BP bought deal. The establishment firm had agreed to buy the BP shares from the British government at a price set on October 15, four days before the global stock-market crash. On Black Monday, BP shares tumbled 30% below that price. Late in the afternoon of Friday, October 23, Medland stunned the other members of the Canadian syndicate when he announced that Wood Gundy was going to "tear up the agreement." Unlike a Canadian agreement, there was no "out clause" that let the BP underwriters withdraw if there was a substantial change in the market.

Bank of Canada Governor John Crow and other global central bankers entreated British Chancellor of the Exchequer Nigel Lawson to postpone the BP issue. But Lawson rose in the British Parliament on October 29 to announce, at 5:00 p.m. Toronto time, that the British government planned to go ahead, although it had set a floor price below which the Bank of England would buy back shares. The deal was set to close at 10:00 a.m. the next day, Toronto time.

After listening to Nigel Lawson's announcement in their board-room, Wood Gundy's senior executives turned to Jack Cockwell and Ken Clarke and asked for a $137 million loan to pay the British government the first instalment the next morning and to report-edly "handle [the] liability in the event [the BP shares] were worth zero." They offered the BP shares and Wood Gundy's holding-company shares as collateral. Cockwell and Clarke agreed, then set off through the 10-kilometre maze of underground tunnels beneath the financial district toward the Edper Group offices at Commerce Court West on Bay Street, to report back to their partners.

An hour later, Cockwell and Clarke returned to Woody Gundy with the news that Great Lakes Group would make the loan, charg-ing one percentage point above the prime lending rate, and forgo-ing its customary 20% of profits to sub-underwrite the deal. Later that night, Wood Gundy and Great Lakes Group signed a two-page agreement, and the merchant bank paid the money to the British government the following morning.

By any standard, the BP deal was a monumental flop around the world. Some even tried to pin the blame for the Crash on the British government. As one Goldman Sachs partner in New York City re-portedly shouted at a British counterpart, "Your people damn well better pull it [the BP issue]. If it wasn't for us, you'd all be speaking German." Whenever Wood Gundy sold BP shares, it turned over the proceeds to Great Lakes Group, repaying $100 million of the loan by the end of January — the same week the thrice-spurned bro-kerage firm announced a merger with Canadian Imperial Bank of Commerce. Ultimately, Wood Gundy took an estimated $20 million to $40 million loss on the BP share issue.

The Great Lakes Group bailout of Wood Gundy proved how fast the Edper Group merchant banks could come to the rescue of a distressed business. Canadian investment dealers could move quickly, but they lacked capital. (With an eye to their meagre cap-italization, *The Economist* had dubbed them the "Bay St. babies.")

But once the dealers were swallowed up by the big banks, in the months following Ontario's Mini-Bang of securities deregulation in June 1987, many would set up merchant banks that competed with the Edper Group. In the meantime, the big banks had the capital but found it difficult, given their bureaucratic structures, to make investment decisions quickly. Indeed, several Canadian banks reportedly had turned down Wood Gundy's request for an emergency credit line before chairman Ted Medland called Jack Cockwell and Ken Clarke, less than 24 hours before Wood Gundy's deadline. After its Good-Samaritan rescue of Wood Gundy, the Edper Group was convinced it had found a timely way to chase profit: Its merchant banks, Hees, Great Lakes Group and Carena, had both the capital and the management expertise to act as principals in the restructuring of hemorrhaging businesses.

Paul Reichmann initially viewed the Crash as a contrarian opportunity: Olympia & York was in the markets during the first two days of the bloodbath, buying large share blocks of developer-retailer Campeau Corp. — trading at around $15, almost 50% below its summer high of $30 — and American railroad company Santa Fe Southern Pacific Corp.

Still, Olympia & York had experienced carnage from the Crash. Its recently issued Gulf Canada Resources shares fell $2 5/8 on Black Monday to close at $17 5/8 (36% below their August peak of $27 3/4), and Abitibi-Price shares tumbled $3 3/4 to $29 (33% below their high of $43). And Olympia & York's interlocking investments with the Edper Group had lost about a third of their market value. There were also big fears in the capital markets of the world that the Crash would kill Olympia & York's leasing prospects for Canary Wharf.

Paul Reichmann reminded the fearmongers that Olympia & York had built the first four million square feet of the World Financial Center in Manhattan during the 1981–82 recession, on the strength of a pre-let rate of only 16%. Credit Suisse and Morgan Stanley had agreed to lease space when the Reichmanns salvaged the project, so Canary Wharf had a pre-let rate of 12%. "When we built the World Financial Center, I thought there'd be no repeat of that," Reichmann later told *The Globe and Mail*. "Then the San Francisco redevelopment came along. But something like this...I can't imagine anything like Canary Wharf coming up again. It's exciting, lots of fun." All of these projects had the potential for what Reichmann called "critical mass": a development so big it could change the character of an area, even a landfill at the foot of Manhattan or a semi-derelict district in east London.

By the end of October, Olympia & York had accumulated 1.2 billion shares of Santa Fe Southern Pacific in 10 trading sessions. Even though the Reichmann brothers hadn't made a formal offer for Santa Fe Southern Pacific, a U.S. company with five operating divisions — real estate, petroleum, minerals, pipelines and rail — Paul Reichmann had sent Olympia & York lieutenant Mickey Cohen to its Chicago headquarters in August 1987 with a letter offering to help restructure its undervalued real-estate and energy resources. Santa Fe Southern Pacific rebuffed the Reichmann advances and wooed California's Henley Group, which subsequently made a US$9.9 billion offer of cash and shares for the company. In November 1987 Sante Fe Southern Pacific asked the Reichmanns to consider making an all-cash US$9.9 billion counter-offer, which would have been the largest-ever takeover of an American company by a Canadian one. Olympia & York's advisers began to examine the railway company's confidential financial data.

By that time Olympia & York had also assembled almost 11% of Campeau Corp.'s subordinated voting shares, using some of the proceeds from the November 2 closing of the sale of its 23% stake in Cadillac Fairview to Chicago's JMB Realty Corp., for about $650 million in cash and warrants. On Monday, November 23, 1987, Robert Campeau assured reporters, after a rubber-chicken luncheon speech to the Canadian Club in Toronto, that he wasn't concerned by reports that the Reichmanns were stalking his company. "They are good people," said Campeau, although he conceded that he didn't know what their plans were.

By then the vainglorious and insecure Campeau was too distracted by his own plans. Puffed up from his out-of-nowhere takeover of Allied Stores in late 1986, the deal junkie needed another ego fix. His American financial advisers at First Boston were only too happy to oblige after their top takeover adviser, Bruce Wasserstein, reminded them that their fees from the Canadian — whom their CEO secretly called a "living water torture" — had accounted for half of the firm's profit the year before. Over the hot summer of 1987, First Boston identified the Cincinnati-based American retailing giant, Federated Department Stores, owner of the Bloomingdales chain, as a potential takeover target for Campeau Corp. At the beginning of October, Campeau secretly began buying shares of Federated at US$45 each. When the Crash knocked down the stock to US$34 a share, Campeau reportedly placed a frantic to Bruce Wasserstein and urged him to get First Boston to grab all the loose Federated shares. "We ought to launch a bid for Federated now," Campeau reportedly agitated. "Let's make an offer while the shareholders are still desperate." But First Boston hesitated; Wasserstein didn't think a full takeover was feasible, because Campeau Corp. had no financing. It was more likely that once Federated was in play, Campeau Corp. would be able to pick up some prime department-store assets. Campeau's advisers also wondered if their client's notoriously short attention span could stay the course through yet another multi-billion-dollar takeover battle. Campeau in-house adviser Carolyn Buck Luce later told author John Rothchild that the sense she got from a Manhattan summit meeting in mid-November "was that Bob saw it as a choice between taking over Federated right [then], or going skiing."

Around the same time, on Wednesday, November 25, 1987, the Reichmann brothers agreed to swap their 49% stake in liquor and resources conglomerate Hiram Walker for cash and convertible preferred shares in Allied Lyons, making them the biggest single shareholder in the British food giant, with a 10% stake, fully diluted. Bay Street considered that move a prelude to further restructuring of GW Utilities, which held 83% of Consumers Gas.

In early 1988, the Reichmanns also reached a rapprochement with Santa Fe Southern Pacific, after the railroad company thwarted a takeover by paying out a US$4.7 billion special dividend that buried it in debt. Paul Reichmann and Mickey Cohen joined the Santa Fe Southern Pacific board to see what could be done.

By that time Robert Campeau had secured the support of Campeau Corp.'s board of directors for his proposed takeover of Federated Stores. On Monday, January 25, 1988, Campeau Corp. made a formal offer of US$4.2 billion for Federated Stores, or US$47 a share — with no financing in place, not even a "highly confident" letter from a commercial bank. One week later, Campeau's celebrated takeover adviser, Bruce Wasserstein, left First Boston to set up his own firm called Wasserstein, Perella & Co. Campeau was furious, although he ultimately decided to pay advisory fees to Wasserstein as well as to First Boston. On February 5, Federated rejected Campeau Corp.'s bid because of its lack of financing commitments.

On February 2, 1988, Robert Campeau met with Paul Reichmann in the Waldorf-Astoria Hotel apartments in Manhattan to try to charm Reichmann into putting up money for his Federated bid. The outcome was similar to the two developers, November 1986 meeting in Toronto, when Campeau had sought Reichmann's backing for the Allied Stores takeover. Again, Reichmann reminded Campeau that he didn't know anything about retailing and recommended that Campeau find a retailing partner to help fund the Federated takeover.

In fact, Campeau was negotiating with Edward DeBartolo, his equity partner on the Allied Stores takeover, in a separate room at the Waldorf. Campeau made sure Reichmann and DeBartolo did not meet. A week later, DeBartolo agreed to make a US$480 million loan and to form a development partnership with Campeau in the U.S., and Olympia & York agreed to buy US$260 million of convertible debentures in Campeau Corp., the proceeds of which could be used for the Federated takeover. On February 11, 1988, Campeau announced that DeBartolo and the Reichmanns were backing his Federated bid and upped his offer to US$61 a share.

"We are investing in Campeau Corp., not the particular as-sets," Paul Reichmann told Eric Reguly for *The Financial Post*, ex-plaining that Olympia & York's interest in Federated Stores would be limited to a passive stake in Campeau Corp. Reichmann did concede that he was captivated by Robert Campeau's sales spiel about the synergies between real estate and retailing: how Campeau was going to use the department stores as flagships for the shopping malls he planned to erect around the globe. Some speculated that Olympia & York saw an opportunity to ultimately own some of Federated's real-estate holdings, which then carried a book value of US$2 billion. But Paul Reichmann later told arbitrageur Andrew Sarlos that he was simply fascinated by Campeau and believed then that Olympia & York's investment in Campeau Corp. was well secured. Sarlos felt that Reichmann "hadn't comprehended that Campeau would gamble as much as he did on the Federated deal."

Within days Campeau Corp. had bumped up its Federated offer to US$65 a share, US$10 a share above a personal limit Robert Campeau had established in November. Traders called it the "Wasser-stein Premium" — to pay Bruce Wasserstein's fees. On February 16, 1988, Campeau Corp.'s Federated bid went up again to US$66 a share, as Robert Campeau flew to London to raise cash by selling Allied's Brooks Brothers to Marks & Spencer for an unexpectedly rich US$750 million. On Friday, February 26, Campeau Corp.'s team of advisers met with the Federated board and agreed to raise the offer still higher to US$69 a share, but they couldn't reach Campeau for approval. Finally, at seven p.m. their time, they found him in a restaurant in Austria. From the restaurant's payphone, Campeau agreed to the US$6.2 billion price, spoke to Federated's CEO and then went back to his midnight meal. But the frazzled Federated di-rectors stalled and decided to wait until Monday to sign off on the deal, mainly because there was still no letter of commitment from a com-mercial bank. Campeau had been dithering between two American banks: Citibank NA and Security Pacific Bank.

As Robert Campeau jetted back from Europe in the Allied Gulfstream III, a bidding war exploded. Over the weekend Federated had been secretly negotiating with R.H. Macy & Co., and that Monday Macy had offered a US$73.50 share package of cash and Macy shares. "I know what they're doing is illegal," a livid Campeau told Richard Siklos for the *Financial Times of Canada* from his Manhattan suite. "What those guys [Federated] have done is they've given them [Macy] an option to get out and not risk anything, and they've made a deal full of ifs, buts and maybes. I've never seen anything so ridiculous and so notorious." Still, the Macy threat didn't stop the Campeaus and their youngest son from going on a ski vacation in Vail, Colorado, followed by a little holiday at their home in Palm Beach.

On March 21, 1988, Campeau and Olympia & York signed their deal. The following day, Campeau Corp. raised its Federated offer to US$73 a share, all cash, unleashing a volley of offers and counteroffers — US$74.50 a share from Macy, US$75 a share from Campeau Corp., US$77 a share from Campeau Corp., US$77.50 a share from Macy, US$79 a share from Macy.

On March 29, Skadden, Arps, Slate, Meagher & Flom's Joseph Flom, the U.S. securities lawyer and expert on hostile takeovers, stopped the out-of-control bidding by negotiating a truce between the warring camps.

On Good Friday, April 1, Campeau Corp. agreed to pay US$73.50 a share, all cash, or US$6.6 billion for Federated Stores, and to sell certain divisions of Federated to Macy for US$1.1 billion. Federated Stores would be the largest-ever takeover of an American company by a Canadian, double Campeau's US$3.6 billion takeover of Allied Stores.

The following Monday, the Reichmanns completed their purchase of US$260 million of Campeau Corp. convertible debentures, boosting Olympia & York's interest to 22%, fully diluted, from 11.2%.

A week after Robert Campeau took control of Federated he changed his mind about hiring experienced retail executive Robert Morosky to run operations, instead naming himself CEO of Federated and Allied.

During Olympia & York's overlapping negotiations with Campeau, Santa Fe Pacific and Allied Lyons, the three Toronto-based Reichmann brothers and their mother, Renée, took time out to launch a $100 million libel lawsuit against *Toronto Life* magazine. The family was outraged by a November 1987 article which examined the origins of the family and its fortune in Europe and North Africa. Before launching the action in 1988, the Reichmanns had hired private investigator Jules Kroll of Kroll & Associates in New York City to review the magazine's allegations, spending $6 million on the investigation. Freespeech activists protested against the Reichmanns for their lawsuit, but in March 1991, *Toronto Life* printed an apology: "An exhaustive review, since the action started, of thousands of archival documents from various countries as well as the pre-trial testimony by members of the Reichmann family and others and a review of the family's own papers have confirmed that none of the allegations and insinuations should ever have been raised." All the negative insinuations about the Reichmann family and Olympia & York were "totally false," said the magazine, which had reached an out-of-court settlement with the Reichmanns, a large amount of which was donated to charity.

While all this was going on, the Reichmanns were also jetting to London and back to oversee the development of their mega project on the Thames. Olympia & York's team of architects and planners had enlarged Travelstead's master plan for Canary Wharf to more than 13 million square feet — one-and-half-times larger than Manhattan's World Financial Center — but softened its North American character. Instead of a shockingly modern trio of 85-storey skyscrapers, the revised master plan called for 26 buildings in a more familiar classical style, all less than 35 storeys, except for one stainless steel-clad, 50-storey skyscraper with a pyramid-shaped hat, designed by architect Cesar Pelli. It was still too much for the blue-bloods. "I personally would go mad working in a place like that," complained Prince Charles to Paul Reichmann, in front of television cameras, after viewing the model. "There's no need for us to ape Manhattan." Certainly it was a disappointing reaction from the king-in-waiting, but not unexpected given his quaint architectural views. Reichmann was counting on British Prime Minister Margaret Thatcher to push the project forward, particularly after the House of Commons' Public Accounts Committee lambasted the London Docklands Development Corp. for selling the land to Olympia & York so cheaply. In mid-May 1988, Paul Reichmann stood by as the indefatigable Thatcher, dressed in a tweed suit, white earrings and a matching hardhat, drove a ceremonial pile into Canary Wharf from the cab of a piledriver.

A month later Margaret Thatcher was in Toronto with U.S. President Ronald Reagan and Canadian Prime Minister Brian Mulroney — her compatriots in the neoconservative revolution — for the annual economic summit of the Group of Seven industrial nations. Canada was the host country to the coveted international schmoozefest. Trevor Eyton had even raised corporate donations for lavish media tents and pavilions on Summit Square, offering free food, liquor and entertainment, in a bid to influence the world's hacks to write glowing reports about Toronto, as part of the city's drive to get the 1996 Olympics. The Reichmanns had contributed $100,000 to the cause.

To cap off the four-day summit, Thatcher spoke as the guest of honour at Conrad Black's annual black-tie Hollinger Dinner (until then, stag) at the Toronto Club, to a standing ovation from 170 of Canada's right-of-centre elite, including Eyton, Jack Cockwell and the Reichmann brothers. The next day in Ottawa, Thatcher lauded both Black and Paul Reichmann as constructive, entrepreneurial forces much admired in Britain.

By mid-summer the Reichmann brothers found themselves in business with a different sort of character — a so-called vulture investor — when the Henley Group sold its interest in Santa Fe Southern Pacific to Sam Zell's Itel Corp. of Chicago for US$1.2 billion and some of Henley's assets. Zell, who called himself "The Grave Dancer," liked to flout convention: He wore jeans and cowboy boots to the office, rode a Ducati motorcycle, and had enough energy to power a small city. Bearded and balding, he was famous for his "war at four" parties at his house in Sun Valley, Idaho, where up to 20 people would shoot paint pellets at each other for fun. If a Reichmann-Zell partnership had proved compatible, Olympia & York and Itel could have pushed for effective control of Santa Fe Southern Pacific, since the two companies together owned almost 40% of the company, with its real-estate and energy resources, which O & Y considered "undervalued." But it didn't prove compatible.

The Reichmanns' $10 billion diversification hadn't worked, and they had decided to move away from investments in the resources sector. The Reichmanns hired investment banker Morgan Stanley of New York City to analyze Olympia & York's holdings and compare the relative performance of its real-estate and investment portfolios. The conclusion: They had underestimated the potential of their global real-estate projects, ones with "critical mass" like Canary Wharf, which promised better returns than a Canadian Pacific-like conglomerate.

Meanwhile, as the Reichmanns took steps to return to their real-estate roots, the senior managers at the Edper Group seemed almost giddy at the potential of their latest strategic thrust, a return to the corporate workout business.

Chapter 7

Workout Wizards

"We're the only guys on Bay Street praying for a recession," Bill L'Heureux crowed to reporters, after Hees's standing-room-only annual shareholders' meeting in Commerce Hall in Toronto on Tuesday, April 5, 1988. In an economic downturn, Hees expected to use its vaunted management expertise and capital to rescue distressed companies and then walk away with a large chunk of the value it salvaged.

Workouts weren't a new business for the Edper Group. In the early 1970s, Jack Cockwell began to set the pattern for future workouts when Edper exercised its option to swap debt for equity in Marigot Investments, after the Caribbean real-estate company missed several payments on its loan from Edper. Cockwell then dropped in an Edper executive, Tim Price, to replace Marigot's former majority owner as president in Montreal. To sort out Marigot's investment in a trading company called Brysons, Cockwell also sent Tim Casgrain and David Kerr down to Antigua for two years. To participate in the Marigot turnaround, Cockwell and Price borrowed money from their bosses, Edward and Peter Bronfman, to buy stock in the renamed Mico Enterprises — with Cockwell reportedly borrowing an astounding $1.2 million, 60 times his then annual salary of $20,000. It was in the Mico Enterprises annual reports that Cockwell began to articulate his philosophy of corporate redemocratization.

David Kerr had joined the Edper circle in 1971 when Jack Cockwell wooed him from Touche Ross to help manage cash flow and general financial planning at the Montreal Forum, home of the Canadiens hockey club.

In 1975, Jack Cockwell recruited another former colleague, Michael Cornelissen, to join his cadre of ex-Touche Ross accountants at Mico. Not long after, Cockwell parachuted Cornelissen into financially distressed Trizec to replace its vice-president of finance. Trizec was a textbook workout that began with Cockwell's classic "book" on the financial situation, which evaluated the company and the managers' plans for dealing with its problems. But it was Cornelissen who executed the Trizec turnaround in the late 1970s, applying Cockwell's formula of matching assets and liabilities. And it was Cornelissen who got the credit for the workout, which proved to be Edper's most successful.

Late in 1978, David Kerr, who had become one of the trustees for Edward and Peter Bronfman's trusts, organized Edper's move from Montreal to Toronto, where he took over the management of Hees, while Jack Cockwell and Trevor Eyton went after Brascan. Mico merged with Hees in 1980, and Tim Price, Tim Casgrain and Bryan McJannet joined their friends at Edper's new base of operations in the I.M. Pei-designed Commerce Court West, just in time for the recession of 1981–82.

Trevor Eyton introduced the Hees team to its next workout assignment: Dylex co-founder Jimmy Kay and his non-Dylex investments in real estate, restaurants and oil and gas. The Bank of Montreal planned to push Kay into personal bankruptcy, until Hees offered to buy out his $22 million of loans at a substantial discount. Eyton was one of a group of investors, including Trizec's Harold Milavsky, who had pooled $16 million with Kay for a 26% interest in North Canadian Oils in 1977. Eyton also had been Kay's personal lawyer for several years. After Hees's 1981–84 workout of Kay's private assets, known on Bay Street as the "Jimmy Kay bear hug," Hees ended up with a 33% stake in Dexleigh Corp., formed out of its reorganization of Foodex Inc. (Kay's restaurant and racetrack venture) and Hatleigh Corp. (Kay's real-estate and oil-and-gas holding company), as well as a 30% interest in North Canadian Oils. A year later, Hatleigh and North Canadian Oils participated in the Edper-backed takeover of Union Enterprises, buying a quarter of the almost $200 million in preferred shares that Unicorp used to bankroll the takeover. Elsewhere in 1985, a company registered in Kay's name bought $1.4 million, and Noranda $74 million, of an initial public offering by the federal government's Canada Development Corp., with its rich Kidd Creek Mines, when Eyton was director of its parent, Canada Development Investment Corp., and a member of CDIC's special Divestiture Committee. By 1987, Hees had swapped its interest in North Canadian Oils, along with its stake in Norcen Energy Resources (from Conrad Black's Hollinger), for shares in Noranda. Hees then swapped the Noranda shares for cash and shares in Brascan, as well as a preferred-share portfolio, in a serial transaction.

Hees's accounting policy, in accordance with generally accepted accounting principles, was to defer gains on asset exchanges until Hees was free to deal with them and could be assured of the value that could be realized from them. Hees's deferred gains from options, equity-conversion privileges and recapture (where Hees bought loans at significant discount) were its inner reserves. Bay Street argued that Hees set up computerized profit objectives and then managed their earnings to meet those targets. Hees did take reserves against high-risk assets, which effectively reduced its reported earnings, but the Hees partners claimed that the merchant bank had never drawn down on its inner reserves in order to support its reported earnings.

Financial services were the cornerstone of Hees's operations during much of the 1980s. For example, Hees acted as a sub-underwriter on some bought-deal financings at the beginning of the 1983–87 bull market, before Great Lakes Group assumed that function. These were 80:20 deals, or structured partnerships, where Hees earned the spread between the rate it charged on the short-term loan and its own cost of funding, as well as taking 20% of the profit. Hees made similar 80:20 deals with high-net-worth individuals, putting up 80% of the money for their business ventures in exchange for 20% of the profit. To limit the risk that the principal wouldn't be repaid, the loans were of a short duration (sometimes up to a year, but usually three to six months) and Hees insisted on full collateralization, usually with an equity component. Hees's financial-services loans were meant to be confidential; the partners did not disclose the names of their clients nor the amount of their indebtedness.

For example, when Hungarian-Canadian arbitrageur Andrew Sarlos faced a financial crisis during the recession of 1981–82, Trevor Eyton and First City's Sam Belzberg secretly came to his rescue with two $10 million cheques. "I know without Trevor's insistence, Jack Cockwell would never have approved the [Hees] loan," Sarlos recalled. Sarlos was loaned the $10 million in 1982 at prime plus three-quarters, plus a slice of his future trading profits. Sarlos was able to pay back the principal by April 10, 1983. The following day Sarlos's heart stopped and he was rushed to Toronto General Hospital, where he underwent a triple bypass operation.

In early 1984 a recovered Sarlos launched the Sarlos & Zuckerman Fund and later two other arbitrage funds, whose investors, at $100,000 a pop, included some high-profile friends of Edper: Sam Hashman (Edward and Peter Bronfman's partner in Great West Saddlery, which was ultimately rolled into Trizec), the Cummings family (early joint-venture partners with Edward and Peter Bronfman), Patrick Keenan (one of Trevor Eyton's cronies from the Canyon Beauport Investment Club and the Patino family's Canadian representative), the Shiff family (who had flipped their investment in Bramalea into Trizec preferred shares during 1984–85), Lionel Schipper (a trustee of the Peter Bronfman family trust), Peter Widdrington (CEO of Labatt and a close friend of Peter Bronfman's), Peter Munk (an old friend of Sarlos's, a former law client of Trevor Eyton's and someone who had benefited from a timely Hees bridge loan in the early 1980s), and many other Bay Street luminaries. In 1985, Sarlos's funds pocketed almost $8 million of arbitrage profits from the Reichmann takeover of Gulf Canada. These funds also participated in the Edper-backed takeover of Union Enterprises that year.

Sarlos was riding high until the Crash of 1987 trashed the market values of his arbitrage plays. But the party wasn't over — not yet. With the across-the-board drop in share prices, many companies became attractive takeover targets. In 1988, Sarlos's funds made almost $7 million of arbitrage profits from Robert Campeau's assault on Federated Stores, Nova Corp.'s battle for Polysar Energy & Chemical Corp. (the former Canada Development Corp.), and the fight to control RJR Nabisco, the ultimate business drama in the twilight of the Reagan era. Fortunately Sarlos had wound up two of the three funds before he took a $5 million hit on the aborted management buyout of the parent of United Airlines on October 13, 1989. The Dow Jones Industrial Average plummeted nearly 200 points that Friday on news of the busted deal, prompting fears of another market crash. That was the end of the feast, and Sarlos wound up the remaining fund.

Hees had expected to begin salvaging the Roaring '80s immediately after the Crash of 1987, so it cut back on the capital it allocated to Bay Street dealmakers in order to concentrate on the workout business. Hees got its first post-Crash management-services assignment in January 1988, when it was called in to rescue credit-card manufacturer National Business Systems on less than 24 hours' notice, amid allegations of financial wrongdoing by the company's management. Hees did an exploratory two-week walkaround, but underestimated the severity of NBS's problems. "We had no idea how deep the worm went. We dig through layers and layers and it's still rotten," Bill L'Heureux later conceded. Hees put up US$10 million for a standby credit facility with NBS's banking group and installed Hees partner Tim Casgrain as temporary CEO, at an annual salary of $10. Not long after, former NBS executives were charged with criminal offences ranging from inflating revenue and profit figures to stealing almost $10 million. NBS's two major client groups — banks and governments — were understandably skittish about the criminal allegations. Casgrain tried to distance NBS from its past, as he negotiated with NBS creditors and regulators to get a refinancing plan approved. Hees decided to waive its usual practice of taking payment for its services in the form of an equity stake; instead, it took $5 million in management fees.

Hees's workout of Vancouver-based Versatile Corp. was more of a textbook restructuring. Fund manager Peter Cundill, a jazz pianist, judo expert, marathon runner and former financial adviser to the CEMP Bronfmans, called Hees in the spring of 1988, after Versatile's Burrard Yarrows shipyards in Vancouver and Victoria, as well as its nonshipbuilding investments, hit bottom. To meet debt payments, Versatile was liquidating assets. The banks planned to push Versatile into bankruptcy, until Hees came in as a vulture investor and bought them out at a discount, offering only $19 million for Versatile's $92 million of bank debt. A company executive later recalled that the banks felt that Hees was "lowballing them," but it agreed to be cashed out at 21 cents on the dollar. Peter Cundill hoped that a financial restructuring of Versatile would help the Cundill Fund recoup some value from its holdings of Versatile shares and debentures. It did. Hees later converted Versatile preferred shares to common shares and consolidated them one for ten. Then it raised $162.5 million for the renamed B.C. Pacific Capital in two rights offerings with warrant options. "The reality is, when you have nothing, the only way [forward] is if somebody comes in with significant money," B.C. Pacific Capital president Brian Kenning told merchant banker Brian Baxter, then a journalist with *The Financial Post*, but "in the workout business, a lot of shareholders have lost a lot of money, and it's a bitter pill to swallow."

What kind of people would choose to become mired in the contentiousness and complexities of a corporate workout? Unlike takeovers or mergers, the work wasn't glamorous. A Hees partner was often stuck in the same company for years, dealing with one crisis after another. "I often feel frustrated at the end of the day," Tim Casgrain later conceded about National Business Systems, "but I like the do-or-die immediacy of this work. There is no time for a bureaucracy when you're fighting fires." Since it was Jack Cockwell's program, he handpicked the people to execute it. In 1988 six of Hees's seven managing partners were ex-Touche Ross accountants:

silver-haired Bryan McJannet, then 50, was Cockwell's former mentor from Touche Ross in Capetown; Tim Price, 45, and Tim Casgrain, 39, were Cockwell's colleagues from Touche Ross in Montreal; and South African-born Manfred Walt, 35, Ukrainian-born George Myhal, 31, and Robert Harding, 30, had been plucked from Touche Ross in Toronto. The odd one out was freckle-faced Bill L'Heureux, 40, a law partner from Tory Tory DesLauriers & Binnington, who had been part of Trevor Eyton's cluster and later inherited much of Eyton's work for the Edper Group when Eyton left to join Brascan in 1979. Four years later, L'Heureux followed his mentor to the Edper Group, but not to Brascan.

Bill L'Heureux joined Hees because the merchant bank had become the boot camp for future Edper Group executives — the place where they were schooled in the Edper way of doing things. After all, one of the Edper Group's business principles was to parachute in its own executives "should the performance of a group company be below standard or should the management of a group company fail to conform to group values." Thus Michael Cornelissen, one of Cockwell's colleagues from Touche Ross in Montreal, was dropped into bureaucratic Royal Trustco in 1983, after spending six years on the Trizec workout. At Royal Trustco, Cornelissen hired Courtney Pratt, a human-resources expert from Touche Ross Management Consultants in Calgary, whom Cornelissen had used to instil the Edper values at Trizec. In 1983, Hees partner Bryan McJannet was installed as president and CEO of the newly reorganized Dexleigh Corp., known on Bay Street as a "son of Hees." In 1984, British-born Ken Clarke, a former Merrill Lynch Canada corporate finance executive who had worked with Cockwell at Touche Ross in Montreal, was appointed president and CEO of the Great Lakes Group, another "son of Hees." In October 1986, Hees managing partner David Kerr, yet another of Cockwell's contemporaries from Touche Ross in Montreal, was parachuted into Noranda as a senior vice-president of corporate planning; in early 1987, he was named president. That November, Pratt left Royal Trustco for Noranda, to help Kerr infuse the reluctant resources giant with the

Edper ethos. "We [Hees] help other companies in the group and lead them by example," L'Heureux later boasted to *Euromoney*.

Jack Cockwell was the principal author of the famous Edper Group credo outlined in a formal document called *Statement of Beliefs and Shared Values* — first articulated by Cockwell in tracts on the back of Mico Enterprises annual reports and later honed in essays inside the 1985–88 Hees annual reports. Cockwell prohibited Edper Group executives from enjoying the traditional perks of corporate jets, company apartments, chauffeured cars and palatial offices, and from becoming rich on big salaries and stock options; they were supposed to reap most of their reward in the same way their shareholders did, from share appreciation in their group companies. The disembodied principles looked good on paper, but not even Cockwell could abolish the human element. For example, when Trizec moved its headquarters to Calgary from Montreal in the late 1970s, president Harold Milavsky, a half-bald and bespectacled near-twin of Peter Bronfman, operated out of a plush office suite with three corner windows, velvet wallpaper, leather couches and a private dining room, "furnished to resemble an eighteenth-century Quebec kitchen parlour." Cockwell and Milavsky battled for years over his office and over Milavksy's use of a corporate jet. Later, Labatt's CEO and president Peter Widdrington, a flamboyant executive with flowing locks, scoffed at the idea that Edper would stop his senior managers from throwing lavish parties in their owners' box when SkyDome opened in 1989. Schmoozing was part of the corporate culture in the beer business.

Trevor Eyton was another exception to the rule. Still the group's networker without peer, Eyton was a welcome guest at gala dinners at 24 Sussex Drive in Ottawa, the Prime Minister's residence, and was front and centre among Toronto's power brokers. For example, Eyton and Galen Weston — who controlled Canada's biggest grocer, Loblaw's, and played polo at Windsor Castle with Prince Charles — were directors of the Toronto Ontario Olympic Council, set up to bid for the 1996 Games (Atlanta won the bid over six competing cities). And Eyton claimed to have the most jobs in Canada: sitting on the boards of two dozen companies (almost all Edper Group boards, except for Allan Slaight's Standard Broadcasting Corp. and a few others) and at least six public-service organizations, including the federal government's International Trade Advisory Committee. But despite Eyton's almost constant travel, he did not use a corporate jet. And although Eyton and Jack Cockwell both preferred to get around Toronto in their Jaguars, they were also seen on public transportation such as the Go Train or the subway.

Edper Group executives were expected to live modestly outside of work, belying their wealth. "There are certainly a lot of people who view [the Edper Group values] as a religion," George Myhal said in *Euromoney*. "It goes beyond work and extends to the way we live and behave." Peter Bronfman, a child of one of North America's great fortunes, set the tone with the frugal lifestyle of a man who had struggled; Bronfman said he had already done the "big house thing" and social whirl with his first wife in Montreal and had no desire to do it again in Toronto with his third wife, Lynda Hamilton. In a rare social sighting at Conrad Black's party to celebrate the 100th anniversary of *Saturday Night* magazine in January 1988, Peter Bronfman was spotted in conversation with novelist, feminist and anti-free trade activist Margaret Atwood, not a Bay Street mogul. The wryly self-deprecating Bronfman assiduously avoided the charity balls of Toronto's glitterati, preferring to support less-fashionable causes like Jessie's, a home for unwed mothers.

Jack Cockwell, like Peter Bronfman, wanted a low-key social life, but he'd struck a compromise with his common-law wife, Wendy Cecil-Cockwell. Their $1 million-plus Rosedale home, purchased from Merrill Lynch Canada's Michael Sanderson in 1986, was understated but exclusive. Cockwell developed his own master plan for planting the garden and then reportedly spent hours cultivating roses. He even claimed that his favourite vacation spot was his garden. If something broke around the house, Cockwell took it apart and repaired it himself; apparently the corporate fix-it artist needed something to fix even when he was away from the office. During

the winter of 1988, when their first son was born, Cockwell took on
City Hall after he was fined for not clearing the snow from the side-
walk in front of their house. Even when Wendy managed to drag him
out to black-tie events, he was sometimes spotted reading documents by penlight during the performances. But it didn't really
matter if Cockwell set a bad example. Peter Bronfman had articulated the business principle that Edper Group executives devote a
chunk of their off-hours to their communities: "Edper encourages
the sharing of the wealth created by its affiliates with the communities in which they operate." The group even matched the time
contributed by its executives to charitable organizations with financial contributions. Thus Royal Trustco's Michael Cornelissen
headed Toronto's fund-raising campaign for the United Way in
1984. And when Cornelissen moved off the United Way board,
Royal Trustco's Courtney Pratt took his place and went on to serve
as the 1986 chairman. Peter Bronfman also decreed that the Edper
Group be "environmentally conscious in all of its operations."

But at Hees, where the "Edper clones" were manufactured, there
was little time for do-good committees or outside board appointments. Hees junior partners routinely worked 16-hour days; managing partners, minimum 10-hour days. Hees partners were also
expected to give up weekends and holidays during a workout.
Cockwell set the pace, often labouring in his Brascan office on the 48th
floor of Commerce Court West until well after midnight. Although
in theory any three Hees partners could commit to a deal as long as
they informed the other partners before the end of the day, in prac-
tice they often ran it by Cockwell. After all, it was Cockwell's program; he may have handed over the work to the Hees partners but
Cockwell monitored the execution of each assignment and provided
daily counsel, often taking the elevator down to the 44th floor to eat
lunch in Hees's glass-walled boardroom. The Hees partners ate lunch
together every day, usually sandwiches grabbed from the fridge. On
Fridays, selected Hees board members such as Cockwell, Peter
Bronfman, Trevor Eyton, David Kerr, Michael Cornelissen and Ken
Clarke joined the lunch-box crowd for weekly catch-up meetings.

Peter Bronfman's influence at these lunch meetings was said to be subtle; he left few fingerprints. Edward Bronfman had stopped attending.

The lunchroom had the feel of a grown-up boys' club, with plenty of fuckspeak and sports talk flying back and forth. That wasn't unusual in business, where most of the players were men. Indeed, if figures of speech based on fornication and sports were suddenly banned, North America's informal business communication might be reduced to pure mathematics. Most of Hees's managing partners were ex-Touche Ross accountants, so they could communicate very quickly. That took a lot of the stress out of human relations. Lawyer Bill L'Heureux later explained why he felt so at home among the CAs. Big professional firms like Tory Tory DesLauriers & Binnington or Touche Ross were all organized like pyramid schemes, with a constant influx of young lawyers or CAs at the bottom, toiling round the clock, eating hundreds of takeout meals and earning far more for the partners than they ever took home. So the Hees partners had experienced parallel universes as young lawyers or CAs. They also had contact sports in common.

The flat-bellied jock culture was an integral part of the Edper ethos. Bill L'Heureux was a former star defenceman for the University of Toronto's Varsity Blues hockey team; he had even played with a broken hand one year during the national championships. Noranda's David Kerr, 44, who didn't smoke and seldom drank, played hockey for the Toronto Bionics in an oldtimers' league and coached his daughter's hockey team. Trilon's Gordon Cunningham, 43, another former hockey star and law partner from Tory Tory DesLauriers & Binnington, revealed his competitive streak at a charity squash match in Toronto against one of the world's top professional players, Sharif Khan. "Khan walked out with hardly any warm-up, just to shoot a few balls around. Next thing you know, the sweat was really starting to pour off him. Damned if Gordon wasn't trying to beat him," one of the fund-raising directors told Brian Baxter for *The Financial Post* in early 1988. Wendy Cecil-Cockwell later confessed how intimidated she was by the group's high testosterone count — until she took up long-distance running in her early 30s and won the Toronto Marathon, as well as the respect of her jock colleagues. Model-handsome Robert Harding was another marathoner. L'Heureux kept in shape with biking holidays in Europe and regular aerobics classes at the Royal Canadian Yacht Club's building near the York Club; he was a member of the Royal Canadian Yacht Club, even though he didn't own a yacht. Royal Trustco's Michael Cornelissen, 45, who regularly bounced to the beat at The Fitness Institute's aerobic classes, was the competitive sailor in the group, with his yacht *Psychopath*. Trevor Eyton was a member of the Royal Canadian Yacht Club, but he preferred to golf or play tennis with Bay Street tycoons like Toronto Dominion Bank's Richard Thomson and Wood Gundy's Ed King, as well as Trilon Financial's Gordon Cunningham, at weekend camps held at Ontario resorts, such as Manitou's Inn & Tennis Club. That befitted Eyton's statesman-like status within the group. At Eyton's annual Brascan staff picnics on his Caledon country estate, however, the free-for-all soccer games were so savage that one year Jack Cockwell reportedly broke his collarbone. The "Edper clones" may have been decent guys off the field, but many of them were terrors in sports and in business.

Although the Hees partners worshipped Jack Cockwell as their spiritual leader, he was no saint. His temper tantrums were the stuff of Bay Street legends. Cockwell had such a puritan faith in the divine specialness of the Edper Group and its managers that he would explode into a tirade if someone challenged their business code. Any opposition was personal. On Edper's enemies list were Bernie Ghert, Austin Taylor and Tom Kierans, among others. Before the Unicorp takeover of Union Enterprises in 1985, Cockwell had tried to persuade Union Gas adviser Kierans that the utility should refinance by buying $300 million of preferred shares issued by the Edper Group. Kierans said no. Later he recalled how Cockwell screamed, cursed, struck the table and pushed chairs around the room because he couldn't get his way. Then at the Ontario Energy Board hearings, Kierans called Unicorp's preferred shares "the Canadian equivalent of American junk bonds." To

challenge the technical genius of preferred-share financing was to
toy with one of Cockwell's obsessions.

But by the spring of 1988 Jack Cockwell was worried that problems at Unicorp Canada might erode the value of the Edper Group's
$135 million-plus investment in Unicorp preferred shares. A seriously
ill George Mann, then 56, had approached Hees about his need to re-
capitalize his public and private holdings, held through Townsview
Properties Ltd. Hees referred Mann to Ian Cockwell, Jack's youngest
brother, who on May 6, 1988, had set up a new company called
Townsview Investments Ltd. to hold Mann's control block in Unicorp.
As Kimberley Noble and Dan Westall later reported for *The Globe and
Mail*, Ian Cockwell had rounded up his own Westcliff Management
Services Ltd. and three other private investors — Andrew Sarlos's
Barnwood Investments (named after Sarlos's home address in Don
Mills), Northstar Investment Corp. (a subsidiary of Canadian North
Star Corp., which boasted former Hees managing partner David
Kerr as a director and had once controlled a block of Union Gas
stock) and Realwest Energy Corp. (among its principals were Hees
partner Tim Casgrain and Vancouver acquisitors Jack Poole, Edgar
Kaiser Jr., Peter Brown and Charles "Chunky" Woodward) — to in-
vest $28 million in Townsview Investments, for a 38% stake.

Bay Street was suspicious of the deal, arguing that it was a
sneaky way for the Edper Group to gain control of Union Gas,
which it had long coveted. Even though Ian Cockwell's companies
were at arm's length from Hees in a legal sense, they seemed en-
tangled in every other sense. Out of Hees's old office space on the
15th floor of Commerce Court West, Ian Cockwell's Westcliff
Management Services ran several private companies, including
Arteco Holdings, whose directors on incorporation included Hees
managing partners Bill L'Heureux and George Myhal, as well as
two Trilon Financial officials, and ATI Corp. and its subsidiary
Waruda Holdings, which had once boasted Kerr and Casgrain on its
three-man board. During the 1980s, Hees reportedly had even
loaned ATI and Waruda almost $300 million. Yet years after

Townsview Investments Ltd. appointed Ian Cockwell and L'Heureux to its three-man board on May 19, 1988, an ingenuous L'Heureux claimed not to know the identities of Townsview Investment's investors because they were Ian Cockwell's "private clients."

As the Townsview Investments deal was set to close, Mann went into Toronto General Hospital in June 1988 to undergo quadruple-bypass heart surgery. He returned to work 10 days later. Bay Street expected L'Heureux to lobby Mann, whose two children weren't interested in succeeding him, to pass on his controlling 62% stake in Townsview Investments to an Edper affiliate or, at the very least, to stop Townsview from selling its Unicorp stake to a non-Edper company. Ian Cockwell joined the Unicorp board that summer.

Meanwhile, Hees got another distress call from Jimmy Kay, who had engineered a leveraged buyout a year earlier of Red Carpet Distributors Inc., a wholesale food division of Hudson's Bay Co., with a $70 million loan from National Bank of Canada and a $60 million promissory note to Hudson's Bay, part of the Thomson corporate empire. On July 6, 1988, Red Carpet Distributors was on the brink of financial collapse when Kay kicked out his partner Norman Paul and installed Hees's Bryan McJannet as president. McJannet began to analyze the business and its problems and to prepare a new operating plan. Hees offered to inject working capital into Red Carpet Distributors in return for a significant equity stake, but Hudson's Bay and National Bank both rejected the plan. Then National Bank called its loan to Red Carpet Distributors, moving in on Friday, August 12, to change the locks and seize the inventory. In its 1988 annual report, Hees scolded National Bank for "acting precipitously in enforcing its security. The unnecessary destruction of a valuable business and the loss of over 1,000 jobs has led to a major lender liability claim. The pursuit of this claim is certain to make lenders in Canada act more carefully in the future before calling their loans."

That summer, Hees was also caught in the crossfire between Kay and his Dylex partner Wilfred Posluns, who forced Kay out of their retail empire in mid-July 1988 and sued him for breaching their

partnership agreement by allegedly pledging his Dylex stock to
Hees in 1983. Dylex, an acronym for "Damn your lousy excuses,"
was then Canada's biggest retail clothing chain. To complicate mat-
ters, Kay's personal lawyer at the time of the Hees workout was
Bill L'Heureux, who had inherited most of Trevor Eyton's clients at
Tory Tory DesLauriers & Binnington.

Some of the friends and associates in Edper's orbit came into
view again in September 1988, when Varitech Investors Corp., a
preferred-share investment fund run by Hees's preferred-share specialist, George Myhal, was taken public after eight months of preparation. Arbitrageur Andrew Sarlos, Trizec director Dick Shiff and
Northstar Investment Corp. each bought almost one-third of the
$10 million common-share offering, and Edper affiliate B.C. Pacific
Capital Corp. took $40 million in junior participating shares ahead
of the $200 million preferred-share offering. Like a split-share fund,
Varitech investors had a choice between capital appreciation or
dividend income. Varitech was a smaller version of private Mico
Investments, but Varitech investment guidelines limited the value
of Edper Group stocks to 50% of its total portfolio.

That autumn Prime Minister Brian Mulroney sought reelection on
the issue of free trade with the United States. It was an unusual campaign because business leaders, such as Galen Weston, Trevor Eyton,
Paul Reichmann and Noranda's Alf Powis, took a public position in the
free-trade debate. Eyton and John Bitove Sr., at Mulroney's personal
request, also co-chaired the election-year fund-raising drive that
raised a record $25 million for the Tory cause. Meanwhile, in New
York City, Ross Johnson lobbied American companies with Canadian
branch plants to donate to his friend's campaign.

A few days before the election, Trevor Eyton bought hundreds
of copies of *The Financial Post*'s special supplement on free trade
and distributed them to Edper Group employees. The eight-page report, entitled "Everything you want to know about free trade, but
no one's telling you," was co-authored by neoconservative journalist Andrew Coyne and McGill University economist William
Watson, and illustrated with editorial cartoons by Phil Mallette,

including one depicting a group of panicked Americans, running from an innocuous-looking Canadian, while shouting: "Phone Congress! Lock up your shares! It's another crazed Canadian businessman with money to burn!...and he's in a takeover mood!!" Inside, Coyne and Watson responded to the public's concerns about Mulroney's character: "You don't have to trust in his integrity, or his judgement or his backbone. Just in his love of power." In other words, Mulroney wouldn't dare cut Canada's cherished social programs because he would be "dead meat at the polls." To reassure the public that social programs weren't in the draft agreement, Coyne and Watson provided a list of up to 200 "things that weren't on the table," including the beaver, the Group of Seven, igloos, mukluks, toques, "eh," deference to authority, reserve, July 1, the summer cottage, the retractable roof, Thanksgiving in October, separatism, Mordecai Richler, Grey Cup parties, Paul Henderson, the Montreal Forum, Conrad Black and social programs.

Black was the "godfather" of *The Financial Post* business daily, inspired in part by Jack Cockwell. At the height of the bull market, Black had set out to create a Canadian newspaper with a less "adversarial" attitude towards business than what he called the "toadying to the left" Report on Business of *The Globe and Mail*. Over lunch at Winston's with Toronto Sun Publishing chairman Doug Creighton in late May 1987, Black enlisted his support for the new venture. Three months later Black sued *The Globe and Mail* for libel. Two months later and two weeks before the Crash, Maclean Hunter agreed to sell its Financial Post division, with its venerable 80-year-old *Financial Post* weekly, in a share swap with Toronto Sun Publishing, a pro-Conservative, pro-business, prodevelopment and supposedly pro-Israel tabloid newspaper chain launched in 1971 with financial backing from lawyers Rudy Bratty, Eddie Goodman, Herb Solway and Lionel Schipper, the Bronfmans, Cadillac's Jack Daniels, and Labatt's Peter Widdrington, among others. The *Sun*, best known for its page three Sunshine Girl and ample sports coverage, sold 25% of Financial Post Co. to the *Financial Times* of London and 15% to Black's Hollinger. Cockwell was appointed a member of *The Financial Post*'s new national advisory board, along with Burns Fry's Peter Eby (who ran Mulroney's Toronto campaign in 1983). Shortly before the launch of the new *Sun*-style daily on February 2, 1988, Mulroney dropped by the newsroom to gladhand *The Financial Post* staff. Ten months later, on November 21, 1988, Mulroney was elected to a second term as prime minister, ensuring the passage of free trade.

Chapter 8

The Edper Puzzle

Within days of Brian Mulroney's reelection, Edward and Peter Bronfman's private holdings were reorganized to facilitate a public listing on the Toronto Stock Exchange in 1989.

Their public vehicle would be Edper Enterprises, owned 50% by Broncorp (a new private company controlled by the Edward Maurice Bronfman Trust) and 50% by Edper Investments (now controlled by the Peter Frederick Bronfman Trust). Jack Cockwell, Trevor Eyton and David Kerr were trustees of the Peter Frederick Bronfman Trust, along with Peter Bronfman, his son Bruce, his daughter Linda, Toronto Sun director Lionel Schipper, John Scrymgeour and Sheila Zittrer. However, in 1986 Edward Bronfman had replaced Cockwell and Eyton as trustees of the Edward Maurice Bronfman Trust with Toronto Sun director Herb Solway (who later married Ann Shortell, co-author of *The Brass Ring*) and Four Seasons Hotels executive Arnie Cader, along with Edward's three sons, Paul, David and Brian. "To some extent we'll be heading in different directions," Edward Bronfman said of his brother Peter in *The Brass Ring*.

While Edward Bronfman sought "liquidity" for his 50% holding in Edper, the Hees managers had spent months searching for a "liquid" company they could use to cash out the family without making the Edper empire vulnerable to an outside takeover. By the autumn of 1988, they had found one. Multimillionaire broker,

publisher, art dealer and Hees direc
approached Hees about taking over
traded company, Pagurian Corp.

Christopher Ondaatje was born i
ager of a tea plantation in the forme
now Sri Lanka. At age 12 he was sent
boys' school in England. In 1948, his a
tune and his family, later turning into ~~~~~~se. Ondaatje,
who had not seen his father since being sent to England, had to
leave school early. He joined the National Bank of India in London
as a trainee, studying at night at the left-leaning London School of
Economics. At the age of 22, with $12 in his wallet, Ondaatje em-
igrated to Canada with his brother Michael. In Canada, Christopher
Ondaatje sold advertising for *The Financial Post*, then stocks for
Pitfield MacKay Ross, joined Trevor Eyton's Canyon Beauport Club
in 1960, published and partially wrote a bestselling series of books,
Prime Ministers of Canada, and raced with Canada's second bob-
sled team at the Innsbruck Olympics in 1964. Monty Gordon, one
of the co-founders of Gordon Capital, was a member of the gold
medal-winning first team.

In the middle of his second decade in Canada, the renaissance
man co-founded Loewen, Ondaatje & McCutcheon with his co-
workers and Canyon Beauport Club friends Chuck Loewen and
Fred McCutcheon. Ondaatje's volcanic temper became legendary
among the staff at the institutional brokerage firm. In 1974 Ondaatje
skewered the Bay Street village in his hackneyed novel titled *Fool's
Gold: The First $1,000,000*, which he published under a pseudonym.
It was a morality tale about an upstart Bay Street speculator and sexual plunderer, driven to madness and near-suicide by his relentless quest for wealth. After losing his hard-won fortune, the anti-hero
tries to throw himself under a Toronto Transit Commission subway
train, but is rescued by Bay Street friends who cover his margin
call. Ondaatje's novel prefigured the spate of morality tales, like
Oliver Stone's 1987 film *Wall Street*, which attempted to pronounce
judgment on the Greed Decade of the 1980s.

around the time Christopher Ondaatje was imposing his own sense of moral propriety on the saga of Bay Street, he formed investment company Pagurian Corp. from his book-publishing base, Pagurian Press. Like the hermit crab after which it was named, Pagurian proved to be a difficult company to grasp. In 1983, Pagurian picked up a 17.5% equity interest in Hees, after Ondaatje spent nine months rounding up shares in Edper Equities owned by three generations of the Patino family, spending $45 million in cash. Ondaatje then swapped the Edper Equities (later renamed Brascan Holdings) shares for the stake in Hees. And he began to apply the asset-shuffling lessons he had learned from the Edper Group to Pagurian and its minority investments in American Resources Corp. and Consumers Glass Co.

In April 1984 Ondaatje's Pagurian and Ben Webster's Helix Investments provided financial backing for a new manufacturing merchant bank called Enfield Corp., which later bought Pagurian's shares in Consumers Glass. In mid-1984, Pagurian announced the formation of AXE Canada Inc., an investment management company, in partnership with American Resources of Bermuda. That October Ondaatje moved back to London. In 1985 Enfield acquired an interest in Pagurian through a convoluted share swap with Pagurian, AXE Canada and American Resources. Later that year, Pagurian co-founded a Bermuda-based investment banker called Canadian Express Ltd., then bought out its partner in 1986 and rolled Canadian Express into a new company called International Pagurian, financed with a $75 million private placement and a $112 million public share issue, one year before the Crash.

Bay Street dubbed Ondaatje the "slippery Ceylonese" for his financial engineering. Like Argus and Edper, he took advantage of a section in the Income Tax Act, which allowed him to roll assets into companies without paying capital gains tax. Bay Street said Pagurian was piggybacking on the success of Hees and Enfield. "Pagurian was always very difficult for an ordinary securities analyst to follow," wrote money manager Ira Gluskin in the *Financial Times of Canada*. "Besides, Chris always made lots of money for the shareholders, so only a nit-picker would have bothered to try and figure out what the company actually did to generate earnings per share. It turned out that whatever it was could not be kept up. Inevitably, the balloon collapsed — as did the stock price."

Within months of the Crash, Ondaatje quit as vice-chairman of Loewen, Ondaatje & McCutcheon and sold his 12% interest. (In 1986, an $83 million deal that would have put the firm under the control of Pagurian fell apart.) Later in 1988, International Pagurian, which had already bought Pagurian's interest in Enfield, changed its name to Canadian Express and bought Pagurian's investment in Hees. That left Pagurian with roughly $500 million in assets: half in convertible preferred shares in Canadian Express and half in cash and treasury bills. Pagurian had turned into the equivalent of an income fund, as Ondaatje went through a life crisis. Married, with three grown children, Ondaatje was tired of his jet-lagged life, of zooming back and forth between London, Bermuda, New York City and Toronto. "I began to liberate myself from deals and telephones," he later wrote.

In early May 1988, Tessa Wilmott and I interviewed Ondaatje for *The Financial Post*, over an elegant lunch on fine bone china prepared by his personal chef in his Toronto office suite at Loewen, Ondaatje & McCutcheon. Christopher Ondaatje related how frustrated he was by the constant carping about Pagurian shares, then trading at $10, almost 50% below their 1987 peak of $19. Ondaatje, a man of well-worn grace, said he longed to become "a major publisher" by making a large acquisition in the communications sector, such as a takeover of Canadian publishing giant Maclean Hunter. A week later at the Pagurian annual meeting on May 19, 1988, Ondaatje was under fire for Pagurian's declining share price and its unchanged dividend payout. Accused one shareholder, "If we were playing cards, Mr. Ondaatje, I would call that a renege." Ondaatje replied, "I'm dancing as fast as I can."

That summer Pagurian bought one of Canada's top literary publishers, the financially troubled Lester & Orpen Dennys. It was a prestigious acquisition, but it fell far short of Christopher Ondaatje's grand ambition to own a publishing giant. He decided he wanted out of Pagurian and began shopping its assets to potential purchasers at an overall $100 million price tag, to be split 50/50 between Revenue Canada and himself. David Hennigar of Crownx Inc. reportedly flew to Bermuda that autumn to meet with Ondaatje, who was recovering from an operation, to discuss the terms of a sale.

But since Pagurian was the answer to Hees's search for a cash-rich company, Ondaatje made a deal with Hees instead. Hees established a structured partnership with Ondaatje in Canadian Corporate Services Ltd., a private company formed to hold Ondaatje's control block in Pagurian (which consisted of 66% of Pagurian's special multiple-voting B shares). Hees would get Canadian Corporate Services' senior preferred shares; Ondaatje, the junior preferred shares. In turn, Ondaatje would receive 1.5 million Hees shares and be named a Hees vice-chairman, along with Jack Cockwell and David Kerr. Hees shared a management contract with Ondaatje through their joint ownership of Canadian Corporate Services' common shares, whose share value "was very minimal" compared to the dividend-rich preferred shares. The tax-efficient $37 million share swap was formalized on December 16, 1988.

The Hees managers immediately dropped in Bill L'Heureux as Pagurian's new president. Earlier, Tim Price had replaced Edward Bronfman as chairman of Hees, and L'Heureux, a Trevor Eyton-in-waiting, had been named president of Hees, becoming the visible face and public voice of the merchant bank.

Born in Ottawa in 1947 and raised in London, Ontario, around the corner from future Liberal Ontario premier David Peterson, L'Heureux attended a Roman Catholic school and then majored in English literature at the University of Western Ontario, where his mother had been one of the first women to graduate from the renowned business school. L'Heureux later went to the University of Toronto's Law School with *Toronto Star* scion John Honderich, graduating in 1971. At Tory Tory DesLauriers & Binnington, L'Heureux rose to partner, earning an annual salary of $250,000, before leaving in 1983 to join Hees at an annual salary of only $100,000.

But after five years at Hees, L'Heureux owned Hees shares worth about $10 million (Hees stock had recovered from the Crash), purchased with a $2 million-plus stock-loan. He led the good life, with a $1 million house in Toronto's Moore Park, a farm in the country and private schools for three children. He and his wife Janet reportedly hoped to buy a place in the south of France ("cheap") during the summer of 1989. As part of his new mandate at Hees, L'Heureux planned to shop internationally for financial services firms as well as vacation homes — expanding on Pagurian's base in Bermuda and London. L'Heureux also announced plans to untangle the Pagurian Group's cross-ownerships and to simplify Canadian Express, giving it a new purpose as a manufacturing merchant bank, and installing a low-profile Hees partner, Manfred Walt, as president.

Manfred Walt was a regular guy, if bit of a nerd. In that, he was not alone at Hees. The Hees boys, usually photographed in crisp white shirts with ties but without jackets, sometimes resembled those kids in high school that no one wanted to hang out with. Sharp-tongued Liz Tory, a former Jarvis Collegiate classmate of Trevor Eyton and the wife of establishmentarian John Tory, nicknamed Bill L'Heureux "the farmer" after she saw him at a social function wearing a short-sleeved shirt. Walt, who also favoured short-sleeved shirts, was a devoted family man with three young children. He played doubles tennis every Thursday night with his wife, Michelle, mowed his lawn in Thornhill on weekends and worried about his ailing father in faraway Capetown. Equipped with a business degree from the University of Capetown and a CA, Walt had arrived in Canada in 1979. A tax specialist, he had a reputation for a sharp temper, a "sometimes brusque social manner" and a brilliant financial mind.

Walt's relationship with L'Heureux echoed the Trevor Eyton-Jack Cockwell alliance. As the Hees partner in charge of the Bronfman family interests, Manfred Walt had played a key role in the reorganization of the family's private holdings in late November and would be the chief architect of the Edper empire's repositioning in 1989. Already he was reportedly at work on the financial statements in preparation for a preliminary prospectus. Bill L'Heureux would be the chief spokesman.

The Edward Bronfman family had hoped to liquidate all of its investment in Edper Enterprises when it went public, but that would leave Peter Bronfman vulnerable. As L'Heureux later told Philip Mathias of *The Financial Post*, the question became, "Is there going to be…[a third party] who might creep up and buy a lot of the stock [after Edward Bronfman had cashed out] and walk into [Peter Bronfman's] office one day and say, 'Hi! I own 49% of Edper….'" A more secure plan had to be developed. Peter Bronfman privately agreed that the senior Edper managers would replace Edward as his partner. Not with their own money, though. Initially, Peter would be partnered by cash from Pagurian Corp., now jointly controlled by Hees and Hees vice-chairman Christopher Ondaatje. Single-mindedly focused on their Pagurian strategy, the Hees partners did not consider maverick businessman Michael Blair in their plans, assuming the Enfield president and CEO would be content with a senior slot at an Edper affiliate.

Blair, a long-time Pagurian representative on the Hees board and a trusted member of Hees's audit committee, had different ideas. He made moves to preserve his independence. On December 13, 1988, the Enfield board of directors, led by Blair, had quietly approved plans for a private placement of Enfield shares, an exercise that took almost two months and excluded Canadian Express. On January 25, 1989, Enfield formally notified the Toronto Stock Exchange of its intention to do the issue at $6.50 a share, which Hees thought was priced too low.

Jack Cockwell and the Hees partners were furious when they picked up the business papers on Thursday, February 9, 1989, and read that Enfield had completed the $32.5 million private placement of equity — five million shares at $6.50 a share — that had diluted Canadian Express's 30% stake. Through Bart MacDougall's brokerage firm MacDougall MacDougall & MacTier, Enfield had privately placed four large share blocks with Blair's aptly named personal company Renegade Capital, Ben Webster's Helix Investments, Fred Thompson's

FW Thompson Investment Counsel and MacDougall's cousins at the Molson family trust, excluding Canadian Express and the other Enfield shareholders. Blair had effectively given Hees the finger. Three angry institutional shareholders — Fidelity Investments, Mackenzie Financial and the Ontario Municipal Employees Retirement Board — asked Hees what it was going to do about it. Hees said it was a matter of principle; the rebellious Blair had to be taught a lesson.

Meanwhile, the balding, diminutive, bespectacled Michael Blair had been mocking the Hees boys and their famous business principles, handing out copies of his own corporate philosophy, "Rules of the Sandbox." Business principles don't have to be complicated, it said. Remember the rules in nursery school: share your toys, play fair, don't hit people, clean up your own mess, don't take things that aren't yours, say you're sorry when you hurt somebody, don't tell lies, live a balanced life, and learn some and think some and draw every afternoon.

The son of a Royal Canadian Air Force sergeant, Blair was educated at Royal Military College in Kingston, Ontario, where he was a featherweight boxing champ, and then flew CF-107 Voodoo jets for the RCAF. After ten years, Blair left the military to attend the University of Western Ontario's business school, graduating with an MBA in 1976. He was recruited by the world's most elite management-consultancy firm, McKinsey & Co., where he worked as an associate for two years before leaving for a vice-presidency at Canadian General Electric Ltd. In 1984 Blair orchestrated a management buyout of Canadian General Electric's plastic auto-body manufacturing unit.

That same year, with financial backing from Ben Webster's Helix Investments Ltd. and Christopher Ondaatje's Pagurian Corp., Blair formed Enfield, a manufacturing merchant bank. Enfield went on to acquire electrical equipment distributor Federal Pioneer Ltd. and glass-container manufacturer Consumers Glass, as well as an investment in Numac Oil & Gas Ltd. — altogether about $1.2 billion in industrial assets. Along the way, Blair had a falling out with Ondaatje over Enfield's sale of its 30% ownership in Pagurian. By late

1988, Blair, recently separated from his wife of 10 years, was commuting from his condominium in Collingwood, on the south shore of Georgian Bay, to Enfield's penthouse offices atop the Inn on the Park (Four Seasons), where he could spy on Bay Street through a high-powered brass telescope. Blair didn't have a lot of friends on the Street since he had sued an investment dealer, apart from Burns Fry chairman Jack Lawrence, who, along with CityTV's Moses Znaimer, accompanied Blair on California hiking holidays. Unlike the Hees boys, Blair claimed to work only 40 hours a week, spending the winter weekends skiing with his two young sons on Collingwood's privately owned ski hills.

Thus, when an irate Manfred Walt called Michael Blair on Friday, February 10, 1989, about the private placement of Enfield shares, Blair was out of town skiing. Walt got hold of Blair on Monday, demanding that Canadian Express be allowed to buy its pro-rata share of the placement and that a recently vacated seat on the Enfield board be filled by a Hees representative. Blair refused. "The cash is in the bag," he told Walt. A few days later, Walt and Bill L'Heureux went to see Blair, whose son was in the same class at a Toronto school as one of L'Heureux's children, at his office. L'Heureux claimed that Blair told them he couldn't open up the placement or raise the issue price because the financial demands of his pending divorce were making it difficult for him to maintain his 11% stake in Enfield.

So went the corporate dogfight that dominated Canadian business headlines for months. Behind closed doors there were hot-tempered speeches, bouts of name-calling, threats of retaliation and "spirited cries of shareholder justice" on both sides. Manfred Walt began showing up uninvited at board meetings of Enfield subsidiaries to make Canadian Express's pitch to buy Enfield shares and for seats on the Enfield board. He was asked to call first. On Valentine's Day, Walt made a guest appearance at an Enfield board meeting and presented his case. But the directors spurned him, ratifying the private placement and eliminating the vacated board seat. They also decided to use the money raised from the private placement to redeem a class of convertible debentures held, in part, by Michael Blair's Renegade Capital. When the Enfield board voted to pay down the convertible debentures, Blair left the room because of his conflict of interest.

Over the next two weeks, Walt reportedly stepped up his campaign, sometimes in tandem with L'Heureux, at other times with Tim Casgrain, chairman of Canadian Express, or Jack Cockwell. Canadian Express sent two letters to Enfield's major shareholders outlining its opposition to the private placement and seeking support for Walt and L'Heureux, its nominees to Enfield's board. Among other things, the letters claimed that the buyback of convertible debentures was used to finance Blair's Enfield stock purchases, and that Blair's reputation as an innovative manufacturer was overblown. Canadian Express claimed Enfield was losing money on its manufacturing operations, that its profit came from income on investments. Enfield's lawyers, Osler Hoskin & Harcourt, informed Canadian Express that the letters were "libelous" and that litigation was pending.

Michael Blair, played balls poker with the Hees partners, upping the ante in early March. Assuming that Hees was only interested in stripping out the oil side of Enfield's business, Enfield's board approved a plan on Monday, March 6, 1989, to issue warrants to its common shareholders that entitled them to purchase Enfield's 39% stake in Numac Oil & Gas, in order to keep Numac out of Hees's hands. The board also approved a proposed Enfield common-share rights issue at $7.50 a share. But if Blair wanted to play big boys' games, then he would have to play by big boys' rules. The next day, Tuesday, March 7, Hees wiped out most of the dilutive effect of Enfield's private placement when Gordon Capital rounded up a $42.5 million block of Enfield equity — five million shares at $8.50 a share — and quietly distributed it to Hees, Canadian Express and two Hees allies, Conrad Black's Ravelston Corp. and Andrew Sarlos & Associates. On Wednesday, Enfield rejected an opportunity to buy out Canadian Express's 30% stake at $9 a share (a price $2.50 a share higher than Enfield's private placement).

Manfred Walt met with Michael Blair on Thursday, March 9, 1989, but the two men were unable to come to a resolution. Blair dismissed his younger adversary as "an overzealous junior going outside the bounds of propriety." And Blair continued to reject Walt's demands for two seats on the Enfield board. Big mistake. By rejecting Canadian Express's request for proportional board representation, Blair was openly defying one of Jack Cockwell's sacrosanct business principles.

A spitting-mad Jack Cockwell instructed Canadian Express to launch a civil suit against Michael Blair and Enfield to gain the two board seats. Canadian Express also asked the Toronto Stock Exchange to disallow Enfield's proposed common-share rights issue and its warrant distribution of Numac. Enfield's lawyer, Peter Dey, a former chairman of the Ontario Securities Commission, argued that there was no discrimination and that any quarrel Canadian Express had with the business judgment of the issue was not a matter for the Toronto Stock Exchange. The Exchange ruled in favour of Enfield.

In mid-March 1989, Canadian Express launched oppression proceedings against Enfield, Blair and Renegade Capital in an Ontario court, seeking to reverse Enfield's private placement. Three weeks later, Hees presented a signed list of shareholders, including Conrad Black's Ravelston Corp. and Andrew Sarlos & Associates, representing 53% of Enfield's stock, who supported Hees's demands for a new Enfield board and a halt to the proposed equity issues.

On the evening of the day that was to have been Enfield's annual meeting, Thursday, April 13, 1989, Michael Blair threw a dinner party for 80 at the Inn on the Park (Four Seasons) to celebrate Enfield's fifth year of business, and coyly invited all his adversaries. Walt and Canadian Express chairman Tim Casgrain sat across the room from the head table.

Not long after the birthday party, Blair met with Walt, Bill L'Heureux and Jack Cockwell over breakfast, where the four men agreed to a six-month ceasefire. Blair said Cockwell, also a former boxing champion, initiated the peace talks. "Jack should be credited with finding a solution; he basically said 'let's forget about the past and get on with running the company,'" Blair told Jacquie McNish for *The Globe and Mail*. Blair agreed to allow two Hees representatives, Walt and L'Heureux, onto the Enfield board, along with one new independent director, Rob Peters (Hees's list of potential directors had included fund manager James Meekinson, Unicorp's James Leech and First City's Brent Belzberg). In turn, Canadian Express agreed to drop its lawsuit. Blair also promised to cancel the Numac offering and proceed with an Enfield rights offering. "After a boxing match, you get to learn a lot about your sparring partner," Blair said. But it was a false peace — a brief respite between rounds in their bloody-minded fight to the finish.

A month after the peace pact, Bay Street buzzed with the titillating news that Jack Cockwell and his boys would take Edward Bronfman's place at the top of the Edper empire through Pagurian, which would become the Peter Bronfman family's new financial partner. "They do put their money where their mouth is," Peter Bronfman told Patricia Best for the *Financial Times of Canada*. But why weren't the managers bringing in an outside investor to replace Edward? Where would these middle-class professionals get the money? And wasn't this a huge conflict of interest for the Hees managers?

"We went through a very formal process with the [Hees] board and legal opinions at that time," Bill L'Heureux later told Philip Mathias for *The Financial Post*, "[and] it wasn't only a question of the [Hees] managers diluting themselves into Pagurian. It was a question of…Hees disposing of Pagurian." L'Heureux said the Hees managers had concluded that "it was in Hees' best interest that Pagurian [and its cash] be made available to Edward and Peter Bronfman to sort out their estate plan. It was not in our interest to have a public squabble [at Edper (Hees's parent)] between families over succession."

Subversive Hees director Michael Blair sought an outside legal opinion from Osler Hoskin & Harcourt's Peter Dey, who recommended that the Hees independent directors seek additional information, outside investment advice and minority shareholder approval of some of the steps in the transaction. But Dey's recommendation was viewed as an informal opinion prepared for a director who was hostile to Hees and therefore *not* relevant, L'Heureux later told Kimberley Noble for *The Globe and Mail*. When the 19-member

Hees board voted on the transaction, the directors involved in the purchase left the room.

In June, Hees instructed Canadian Corporate Services to issue a block of treasury stock to a private company called Partners Holdings — 60%-owned by nine Hees executives: chairman Tim Price, vice-chairman Jack Cockwell, vice-chairman David Kerr, president Bill L'Heureux and managing partners Tim Casgrain, Robert Harding, Bryan McJannet, George Myhal and Manfred Walt — for a nominal sum, to give Partners Holdings a 20% voting and equity stake. A July 5, 1989, prospectus revealed that Partners Holdings also purchased Canadian Corporate Services' $50 million of junior preferred shares from Christopher Ondaatje. By then Partners Holdings had a 40% voting and equity stake in Canadian Corporate Services; Ondaatje, a diluted 30% stake; and Hees, a diluted 30% stake. The managers had taken control of Pagurian from Hees.

"Lost in the Pagurian Shuffle," read *The Financial Post* headline. Certainly it was one of the most complicated reorganizations that Canada had ever seen. A series of in-house deals created a gigantic Edper puzzle, with Pagurian, Canadian Express, Hees, Edper Enterprises and two new structured partnerships, Edper Holdings and Hees Holdings, as the puzzle pieces. First, Pagurian swapped its roughly $250 million worth of convertible preferred shares in Canadian Express for almost $225 million of Hees shares and about $25 million in cash. Then Pagurian exchanged this $250 million package of Hees shares and cash for senior preferred shares and a 25% equity interest in Hees Holdings, to form a new structured partnership between Pagurian and Edper Enterprises. Peter Bronfman had swapped Edper Investments' 50% of Edper Enterprises for junior preferred shares and a 65% equity interest in Edper Holdings, to form a new structured partnership between Pagurian and Edper Investments. On May 24, Edper Holdings purchased 9.5 million Edper Enterprises treasury shares at about $26.30 a share for $250 million. On June 27, Edper Holdings agreed to purchase 3.4 million Edper Enterprises shares at about $27.50 a share from Edward Bronfman (representing a third of his 50% stake) for roughly

$100 million. On June 29, Pagurian cashed in its $250 million of
treasury bills to pay for the senior preferred shares and a 35% equity interest in Edper Holdings. And Edper Enterprises made a
$250 million private placement of shares.

It was time to invite the public to the private party. From the
black depths of the Crash, the Toronto Stock Exchange 300 Composite
Index had finally clawed its way back up within reach of its all-time
record, set on August 13, 1987, and the Dow Jones Industrial Average
was within sight of its spring 1987 peak. Into this bullish market,
Edper Enterprises planned to issue four million class A subordinated
voting shares in a $100 million initial public offering at $27.50 a
share, led by Gordon Capital. The prospectus disclosed that Edper
Enterprises would use the $100 million proceeds from this small 10%
float to hike up its interests in its principal investments, Hees, Carena
and Brascan. A later Pagurian public offering would raise the proceeds to replace the $100 million Edward Bronfman payout.

For investment professionals, trying to solve the latest Edper
puzzle was like being a tourist in the rat-maze of Toronto's downtown underworld. Frequently quoted Stephen Jarislowsky of
Jarislowsky Fraser & Co. in Montreal, then Canada's largest pension-
fund manager, defied anyone to understand the group's web of
holding companies and interlocking ownerships. Minority shareholders of Hees, Pagurian and Canadian Express had difficulty de-
termining whether they had been treated fairly. Bill L'Heureux
argued that all the boards had approved the internal valuations,
citing the example of Pagurian, which had formed an independent
committee of directors that reviewed the transaction and obtained
a fairness opinion from an independent investment dealer.
L'Heureux also argued that the Edper reorganization was well doc-
umented in public presentations.

But there was a barrage of criticism. The Edper Group was already under fire from the minority shareholders of Westmin
Resources, Norcen Energy, Great Lakes Group and Trilon Financial
for swapping assets between affiliated companies. To consolidate
Noranda's energy division, Westmin Resources had agreed to swap

its oil-and-gas interests and some working capital for convertible debentures and shares in Norcen Energy, as well as Norcen Energy's minority stake in M.A. Hanna Co. But Westmin minority shareholders queried the asset shuffle, skeptical about its $0.5 billion valuation. They voted on the plan at the June 12, 1989, annual meeting, under a majority-of-minority rule. (A majority of the minority shareholders had to approve the transaction.)

Meanwhile, Trilon Financial had made moves to become a full-service financial services firm. Great Lakes Group had agreed to swap its securities arm, Great Lakes Capital Markets Inc., for shares in Trilon Financial. Great Lakes Group directors Jack Cockwell and Trevor Eyton sat side by side at the April annual meeting as CEO Ken Clarke told shareholders that he could not reveal his negotiating strategy with Trilon Financial. But a deluge of public and shareholder criticism forced the Edper Group to get approval from the majority of minority shareholders of both Great Lakes Group and Trilon Financial at a special meeting on June 30, 1989. Seven of the Great Lakes Group dealmakers then went over to Trilon Financial, including Clarke, the former Merrill Lynch Canada official, who was named Trilon Financial's new president and CEO. He replaced Gordon Cunningham, who moved on to head the London Insurance Group.

One of the biggest critics of Edper's reorganization was Merrill Lynch Canada analyst Terry Shaunessy. In his comments to Merrill Lynch Canada's institutional clients, Shaunessy questioned the investment merits of the Edper Enterprises offering, thus straining relations between old friends Merrill Lynch Canada and the Edper Group. When Merrill Lynch Canada chairman Michael Sanderson had signed a $25 million cheque to Great Lakes Group in 1984, it reportedly meant that in case of a "tie" in competition for Edper Group business, the business would go to Merrill Lynch because of its investment in Great Lakes Group. But cracks in the highly profitable relationship had appeared in early 1988 when Great Lakes Group sided with Gordon Capital to force a price cut of a Merrill Lynch Canada-led underwriting. That summer, a Merrill Lynch Canada team advised Falconbridge Ltd., the Western world's second-largest nickel producer, on how to rebuff advances from Edper's Noranda. In October 1988, the cracks widened when Merrill Lynch Canada severed its relationship with Edper's Great Lakes Group, selling its equity stake for $38.4 million. Some insiders said Merrill Lynch Canada was asked to sell its investment because it was interfering with the management of Great Lakes Group.

But Merrill Lynch Canada's institutional clients were not alone in shunning the Edper Enterprises offering, although the issue was oversubscribed by retail investors, who bought the Bronfman name. On July 18, 1989, Edper Enterprises began trading on the Toronto Stock Exchange. It had capitalized on a mini-boom in the equity markets. Common-share financings in Canada exploded to more than $1 billion in July 1989, with the partial privatization of Air Canada accounting for half. The Edper Group accounted for the other half, including the $110 million initial public offering from Edper Enterprises, a $100 million offering from North Canadian Oil, a $100 million offering from Carena, a $200 million offering from Trizec and a $100.5 million offering from Bramalea (its first public issue in 10 years). Though they were wary of Edper Enterprises, institutional investors, otherwise known as the "upstairs market," had snapped up the group's real-estate offerings.

Michael Blair enjoyed tweaking Edper's nose. In a remarkable display of perversity, Blair had invited the Winnipeg-born Ross Johnson, his former Canadian General Electric colleague and the recently deposed head of RJR Nabisco, to come on board as the new chairman of Enfield.

If ever there was an antithesis of an Edper clone, Ross Johnson was it. At RJR Nabisco, Johnson was infamous for his Atlanta fleet of 10 corporate jets and 36 pilots, widely known as the RJR Air Force, which he made available to his close friends Brian and Mila Mulroney and his stable of 29 celebrity athletes called Team RJR Nabisco. (A perennial no-show at Team RJR Nabisco events was O.J. Simpson, on retainer for US$250,000 a year.) Johnson was pilloried as a symbol of corporate greed during his failed management buyout of RJR

Nabisco in late 1988, and his free-spending ways were later immortalized in the best-selling book and Emmy-award-winning HBO film, *Barbarians at the Gate*. Leveraged-buyout kings Kohlberg Kravis Roberts & Co. had won the frenzied two-month bidding war for RJR Nabisco with a jaw-dropping US$25 billion offer, the largest financing ever. The golden-parachute-rich Johnson, with US$53 million in his wallet, was at loose ends, so he welcomed Blair's approach. In mid-June, the Hees managers quietly dissuaded the genial Johnson from becoming Enfield's chairman. It was Blair's move.

At an Enfield directors' meeting on July 5, 1989, Michael Blair proposed issuing 1.2 million common-share options, a stake of almost 3%, to Enfield managers. The following day, Blair hiked up his own stake in Enfield from 11% to 15%, fully diluted. Hees wondered what had happened to the promised Enfield rights offering. Almost immediately, Canadian Express boosted its interest in Enfield from 31% to 31.7%. Within a week, Canadian Express had hiked up its stake to 38.7% and filed notice with the Toronto Stock Exchange that it intended to purchase up to 40% of Enfield. Canadian Express was now prohibited from buying any more Enfield shares until September 6.

Just as tensions were about to burst into the open, Blair invited Bill L'Heureux and Manfred Walt to a Blue Jays baseball game in the new SkyDome, a few days before Enfield's July 20 annual meeting. It was friendly and they had a good time, so L'Heureux and Walt asked Blair and an Enfield vice-president to play doubles tennis. While the four were on the tennis court, Enfield subsidiary Federal Pioneer announced a surprise special dividend of $2 a share.

On July 19, the day before the annual meeting, Michael Blair stunned the Hees partners when he announced at an Enfield directors' meeting that he intended to make two proposals to shareholders: first, that Enfield issue another 300,000 stock options to its managers and, second, that shareholders elect a 12th director to the board. Fred Thompson, a Blair ally, suggested former Ontario Securities Commission chairman Henry Knowles as a candidate. Bill L'Heureux and Manfred Walt were outraged. The Enfield directors had already agreed on a slate of 11, and Knowles was not a friend of the Edper Group. Following an OSC hearing into the Unicorp takeover of Union Enterprises, Knowles said, "There is a new type of money being manufactured today. Crap like the Unicorp preferreds, which the Edper group can turn into money by their endorsement." The two Hees partners suggested that Jack Cockwell and Trevor Eyton be added to the board, replacing two managers of Enfield subsidiaries. Blair told *The Globe and Mail* that he objected to Cockwell and Eyton because it was an "attempt by Canadian Express to have controlling influence over Enfield." L'Heureux replied in *The Financial Post*, "We went crazy at the last board meeting. We were tired of [Blair's] surprises. And our allegedly relentless demand for influence [was] really about our request for common courtesy." There would be no more effort to play nice.

On the night of July 19, Jack Cockwell and the Hees partners worked on a defence strategy. They decided to ambush Michael Blair by nominating Hees chairman Tim Price as an Enfield director at the next day's annual meeting, in an effort to bump Blair off the board. At the 8:30 a.m. board meeting before the annual meeting, Manfred Walt and Bill L'Heureux persuaded Blair not to expand the board to 12 directors.

Then the Hees boys stormed into Enfield's annual meeting minutes after it got under way at 10:00 a.m. in a Toronto hotel room. Bill L'Heureux interrupted the proceedings from the back of the room to ask how many shares were represented at the meeting. Michael Blair explained that the special resolution to expand the Enfield board to 11 members from nine would be voted on by ballot. L'Heureux asked that the election of directors also be conducted by ballot, rather than proxy. Manfred Walt then nominated Hees chairman Tim Price as a director.

There were now 12 candidates for 11 positions. Blair had the backing of about 18 million Enfield shares, including four significant blocks: his own Renegade Capital, Ben Webster's Helix Investments, Fred Thompson's FW Thompson Investment and the Molson family trust. But Walt's slate had the backing of about 19 million Enfield shares, including Hees, Canadian Express, Conrad Black's Ravelston Corp. and Andrew Sarlos & Associates, among others. Hees expected to win the showdown. During the one and a half hours of counting after the balloting, Blair remained upbeat, "making jokes and working the room," while L'Heureux conferred gravely with Walt. Then Blair, reading from a statement prepared by his lawyers, Osler Hoskin & Harcourt, announced that Price had received no votes and that he, Blair, had been elected. L'Heureux rushed to the microphone and demanded an explanation. Blair did not disclose that he had disqualified the votes cast for Price on technical grounds, and counted them as his own. By the time the meeting ended, a visibly frustrated, almost shrill L'Heureux was threatening legal action: "We give notice to all shareholders that we intend to continue this meeting after this farce has been concluded and hold a proper election of directors." Blair would not permit discussion about his decision, announcing that the directors' meeting was cancelled "because it was the wrong atmosphere" in which to conduct Enfield business. The following day, Hees secured a court injunction blocking Blair from acting as a director of Enfield until a court hearing ruled on the validity of the election of directors. The gloves were off.

Later, when someone asked Michael Blair what he got out of all his fighting, he replied, "Well, there's things money can't buy. The look on Tim Price's face when I said, 'I'm sorry, Tim, you didn't get any votes at all,' you can't buy that. It's etched in my mind. It's the picture of the powerful chairman of the board of Hees International Bancorp about to wet his pants." In an affidavit, Hees cited Blair's "total disdain for shareholder rights," arguing that Blair had breached the conditions of their peace treaty, signed three months earlier. Although Hees claimed it hadn't picked the fight, it couldn't afford to lose it. "We can't afford to be seen as pansies. A lot of companies are watching this," Bill L'Heureux told Deirdre McMurdy for *The Financial Post*. Price asked Blair for a "graceful resignation" from the Hees board. Blair said he would think about it. Peter Bronfman then sent a letter officially asking for Blair's resignation from the Hees board.

More than three million Enfield shares changed hands on Monday, July 31, 1989. Michael Blair's Renegade Capital bought one million shares, crossed by MacDougall MacDougall & MacTier, for about $10 million, upping Blair's Enfield stake to about 18%, fully diluted. And James Meekinson of JDM Capital bought 1.8 million shares at $9 a share, crossed by First Marathon. Although Canadian Express was temporarily restricted from buying more Enfield shares, Hees's allies were still in the market. That same day, Numac Oil & Gas announced adoption of a poison-pill takeover defence, designed by Goldman Sachs & Co. of New York, which would thwart any advances from Hees or its affiliates.

The next day Garrett Herman, Merrill Lynch Canada's head of institutional trading, got a call from Alan Radlo, portfolio manager in charge of three Canadian mutual funds at Fidelity Investments. Radlo told Herman that he wanted to sell Fidelity's 1.9 million shares of Enfield, representing a 5% interest. Herman immediately called Hees to offer Fidelity's block, but Hees angered Herman by instructing him to have his traders meet Gordon Capital — Merrill Lynch Canada's rival for the Edper Group's affections — on the floor of the Toronto Stock Exchange to complete the transaction. Herman refused, telling Hees he wanted Merrill Lynch Canada to handle both the buy and sell sides of the deal.

During Herman's 20-year rise through Merrill Lynch Canada, he had pushed "Little Merrill" to follow Gordon Capital into principal or liability trading, where brokerages bought stock for their own account, built big positions and then sold the blocks to institutional clients at a slightly higher price, profiting on the spreads. And under Herman's direction, Merrill Lynch Canada had become the market leader in principal trading, out of nowhere. A man of action, Herman lived his life like an appliance: Plug him in anywhere and he operated on full current, either on the trading floor or racing his Porsche Turbo cup car at a track near Belleville, Ontario, or at Daytona Beach, Florida. Herman had been dubbed Darth Vader at Merrill Lynch Canada, for his dark suits, dark Porsches and evident ambition.

On Friday, August 4, 1989, Herman phoned Michael Blair to see if he was interested in the Fidelity block, but when Blair explained that he couldn't buy it, Herman instructed his equity transaction group to shop the block around.

Merrill Lynch Canada institutional trader Patricia Maclean, a scion of the Maclean family of Maclean Hunter, who covered the Fidelity account for Garrett Herman, was told that the Fidelity block of Enfield was for sale in the $8 1/2 to $9 1/4-a-share range. On Tuesday, August 8, 1989, Maclean phoned Eric Molson, the head of the Molson clan, in Montreal, but he wasn't interested. Then she spoke to Bart MacDougall at MacDougall, MacDougall & MacTier (or the "three Macs," as it was known at the Exchange) to see if MacDougall had a client for the block. He did. Early Friday morning, August 11, Michael Blair called Herman at "The Palace," Merrill Lynch & Co.'s world headquarters in New York's World Financial Center, to ask him to sell a 100,000-share block of Enfield at $9 3/4 a share. Blair's shares were a small part of Merrill Lynch Canada's two-million-share Enfield sell order. That Friday, Merrill Lynch Canada and the three Macs crossed the Enfield block at $9 a share on the floor of the Toronto Stock Exchange at the 9:30 a.m. opening, generating roughly $200,000 in commissions, split between the two brokers. Merrill Lynch Canada had managed to cross only half of Blair's Enfield sell order.

But the entire Fidelity sell order was picked up for about $16.5 million by Federal Pioneer Ltd.'s pension fund, on the authorization of Enfield pension-fund manager Carole Penhale, a Blair ally. A year later Penhale was charged with failing to fulfil her fiduciary duty under the Pension Benefits Act and ultimately was fined $25,000 for her actions.

On the Friday afternoon of that controversial Enfield trade, the Hees managers scattered early for a stolen weekend at their country retreats. Hees hoped the Supreme Court of Ontario would decide Michael Blair's status once and for all. Meanwhile, with the help of a deposition from the scrutineers, Manfred Walt had been painstakingly reconstructing the events of Enfield's now-infamous

annual meeting, while he reportedly fretted about missing his summer vacation, as well as his children's puppet show one Sunday.

By mid-August, Walt had composed a letter to Blair offering
him an Enfield board seat, as well as a promise to drop all litigation
against him, if Blair would resign from the Hees board and relin-
quish his position as Enfield president and CEO to Toronto fund
manager James Meekinson. At a meeting at Blair's home in
Collingwood, Meekinson personally delivered the letter, signed by the
usual suspects: Canadian Express, Conrad Black's Ravelston Corp.,
Andrew Sarlos & Associates, Meekinson's JDM Capital and Michael
Nesbitt's Montrose Investment Corp. But Blair rejected the settlement, proposing instead that Enfield seek a new owner (to which
Renegade and Canadian Express would both tender their shares to
any bid of $9 a share or more), using Goldman Sachs to solicit the
bids. There was no response from either Canadian Express or Enfield
to Blair's proposal, although the Enfield board did agree to hold another shareholders' meeting on Hallowe'en, regardless of the court
outcome. Blair was assured of a rematch.

Just as the court challenge was set to start, Michael Blair resigned from the Hees board, Canadian Express sold its 25.7 million
Pagurian subordinate voting A shares in a secondary share offering, which unlocked the two companies' cross-ownership, and
Pagurian issued 37.5 million A shares from its treasury in a separate offering led by Gordon Capital.

Analyst Terry Shaunessy of rival Merrill Lynch Canada questioned the investment merits of the $500 million combined offer-
ings, citing concerns about the cash flow up to Pagurian, now the
primary investment vehicle for the senior Edper Group managers.
Over the summer, Partners Holdings had raised almost $150 million
to buy the lion's share — 18 million A shares at $8.25 each — of the
Pagurian offerings. Partners Holdings also picked up the rest of
Christopher Ondaatje's common shares in Canadian Corporate
Services "for not very much money," to own 70% of the voting and
equity interests in Pagurian's parent.

Separately, an embittered Ondaatje spent about $40 million to buy almost five million Pagurian A shares for himself. Ondaatje, who claimed he had been squeezed out by the Hees managers, later told Kimberley Noble for *The Globe and Mail* how surprised he was when they took control of Pagurian from Hees. Ondaatje said he had believed in late 1988 that Hees would use its vaunted management expertise to add value to Pagurian's assets, and his Pagurian and Hees stock would appreciate as a result. Instead, "somewhere after I did the deal, management got control of the deal from Hees and that changed the whole thing," Ondaatje recalled. By putting their own money into Pagurian, the managers "diluted their ownership and interest and direction. Hees will never have the same magic again," he said.

The Michael Blair court challenge began on Tuesday, September 5, 1989, and ended seven sessions later. In a stern judgment against Blair, Justice John Holland ruled on September 25 that Blair had "failed to meet the quasi-judicial standard of conduct demanded of a Chairman" at the Enfield annual meeting. From the evidence, Holland concluded that Blair had decided to "act as a judge in his own cause" in accordance with a "plan conceived by Blair to protect his personal interests" as early as the July 19 directors' meeting. Holland said "it was no excuse" for Blair to say he "was relying upon legal advice" when he determined that the ballots cast for Hees chairman Tim Price be counted as votes resulting in Blair's election. Holland overturned the election of Enfield directors and handed Blair's seat at the Enfield board table to Price.

On September 28, the Enfield board created an office of the chairman, comprising Bill L'Heureux, David Lewis and Rob Peters, to run the company. The management circular for the October 31 special meeting nominated 12 candidates for 11 slots on the Enfield board, leaving Blair and Price to duke it out. The circular charged that Blair "took a hostile view" to Canadian Express as soon as it moved into the Hees orbit. "We assure you that the inability of Canadian Express to work with Mr. Blair has been a matter of considerable disappointment and frustration," the circular stated. Enfield "has not been properly managed" under Blair, it said. By

early October, Blair was out as Enfield president, temporarily replaced by L'Heureux. On October 14, Blair put his money and
Enfield shares into a new company, Algonquin Mercantile Corp.,
bringing in Henry Knowles as its chairman. (Algonquin paid roughly
$25 million to Blair for his Enfield stock.)

While Michael Blair prepared for his next round with Hees, the
Edper-Merrill Lynch Canada spat reached a crisis point. Hugh Aird,
the only son of a former Ontario lieutenant governor and the new
president and CEO of Trilon Securities (formerly Great Lakes
Capital Markets), had sent a "stiff" letter to Merrill Lynch Canada
chairman Michael Sanderson earlier that month demanding that
Garrett Herman's equity transaction group stop spreading negative opinions to institutional investors on Edper Enterprises,
Pagurian and Canadian Express. Analyst Terry Shaunessy had not
issued a formal research report on the Edper reorganization, but it
was no secret on Bay Street that he was critical of the recent share
offerings. Because Merrill Lynch Canada could not afford to lose
the Edper Group — its biggest source of revenue during the 1980s
— it removed Shaunessy from coverage of Edper Enterprises,
Pagurian and Canadian Express and sent him over to the Edper
offices for a little chat with Jack Cockwell. As a Merrill Lynch
Canada official told *The Financial Post*, "These guys are vindictive." But one rival research manager argued that the spat had
"nothing to do with research." He said Edper was really angry at
Merrill Lynch Canada for taking the side of its enemies in the
group's ongoing takeover battles for Falconbridge and Enfield.

Three days before Enfield's special meeting, Michael Blair
launched a $720,000 wrongful-dismissal suit against Enfield and a $10
million libel action against Bill L'Heureux, Manfred Walt and Canadian
Express. Earlier Blair had accused Jack Cockwell of badmouthing
him at parties and social events, but he did not name Cockwell in the
libel action. Blair, whose 18% stake in Enfield entitled him to two
board seats, planned to open the special meeting by insisting that he
and his nominee, Ben Webster, a former Ravelston partner of Conrad
Black's, be appointed as Enfield directors. In an effort to embarrass

Hees, Blair supporters wore buttons that read "Hees supports pro-*tort*ionate representation." Although Enfield's Carole Penhale did not vote the Federal Pioneer block at the meeting, she discomfited L'Heureux by asking whether Enfield stock would perform the same way that Canadian Express stock had done since Hees had taken over — it had plunged in price since early summer. Blair's remarks were cheered loudly at the meeting, but after a five-hour voting process, he was banished from Enfield.

It was a Pyrrhic victory for Hees. Michael Blair had ignited an anti-Hees backlash. "It's about time they were challenged over the acquisition of assets," said one critic.

Blair characterized it so: "Hey, listen, this was an ambush. What's going on here is this big bloody takeover designed to leave everyone else out and get what they want on the cheap, or to put so much pressure on the company that it yields [up] some prized asset." Blair later sought a judgment against Gordon Capital, Hees, Canadian Express, Conrad Black's Ravelston Corp., Andrew Sarlos & Associates and others who had purchased Enfield stock in March 1989, whom he claimed "acted in concert" in voting to oust him. Blair argued that they should be forced to make a follow-up offer to all shareholders for control of Enfield.

Blair also argued that Hees had been badly damaged by the corporate melodrama. Many agreed with him, contending that Hees had handled the public relations poorly, by reacting rather than explaining. L'Heureux disagreed. "We came of age in 1989," he later told *Canadian Business*. "It may sound like an absurd rationalization, but in a sense I think the publicity told the world that we had grown up and that we're ready to be seen as a force that, whether you like us or not, is going to be reckoned with."

Just two weeks after Enfield's Hallowe'en meeting, Hees had moved on to its next management services assignment: the restructuring of George Mann's Unicorp, following Unicorp's debilitating $66 million nine-month loss. Above all, Hees was concerned about erosion of the Edper Group's $135 million-plus investment in Unicorp preferred shares. Hees sent a private letter to Unicorp promising to assist in refinancing the almost $200 million of Unicorp preferred shares "on terms as favorable" to Unicorp as possible. Unicorp extended the preferred shares' retraction date by five years to 1997 and halved its 40 cent annual dividend on both classes of Unicorp common shares. Mann took a lot of abuse on the holiday circuit of Christmas and Hanukkah parties for making a deal to give up control of his company to the Edper Group. "We hope that we can persuade George, who we view as a partner, to help us transfer control [of Union Gas] to Brascan," Hees president Bill L'Heureux later said. This was exactly what Bay Street was predicting would happen. Hees said it would oversee the sale of Unicorp's U.S. real-estate holdings and Lincoln Savings Bank, a U.S. thrift purchased in late 1987, leaving Unicorp's natural-gas utility as the core business. And Hees gave its affiliate Brascan a two-year right of first purchase on any Unicorp shares it bought under a planned $53.5 million rights offering.

On Thursday, November 16, 1989, senior managers of the Edper Group and Merrill Lynch Canada sat down to try to settle some of their differences. Trilon Securities' letter to Merrill Lynch Canada hadn't changed the group's reputation as the bully boys of Bay Street. Trilon Securities had pushed its way into the underwriting syndicate of almost every bought deal since mid-summer, using its clout as the Edper Group's new in-house investment dealer. One of the few not to be swayed was Royal Bank of Canada chairman Allan Taylor, who blocked Trilon Securities' participation in one of the bank's underwritings, which was led by the bank's new brokerage subsidiary, RBC Dominion Securities. But that was the exception, not the rule.

As part of the Edper Group — the biggest issuer of paper in Canada — Trilon Securities could generally do as it pleased. Despite tough markets, by the end of 1989 the Edper Group had managed to raise $2 billion more of equity financing since the Crash. And the Edper Group was the biggest buyer of the $2.5 billion of preferred shares issued in Canada during 1989, followed by the Toronto-Dominion Bank, which added more than $1 billion to its preferred-share portfolio. "We were forced on the dealers, but I like to think they're getting used to us," Trilon Securities' Hugh Aird later told Deirdre McMurdy for *The Globe and Mail*. "Now we're within Trilon, we're perceived as bigger and meaner and pushier. I know we may never be loved, but we'd like to be respected."

Cockwell & Co. made it a habit to send letters to anyone who acted against the Edper Group, to phone institutional shareholders who dared sell blocks of Edper Group stock and to tell analysts how to evaluate Edper Group companies. As money manager Ira Gluskin put it, "They have no sense of humour." Up until the late 1980s, the Edper managers could get away with these tactics because Trizec, Bramalea, John Labatt, MacMillan Bloedel, Royal Trustco and Hees had all been triple-digit stock performers on the Toronto Stock Exchange over the previous five years, and Hees was one of the most profitable companies that Bay Street had ever seen. And its stock price had responded during the '80s. Hees reached a peak of $31.83 in 1989, up from $2.05 at the beginning of 1981. But after the fireworks with Michael Blair sputtered out, it was clear that the group had seriously neglected investor relations.

At a late November 1989 lunch sponsored by Gordon Capital for Pagurian, Bill L'Heureux and Manfred Walt used a mountain of slides to explain the Edper reorganization to institutional investors. Tim Price and Ian Cockwell provided backup. As L'Heureux said later in *Canadian Business*, "With all the change, we have to go back to basics and get the analysts to understand us again." But Gino Blink was one of several analysts who were not receptive. In *The G-Note Special Situations Market Letter* in late 1989, Blink wrote that Hees managers were "addicted to the concept that there is but one way — the Hees Way. When the arrogance grows and becomes a conviction of infallibility, the possibility of a calamitous event also grows."

Already there was the possibility of calamitous events at Edper's operating companies. Late in the economic cycle, Royal Trustco, John Labatt, Noranda and Bramalea were still in acquisition mode, swept up in the boom euphoria of the Roaring '80s.

Chapter 9

Big Boys' Games

At Royal Trustco's annual shareholders' meeting on Thursday, April 7, 1988, Michael Cornelissen announced plans for a big push into the United States. "If I want to keep my job," the CEO said, "in the next two or three years we will have established ourselves in the U.S. in some way."

Royal Trustco's overtures to Glenfed Inc., parent of the fifth-largest U.S. thrift, had been thwarted in December 1987, when Glenfed adopted a poison-pill takeover defence. Michael Cornelissen had to find another base for Royal Trustco's U.S. operations. A Royal Trustco team, led by chief financial officer Barry Henstock, scoured the U.S., studying 300 savings and loan institutions, about one-tenth of the entire U.S. thrift industry, and examining three or four "in extreme detail."

Meanwhile, Michael Cornelissen was named chairman of the board of Canada's Challenge for the America's Cup, the world's greatest sailing event, after forming a limited partnership in 1988 whose objective was to raise $27 million over four years for Canada's cup entry, named "Force 12 North," through the sale of sponsorship deals. That September, the tall, greying Cornelissen, who was then 45 but still had a long-limbed athletic look, and Royal Trustco's general counsel, Bill Inwood, flew down to San Diego, California, to party at the 27th Challenge Match of the America's Cup. The Force 12 North syndicate had chartered a 78-foot yacht called *Sun Devil*, flying a gigantic Canadian flag, to ferry prospective corporate sponsors around the 40-mile-long race course and ply them with plenty of booze, sunshine and pretty young Californian women.

The Force 12 North syndicate "roadshow" was an unmitigated success, with millions of dollars in corporate funds committed. And the Royal Trustco men had a wild time. It was no secret that after more than 20 years of marriage to his wife, Trina, Cornelissen was busy with extramarital pursuits. In the Bay Street village, Cornelissen's affair with an aerobics instructor at The Fitness Institute later became the subject of quiet sniggering with some speculating that Cornelissen's new sexual appetites were a direct corollary of his ambitious plan to take Royal Trustco's total U.S. assets up to $25 billion.

Not long after Michael Cornelissen whooped it up in California, officials from Pacific First Financial Corp. of Seattle, Washington, were in Toronto to meet with Canada Trust, which briefly considered buying the U.S. thrift. Pacific First, with less than a quarter of Glenfed's US$24 billion in assets, had been looking for investors to buy a 25% stake. The search for a capital infusion brought Pacific First chairman Jerry Pohlman back to Toronto in November 1988 for talks at Royal Trustco, arranged by Pacific First advisors Merrill Lynch & Co. Cornelissen and Pohlman, a former economics professor, quickly established a rapport, chatting for hours about world events. A series of high-level meetings in Toronto and Seattle culminated two months later in a US$27 a share, or US$212 million, takeover proposal.

On Monday, February 6, 1989, Royal Trustco announced the agreement in principle, signed over the weekend. Pacific First had also granted Royal Trustco an option to buy about 25% of its stock through an issue of new treasury shares at US$16.50 a share, to deter potential bidders until approvals were obtained. Pacific First had experienced turbulence during its six years as a public company, with the rapid turnover of three different CEOs, each with a different corporate agenda. Jerry Pohlman had arrived in 1986 as president, and was elected chairman a year later. Another executive managed the day-to-day-operations of Pacific First's 81 branches in Washington, Oregon, California and four other Western states.

"We have earmarked Pacific First as our flagship in the U.S. and it will be our vehicle for further acquisitions," Michael Cornelissen said. "I wouldn't be surprised if in five to 10 years our U.S. operations were as large as our Canadian ones." Cornelissen argued that U.S. savings and loan companies offered the greatest takeover opportunities because the flood of thrift failures had triggered deep discounts on their stock prices. "We have a two-year window of opportunity to acquire healthy thrifts ahead of the U.S. commercial banking industry," Cornelissen said at Royal Trustco's annual meeting on Thursday, March 30, 1989. State banking regulations effectively prohibited major U.S. banks from buying healthy savings and loan companies until 1992. Cornelissen targeted southern California as the first area of expansion.

In the spring of 1989, the savings and loan scandal broke wide open as the Federal Home Loan Bank Board declared Lincoln Savings & Loan of Irving, California, insolvent. Lincoln's chairman, Charles Keating, came to symbolize the debacle. The seeds of the scandal were sown in 1980, during the final months of Democrat Jimmy Carter's U.S. presidency, when Congress boosted the level of deposits that the government would insure from US$40,000 to US$100,000. Then, seven months after the January 1981 inauguration of Ronald Reagan, the Republican president signed into law the Economic Recovery Tax Act, known facetiously as the Developers Retirement Act because it made real-estate investments enormously profitable by shortening depreciation periods and providing special tax treatment for long-term capital gains. The following year, the Reagan administration pushed through a law that loosened the regulatory reins on savings and loans, easing their accounting rules and decreasing the amount of cash they had to keep on hand to cover bad loans. This encouraged the thrifts to expand from stable home mortgages into more profitable — and risky — commercial and real-estate loans. By the time the Tax Reform Act of 1986 dealt a body blow to real estate, yanking away many of its special tax benefits, it was too late. With nearly 200 insolvent savings and loans in 1988, the crisis in the U.S. thrift industry was coming to a head. In the final weeks of 1988, with the presidential election safely past, the lame-duck Reagan administration launched a fire sale of insolvent savings and loans, greased by more than US$50 billion in government subsidies. The most expensive single failure was the bailout of Lincoln Savings & Loan, costing taxpayers US$2.6 billion.

Six months after he left office, former U.S. president Ronald Reagan was the guest speaker at the Hollinger Dinner at the Toronto Club on Thursday, June 29, 1989. Reagan was greeted by Canadian Prime Minister Brian Mulroney and introduced and praised by the host, Conrad Black, who had assembled the usual right-of-centre suspects for the occasion.

That October Royal Trustco picked up certain assets and assumed the deposit liabilities of Pacific Savings Bank of Costa Mesa, a small 11-branch thrift in suburban Los Angeles, for US$26 million, plus US$17 million in additional acquisition costs. It planned to merge Pacific Savings with Pacific First. Then, on December 1, 1989, Royal Trustco purchased all the outstanding shares of Pacific First for the agreed-upon US$212 million, or 1.8 times book value. Critics questioned Cornelissen's push into the scandal-ridden U.S. savings and loan industry, arguing that he had paid too much for Pacific First and Pacific Savings.

Meanwhile, in Britain, Royal Trustco had doubled its loan portfolio between 1986 and 1989 to £1 billion, reportedly positioning itself in "the lower end of the middle band of borrowers," the client base that would be hardest hit by a recession. It had also pushed aggressively for business in its offices outside London, especially in Leeds. The Leeds office, in its second year of operation, upped its commercial banking and property finance business by 400% and residential mortgages by 240%. The British loans were made during "a crazy period of free-wheeling lending," Michael Cornelissen's replacement, James Miller, later wrote to Royal Trustco employees. Such loans were stopped early in 1990, but Royal Trustco paid for the mistakes.

Where were the other Edper senior managers when these decisions were made? Although Michael Cornelissen was a Jack Cockwell disciple, Royal Trustco was in Trevor Eyton's sphere of influence. Eyton, a deputy chairman of Royal Trustco, had personally recruited Hartland Molson MacDougall (brother of Bart MacDougall, a Michael Blair ally) as chairman of Royal Trustco, retired Toronto-Dominion Bank chairman Allen Lambert as group chairman of financial services in the Edper Group, former Fuller Brush president and the 1950–51 quarterback for the Hamilton Tigercats Melvin Hawkrigg as CEO of Trilon Financial, and Gordon Cunningham. These men, along with Earl Orser, CEO of London Life Insurance, were the Edper Group appointees on Royal Trustco's 29-member board. Olympia & York was represented by executives Gilbert Newman and Kenneth Leung. Two-thirds of the board was considered independent.

Royal Trustco had "a sense of infallibility," James Miller said later in an interview. Royal Trustco common shares peaked in 1989, at almost $20. And Miller said he had a copy of a 52-page Harvard Business School case study for the 1988–89 term, which examined Royal Trustco's "wonderful success story." As Miller explained, Royal Trustco executives were "caught up in the belief in something," but the late 1980s were the years when "critical decisions were being made" that led to Royal Trustco's downfall.

Still, Royal Trustco wasn't the only Edper Group company expanding south. Brewer John Labatt had bought a slew of U.S. dairy and frozen-pizza outfits during the 1980s, including Johanna Farms. After the Crash of 1987, Labatt expanded in another direction, picking up interests in rock music talent agency International Talent Group and Michael Cohl's BCL Entertainment, the Toronto-based rock concert promoter for the Rolling Stones. There were more food-related acquisitions in 1989, but for Labatt executives the highlight of that year was watching the Toronto Blue Jays play in the SkyDome on the stadium's opening day, June 5, 1989, from their Skybox, a "corporate playpen fitted out with closed-circuit TV and wet bars." Later in the week, when it rained mid-way through a Blue Jays game, it took half an hour to close the roof, half an hour that the fans spent drinking

Labatt's beer and eating hotdogs. Trevor Eyton, one of the godfathers of the stadium, was a Labatt vice-chairman.

Elsewhere, resources giant Noranda was also in acquisition mode. On the eve of the summer of 1988, Alf Powis thought he had an opportunity to finally end Noranda's 25-year pursuit of Kidd Creek Mines. Noranda had first tried to win control of the Timmins, Ontario, ore body during the 1960s, but a Crown corporation called Canada Development Corp. ended up with the prized copper, zinc and silver mines.

Twenty years later, in 1984, Noranda got another chance at Kidd Creek Mines when Brian Mulroney's newly elected government announced plans to sell off, Thatcher-style, a number of Crown assets, including Canada Development Corp. That September, Industry Minister Sinclair Stevens asked Trevor Eyton to head Canada Development Corp's parent, Canada Development Investment Corp., and to lead the privatization drive. In a memo to his boss, Mulroney, Stevens also suggested that the Edper Group act as "a merchant banker type of advisor" to the government. Eyton declined, but offered Edper Group executive Paul Marshall as an alternative. Eyton and his friend Patrick Keenan then became members of the Canada Development Investment Corp. board and its special Divestiture Committee.

Within a few weeks of Paul Marshall's mid-October 1984 appointment, Noranda president Adam Zimmerman — one of the Gang of Four who had lorded it over Noranda from the late 1960s until the Brascan takeover in the early 1980s — sent a memo to Edper Group executives asking for a general review of the Crown assets. "The obvious candidate that fits with Noranda is the [Canada Development Corp.] or large parts of it," the memo reportedly said. Noranda was interested in a joint venture with CDC's Kidd Creek Mines to consolidate its mining operations in Timmins, and a possible acquisition of CDC's Eldorado Nuclear.

It was no wonder that Canada Development Corp. CEO Tony Hampson was convinced the Edper Group was plotting to take over *his* company and cherry-pick the best assets, specifically Kidd

Creek Mines. At a 1984 Christmas lunch at the York Club in Toronto, Hampson spoke of his fears to Bill James, a former member of Noranda's Gang of Four, who had left Noranda two years earlier to become CEO of Falconbridge Ltd., the Western world's second-largest nickel producer.

In the spring of 1985, Jack Cockwell wrote a memo to Paul Marshall at Canada Development Investment Corp., suggesting that Edper's Great Lakes Group line up two or three major buyers, like Noranda, for a special government bond issue with Canada Development Corp. warrants attached. Meanwhile, Sinclair Stevens had arranged the appointment of Gordon Capital as government adviser to analyze the privatization contacts with other brokers. That May, Burns Fry Ltd. won the brokers' competition for the initial public offering of CDC, slated for September. Since Noranda was a potential buyer, Trevor Eyton declared a conflict of interest and left the room when the divestiture committee met on August 20, 1985, to discuss the pricing of the share issue. Thus Eyton missed the three-hour yelling match between Gordon Capital's Jimmy Connacher and Burns Fry's Jack Lawrence. Earlier that day, Gordon Capital had purchased $1.4 million of CDC shares for a company registered in the name of Jimmy Kay. Lawrence said the trade was more than coincidence, accusing Gordon Capital of deliberately driving up the price.

By this point, Jack Cockwell was advising Noranda not to purchase shares in Canada Development Corp., arguing that the price was too high. But Alf Powis committed Noranda to buying $74 million of shares, payable in two instalments. With a 10% holding in CDC, Powis thought he would have the clout to negotiate an acquisition of Kidd Creek Mines. He was wrong. His old friend Bill James had been busy hustling CDC's Tony Hampson to sell Kidd Creek Mines to Falconbridge. At a Scotiabank-Dofasco dinner that autumn, James and Hampson continued their secret negotiations, reportedly calculating debt, cash flow and tax liabilities on the dinner program. Their talks continued in mid-December in a private room at the King Edward Hotel. CDC soon changed its name to

Polysar Energy & Chemical Corp., selling Kidd Creek Mines to Falconbridge in the spring of 1986.

Jack Cockwell wasn't pleased. He had been working on a restructuring plan for Noranda since the resource giant's annual meeting in 1985, when an analyst had asked why Noranda wasn't slashing debt like Bill James was at Falconbridge. A few months later, Noranda began selling assets to reduce debt. When Noranda's fortunes improved in 1986, Cockwell parachuted in David Kerr as vice-president of strategic planning. Five months later, in March 1987, Kerr replaced Adam Zimmerman as president of Noranda; Zimmerman was sent out west to manage Noranda Forest. At the Noranda Christmas party that year, a video entitled "The New Employee" depicted the "trials and tribulations of a new boy named Dave. In the final scene, Dave, working late on the books, [was] given a lecture by the janitor [Bill James] on how to get ahead at Noranda," according to Patricia Best and Jennifer Wells in the *Financial Times of Canada*. Alf Powis later told Best and Wells that he felt great relief when Kerr showed up: "It gives me some comfort level that if David and I agree to do something I don't have to go running up to Brascan and say, 'Is that all right?'" But a friend of Powis's contradicted him, telling the two journalists that Powis was "being squeezed between Cockwell and Kerr like a piece of baloney in a sandwich."

For example, Jack Cockwell reportedly told Alf Powis to manage Noranda's 1987 earnings. Then on Thursday, May 25, 1988, Cockwell instructed Powis not to vote Noranda's shares of Polysar Energy & Chemical Corp., the former Canada Development Corp., in the nasty proxy fight between Polysar and Bob Blair's Nova Corp. With Gordon Capital's help, Nova had been stalking Polysar since late 1987. Although Noranda had sold its 7.5 million Polysar shares, representing a 10.5% interest, to Gordon Capital in mid-April at $22.50 a share — almost twice what it had paid for them — some of Gordon Capital's buyers did not register the shares in their names, leaving Noranda with two million Polysar shares to vote at the annual shareholders' meeting. Powis intended to vote in favour of Polysar management, but Blair's lawyers demanded he revoke the proxy. So did Cockwell. Powis did as he was told — it wasn't a big issue because his sights were set once more on Kidd Creek Mines.

Noranda got another opportunity to grab control of the rich ore body, when Placer Dome Inc. put its 24.7% block of Falconbridge shares up for auction on June 21, 1988. But Noranda failed to persuade the Ontario Securities Commission to allow its lowball bid "without the offer constituting a takeover bid." Since the commission had granted Falconbridge certain takeover exemptions, the block went to Falconbridge for roughly $1 billion.

That didn't stop Alf Powis. Almost immediately, Noranda started scooping up cheap Falconbridge stock in the open market, paying an average $22.43 a share in a creeping takeover. By early autumn, Noranda had accumulated slightly more than a 20% interest in Falconbridge and announced that it wanted to pay $22.25 a share for an additional 10% stake. A team from Merrill Lynch Canada was advising Falconbridge on how to rebuff Noranda's advances. Falconbridge called in the Ontario Securities Commission, which ruled that any bid made by Noranda must offer shareholders the same deal that institutional shareholders had got in August. In other words, Noranda had to bid $23 a share for 100% of the stock. When the OSC requirement expired in November 1988, Noranda announced a normal-course bid, enabling it to buy 10% of Falconbridge over six months at market prices.

But during the next six months, nickel prices rose, copper prices reached a historic high, and Falconbridge stock followed, soaring above $30 a share. Noranda stayed out of the market, while Falconbridge's Bill James held friendly elevator chats (his headquarters was five floors below Noranda in Commerce Court West) and low-level discussions with Alf Powis and David Kerr to see whether they could strike a deal before Noranda upped its stake and its demands. Already Noranda had asked Falconbridge to expand its board to 14 directors from 11, and to give Noranda the additional three spots. Noranda had also asked Falconbridge to cancel the block of stock it had acquired, to boost Noranda's stake so that it could equity-account its Falconbridge investment.

On Friday, March 3, 1989, Bill James and his chief financial officer met with Alf Powis and David Kerr in Hershel's delicatessen, across the courtyard in Commerce Court East (now the site of Jump restaurant). The four men discussed Kidd Creek Mines over sandwiches at the standup counter. Later that day, James called a second meeting at Hershel's. There Powis made some concessions, and James felt he had the "makings of a deal" for Kidd Creek Mines. Believing that an agreement in principle had been reached, Powis left Toronto that weekend for an extended safari in Kenya, and was out of telephone contact for several weeks. Unfortunately, the follow-up negotiations revealed fundamental differences, and in April talks broke down. Noranda renewed notice of its normal-course bid, but its creeping takeover had ground to a halt.

Then, in the afternoon of Thursday, June 1, 1989, Gordon Capital called Alf Powis to say it had lined up a block of 3.5 million Falconbridge shares at $32 a share, which would boost Noranda's stake to 24%. Would Noranda be interested? Powis thought about it overnight; the answer was yes and the deal was done before lunch on Friday.

Falconbridge's Bill James got a telephone call from the CEO of Amax Inc. of New York City on June 23, to discuss joint nickel-exploration projects. That led to a series of chats about Amax coming in as a white knight to fend off Noranda. On July 6, Amax and Falconbridge signed a confidentiality agreement, and on July 14, James met with the Amax CEO and Amax advisers Merrill Lynch & Co. in New York City to discuss Amax acquiring a control stake in Falconbridge. By Tuesday, August 1, they had struck a deal. The following day, Amax announced a stunning $2.8 billion bid — $36.13 a share — for 100% of Falconbridge. The company also adopted a poison pill to force Noranda to bid for all of Falconbridge if it wanted to buy more shares.

That Friday, August 4, 1989, at 6:45 in the morning, Vic Alboini, an investment banker at Loewen, Ondaatje & McCutcheon in Toronto, who had been searching for a possible partner for Noranda, made his first call of the day, to the mining arm of Trelleborg AB of Sweden, which already had a small stake in Falconbridge and planned to acquire more. Within a matter of hours, Trelleborg had decided it would be interested in a joint venture. The investment banker contacted a vice-president at Noranda, who spoke to Alf Powis. This time it was David Kerr, vacationing with his family on an island off the coast of Vancouver, who was out of telephone contact for several weeks. But Noranda had a scheduled board meeting that afternoon, so the joint venture was discussed by Noranda directors, including Edper Group appointees Jack Cockwell, Peter Bronfman, Trevor Eyton, Bill L'Heureux and Paul Marshall. Late Friday afternoon, Powis and the Trelleborg president began negotiations, in a conference call arranged by Alboini. By early Monday morning, August 7, a four-man Noranda team was in the town of Trelleborg, Sweden, population 35,000. Negotiations resumed at 5:00 p.m. and went on until 4:00 a.m. Tuesday. Noranda's board approved the deal that Friday, and the following Monday, August 14, Noranda and Trelleborg, who together owned 27.5% of Falconbridge, announced their $37 a share bid, which beat Amax's offer by 88 cents a share. That set the stage for a bidding war, until Amax withdrew from the contest on Friday, September 1. The Noranda-Trelleborg partnership ended up paying $39 a share — $16 a share higher than what Noranda had paid a year earlier in its creeping takeover — for the 72.5% of Falconbridge it did not already own.

Once again, the Edper Group had bought control of a resources company at the top of a cycle. It would allow something similar to happen in real estate — at Bramalea.

Kenny Field told a tearful gathering of Bramalea office staff on Friday, June 30, 1988, that he would step down as president and co-CEO at the upcoming annual meeting. The contract he had signed almost two years earlier, when Trizec took control of Bramalea, expired that summer. After months of sparring with

Trizec executives over the management of Bramalea, Field had decided not to renew the contract.

That left Ben Swirsky as the last of the troika of enterprising lawyers — Dick Shiff, Field and Swirsky — who had turned a local Toronto home-builder into one of North America's most successful real-estate companies. Dick Shiff, a smart, penny-pinching operator, and Kenny Field, an ebullient young dealmaker, had borrowed $2.5 million in the mid-1970s to buy 60% of Bramalea's shares. By the time Ben Swirsky, a tax lawyer and senior partner at chartered accountants Peat Marwick & Mitchell, came on board as executive vice-president at the end of 1978, the value of Bramalea's assets had tripled to half a billion dollars, including the two hotels, nine shopping centres and five other properties picked up for roughly $100 million from debt-swamped Trizec three years earlier. But by the time Bramalea's assets had quadrupled to almost $2 billion in 1984, it was facing its own debt crisis, following a disastrous foray into oil-and-gas exploration. A restructured Trizec came to the rescue, infusing $160 million into Bramalea for a minority stake. The following year, Shiff swapped his family's block of Bramalea shares for Trizec preferred shares in a $70 million transaction. Trizec got more Bramalea shares in 1986 in exchange for its shopping centres, pooled in a new Bramalea subsidary, Trilea Centres.

A month after Trizec gained control of Bramalea, Jack Cockwell good-naturedly challenged the chubby-cheeked Kenny Field to prove on paper that Bramalea was a more successful company than Trizec. Cockwell had overseen the successful financial restructuring of Trizec in the late 1970s, and Field was considered the entrepreneurial force behind Bramalea. He was the man who had flown to American Motors' Detroit headquarters in 1984 and refused to leave until the auto executives agreed to consider Brampton as the site for a new car plant. Later, Field sold American Motors some of Bramalea's land for a plant, and Bramalea built houses in the surrounding area and sold them to the new plant workers.

Although Kenny Field had the confidence of Jack Cockwell, he had to fight Trizec executives Harold Milavsky and Kevin Benson every step of the way for operational control of Bramalea. In a last-ditch bid for autonomy, Field asked Bramalea director Albert Reichmann to intervene. Reichmann didn't want Field to leave Bramalea, but after he read the file Field had prepared for a book he planned to write about Trizec's "mismanagement" of Bramalea, he realized it was too late to stop him. Reichmann said Olympia & York would try to find a new project for Field to take on.

At the July 22, 1988, annual meeting, Kenny Field bid the Bramalea shareholders farewell: "Fourteen years ago I stood here at an annual meeting with a vision of transforming an Ontario house-building company to a giant of the North American real-estate industry. It was a big dream and it came through." The divorced Field, then 44, sold his 10% stake in Bramalea to Trizec for $100 million in cash, set up his own investment company and embarked on a year-long sabbatical of playing tennis, sailing and skiing with his three teenaged children.

Months later, Field was paged at a country club in Palm Springs, California. Apparently, Paul Reichmann had a note in his datebook to call Field, so Reichmann's secretary had tracked him down. When Field managed to return the call a few days later, Reichmann talked vaguely about Field getting involved in Olympia & York's restructuring of U.S. railroad Santa Fe Pacific Corp. Later, on a skiing holiday in Vail, Colorado, Field was surprised to receive four cartons of documents on Santa Fe Pacific that Reichmann had sent by Federal Express.

Meanwhile, Ben Swirsky, the last of the Shiff-Field-Swirsky triumvirate, had been left to fend for himself at Bramalea, after suffering a personal tragedy that reportedly left him traumatized. In 1987 Bramalea had reached a milestone of more than $100 million in annual cash flow. It had $4 billion in assets split half and half between Canada and the U.S. Among public real-estate companies, Bramalea's portfolio of income-producing properties, including hotels, office buildings, business parks, 30 shopping centres in Canada and 11 shopping centres in the U.S., ranked second only to Trizec, said BBN James Capel analyst Frank Mayer. When Trizec handed

Swirzky the reins at Bramalea, "it was Ben's moment to show what he could do," a friend later told Kimberley Noble and Margaret Philp for *The Globe and Mail.* "So he went out and bought up the world."

Under Ben Swirsky's stewardship, Bramalea embarked on a $2 billion-plus North American development plan. On the drawing boards were a joint-venture US$400 million downtown Chicago office tower, a US$160 million office and retail development in Oakland, a US$60 million office building in Los Angeles, and a $100 million building at Queen and Yonge streets in Toronto. Another $400 million had been earmarked to modernize and expand the shopping centres. Convinced that Bramalea would soon run out of land to build houses on, Swirsky also spent close to $1 billion over the next two years for 930 acres of land in and around Metro Toronto. "The problem was that Bramalea moved too aggressively buying sites in the Toronto area. It got swept up in the boom euphoria and was among those caught by the unexpected timing of the market downturn," Swirsky's replacement, Marvin Marshall, told the Bramalea annual meeting in 1990.

In mid-1988, Ben Swirsky expected housing to drop to about 20% of Bramalea's operating profit, "but it won't be because we're de-emphasizing housing. Other aspects of the operations are just growing faster." And about 20–30 aquisitions were in the works, Swirsky said in an interview. "We're an opportunistic company and we achieve growth by acquisition and development." In late June, Bramalea spent $100 million to acquire Campeau properties in Ottawa. Seven months later, Bramalea bought Marlborough Development Corp., a home-builder in southern California, for US$250 million. Later in 1989, Bramalea and Trizec jointly paid $240 million for the old post office site in downtown Toronto.

Where was the oppressive Trizec management, which had fought so hard over computer systems, during this spending spree? Trizec was busy building the $300 million Bankers Hall in Calgary, with the first phase scheduled for completion in 1989, and beginning construction of the Bay Adelaide Centre in downtown Toronto, with its elaborate 57-storey design of granite columns, marble lobbies,

32 high-speed elevators and a half-acre garden. But Bramalea's 15-member board, which included Harold Milavsky, Kevin Benson, Gordon Arnell, Peter Bronfman and Jack Cockwell, had approved Ben Swirsky's acquisition plans. Olympia & York was represented by Albert Reichmann and Gilbert Newman. Dick Shiff was also a Bramalea director, but Kenny Field had gone sailing, on his 36-foot yacht called *For Sail*.

Bramalea's boom euphoria was summed up in its corporate sponsorship of Toronto's 1989 Opera Ball, held at the Inn on the Park (Four Seasons) on Thursday, September 21. Jack Cockwell, Wendy Cecil-Cockwell and other arriving guests were "serenaded by a dozen violinists, showered with rose petals by baroque-gowned girls and served antipasto from an Italian gondola." Patricia Appleby, chair of the ball, had insisted it be moved to Thursday evening from Friday, the start of the Jewish Sabbath. To get the right people to attend, Appleby's committee sent out gift packages to the homes of 200 CEOs. Gordon Capital's Jimmy Connacher immediately sent a cheque for $10,000; Olympia & York's Albert Reichmann, a cheque for $5,000. The ball netted almost half a million dollars.

The night of the Opera Ball, Edper's Gordon Arnell had been working late into the night, negotiating a joint venture with BCE in BCE Development Ltd. The Reichmanns had already jetted away twice from the little Vancouver home-builder that took on North America.

Chapter 10

Playing Monopoly

In conversation with Vancouver developer Jack Poole in the autumn of 1988, Paul Reichmann had expressed a casual interest in BCE Place, twin office towers under construction on Bay Street in Toronto, and in BCE Development Corp.

The six-foot Jack Poole had co-founded Daon Development Corp., a predecessor of BCE Development, almost a quarter of a century earlier with Graham Dawson, a man who would have been more at home in puritanical Toronto than hedonistic Vancouver. Daon (the name was contracted from Dawson Housing Developments) was one of North America's highest fliers during the 1970s, and so was Poole. His office in the brick-clad Daon Building at the foot of Burrard Street in Vancouver, reportedly set back so that it did not obstruct the harbour view for members of the neighbouring Vancouver Club, boasted 22 windows.

Most of Daon's real-estate holdings were in the West, but three-quarters of its earnings came from south of the border; in fact, Daon had one of California's largest land banks. At Daon's peak, when Poole's shareholdings were said to be worth $100 million, he travelled by private jet and lived in a $4 million house in West Vancouver. But the recession of 1981–82 put Daon on the brink of bankruptcy and wiped out most of Poole's personal fortune. The handsome 55-year-old with the Steinway smile aged almost overnight, getting involved with a younger woman and splitting up with his wife of more than 30 years, whom he'd married when he was just 17. She moved to California to be near their married daughter.

Just before Christmas of 1982, a journalist stopped Jack Poole on a Vancouver street and asked him what he wanted under the tree. He is said to have replied, "I want my $100 million back." Over the next two years, Poole charmed Daon's bankers into accepting a complicated debt-restructuring plan that kept the company alive. Daon eased its massive debt load by selling off properties like its Vancouver showpiece, Park Place. In early 1985 an executive from BCE Inc., the holding company of Bell Canada, flew west to put a bid on the Park Place office tower. He didn't get it, but he liked Daon so much that he persuaded BCE to buy 70% of the company, renamed BCE Development Corp. Poole was back in business.

Within a year, Don Love's Oxford Development Group, another financially troubled Western developer, put US$1 billion of U.S. properties on the market. Arguing that this was a forced sale and the properties were cheap, Poole managed to push BCE into the deal, financed 90% by debt. It was a big mistake. American real-estate markets collapsed with the savings and loan debacle, sucking up the money needed for BCE Development's Canadian projects such as BCE Place in Toronto. BCE executives started dogging Poole, reviewing his decisions and restricting his autonomy.

The situation worsened for Poole when Raymond Cyr, known as the Human Computer, replaced the free-wheeling Jean de Grandpré as CEO of the parent company, BCE, in May 1988. Not long after, Poole sold 87% of his BCE Development stock and BCE later installed several of its own executives below Poole at the real-estate arm. Cyr wanted to find a partner to share BCE's debt burden before BCE Development was forced to sell the U.S. properties at a loss. After Poole spoke to Paul Reichmann that autumn, Reichmann asked to meet with Cyr to discuss the possibility of Olympia & York making an investment in BCE Development.

Adding BCE Place to Olympia & York's portfolio of trophy properties on Bay Street, which already included First Canadian Place and a half-interest in Campeau's Scotia Plaza, would give the Reichmanns the Toronto equivalent of Park Place, Boardwalk and St. Charles Place on the Monopoly board. Yet Olympia & York's US$260 million investment in Campeau debentures was proving to be nothing but trouble. With Campeau stock trading in the $15-a-share range on the Toronto Stock Exchange and the debentures convertible at $26 a share, Olympia & York was forced to buy 500,000 more Campeau Corp. shares in late 1988 to prop up the stock price.

Campeau Corp. was in a tailspin, and Robert Campeau was in denial. He had not dealt with the enormous US$9.9 billion debt overhang from his back-to-back takeovers of Allied and Federated Stores. Since the spring of 1988, Campeau had been busy building his dream home on the shore of an Austrian lake. Although he did put Allied's Ann Taylor retail chain on the block in mid-May 1988, it didn't sell until the following February, at US$100 million less than Campeau's price. He also turned down buyers for Federated's Gold Circle division, which had to be liquidated in October 1988.

At the same time, Campeau was fighting in court with his two oldest children for voting control of their Campeau shares, which they had gained control of at age 35. If all six children from two wives voted their trust shares independently of their father when they came of age, Campeau's stake would slip below 50%.

By the time a delayed US$1.15 billion Federated junk-bond issue was finally launched in late September 1988, the market was saturated with an expected US$60 billion of junk debt, mostly from RJR Nabisco. Underwriter First Boston was forced to withdraw the issue, cut the size to US$750 million and raise the yield twice, before it sold in late October. The remaining US$400 million was supposed to be sold before Christmas. Inspired by Paul Reichmann's innovative financings, Campeau turned down Citibank NA's offer of a US$1.1 billion mortgage in November that could have been used to pay off a US$800 million shorter-term high-interest takeover loan led by Citibank NA, which was due in January 1990. Campeau envisioned instead a US$4 billion jumbo mortgage, with the lenders participating in Federated's future growth in return for a lower interest rate.

Quick to make judgments that were not always correct, and entirely beyond persuasion once he had done so, Campeau approached Prudential Assurance with his scheme. It said no thanks. In late 1988, Campeau flew to Tokyo in Federated's Gulfstream jet, one of four planes in the Federated Air Force, but the Japanese bankers weren't interested. "You ought to be grateful to America. It's rare that a conqueror treats a conquered country as well as you have been treated," Campeau reportedly told the startled bankers. Back in the U.S., JMB Realty said no. So did The Equitable. Campeau then jetted to Frankfurt, Germany, to see the powerful Deutsche Bank; again he left empty-handed. Campeau couldn't sell his jumbo loan idea anywhere, his two key in-house advisers, then-president James Roddy and finance expert Carolyn Buck Luce, were threatening to quit over the scheme, and he still had US$400 million of junk bonds to hawk. In January 1989, First Boston and two other investment banks bought the remaining junk bonds for exchange notes, which would entitle junk-bond holders to almost 7% of Federated's capital stock. Later Campeau asked First Boston to scrap the deal because he didn't want to give that much equity away.

Paul Reichmann was more successful in his refinancing efforts. By January 1989, Olympia & York had arranged a US$2.5 billion jumbo loan from a global consortium of banks led by Hong Kong & Shanghai Banking Corp. and including Frankfurt's Commerzbank and Tokyo's Dai-Ichi Kangyo Bank, the world's biggest bank. The Reichmann mystique was so powerful that the jumbo loan was originally going to be unsecured, until Osler Hoskin & Harcourt, the Toronto legal advisers to Credit Lyonnais, protested and it ended up being collateralized by Olympia & York's equity stakes in Abitibi-Price and Gulf Canada.

Incredibly, these banks did not get to see the secrets of Paul Reichmann's leather binder. Instead, they got an annual certificate from auditors Price Waterhouse that Olympia & York Developments' net worth was at least US$2.5 billion. (When Price Waterhouse conducted its annual audit of Olympia & York Developments, the work was subdivided into a multitude of small parts, and only one or two senior partners got to see the entire balance sheet.) The Reichmanns reportedly also promised to "make available once annually a senior financing officer to discuss the affairs and finances of Olympia & York Developments Ltd. with officers and lenders." Less than six months earlier, Reichmann had arranged a mammoth refinancing of First Canadian Place in Toronto, with the biggest corporate bond issue in Canadian history, led by Merrill Lynch Canada. The issue raised almost half a billion dollars in the Canadian and European bond markets. Just as it had financed and refinanced its prized Uris properties in New York City to fund the construction of the World Financial Center, Olympia & York was financing and refinancing its prized Canadian assets to fund the construction of Canary Wharf, the biggest development project in the world.

At the same time, Paul Reichmann was negotiating a joint venture in BCE Development with BCE's Raymond Cyr, a short, barrel-bellied Quebecker. In late January 1989, Olympia & York offered to pay $3.75 a share for treasury shares and to pick up additional shares in the market to reach a 40% stake in BCE Development, for an expected $200 million–$300 million in cash. An Olympia & York team that included Albert Reichmann's son Philip set up camp in BCE Development's head office on the 38th floor of the Toronto-Dominion Bank Tower.

That same week, on January 25, 1989, French-Canadian conglomateur Paul Desmarais did the first of two back-to-back deals that put more than a billion dollars in his wallet. First he sold Power Corp.'s 40% interest in pulp and paper company Consolidated-Bathurst Inc. for $1.25 billion in cash. A little more than a month later, Desmarais sold Power Financial Corp.'s 63.8% interest in Montreal Trustco to BCE Inc. for a package of cash and shares valued at $875 million. These were timely dispositions.

Desmarais's strategy was in sharp contrast to BCE's. Since 1983, when Jean de Grandpré had formed BCE to separate Bell's subsidiaries from the telephone utility and the constraints of its government regulators, the conglomerate had been on a buying spree, investing in the pipeline, energy, real-estate, publishing and computer businesses. Money manager Ira Gluskin called it the "floundering empire of BCE," with a "history of incompetence." Raymond Cyr's strategy was to move out of the marginal areas and concentrate on core telecommunications companies and long-term investments that would provide stable profits. Cyr professed to be happier with the Montreal Trustco investment than he was with BCE Development, anticipating a regular cash flow from the trust company. He didn't get it.

By mid-March 1989, Olympia & York and BCE were ready to sign off on their joint venture in BCE Development, but Paul Reichmann was out of the country. He was in London, where Olympia & York was trumpeting a tentative agreement to lease 240,000 square feet of space at Canary Wharf to Merrill Lynch & Co. After several trans-Atlantic telephone calls between Reichmann and Raymond Cyr, the BCE chief reportedly realized the deal wasn't going to work. For public consumption, Cyr explained that there was a disagreement over the long-term direction BCE Development would take and suggested a public company might make a better partner. Insiders said the issue was control: BCE feared that Reichmann would insist on the sale of BCE Development's U.S. properties at a loss, wrecking BCE's carefully managed profits.

Three weeks later, Robert Campeau appeared at Olympia & York's world headquarters in Toronto, begging for cash. "If I don't get it, I don't know what I'm going to do," a frantic Campeau privately told Paul Reichmann on Friday, April 7, 1989. Campeau Corp.'s James Roddy and Carolyn Buck Luce had managed to refinance most of Allied's US$1.2 billion working capital and receivables facility, except for a US$250 million shortfall. The situation was so desperate that Campeau's lawyers had prepared documents for Allied to seek court protection from its creditors. US$100 million was supposed to come from Canadian property sales. Campeau Corp. did manage to draw down US$75 million from a bank operating line, and Reichmann agreed to loan US$75 million to Allied, backed by a second mortgage on Campeau Corp.'s half of Scotia Plaza. After Campeau left, Reichmann called in private detective Jules Kroll to investigate the company's finances. By late April, Roddy and Buck Luce both had quit Campeau Corp., fed up with running interference between Campeau and his bankers.

Then, in Vancouver, Jack Poole surprised the crowd at the BCE Development annual meeting on Monday, May 1, 1989, by announcing his departure from the company he had co-founded. In the wake of the collapsed deal with the Reichmanns, Poole also announced that BCE Development would have to sell its U.S. properties, accounting for 80% of its property portfolio and located mainly in middle America, or the flyover states, as coastal executives disparagingly called them. JMB Realty Corp. of Chicago approached BCE's Raymond Cyr, and a series of talks were held, but they never went very far, Cyr later said. JMB Realty offered to take over management of the U.S. properties for a $100 million cash infusion into BCE Development, but Cyr thought the offer was too low, and secretly used it as leverage to bring the Reichmanns back to the table. Olympia & York made a competing offer, dubbed Reichmann Two, of $557 million, or $2.80 a share, for all of BCE Development, with the provision that a minimum of 90% of BCE Development's common shares had to be tendered to its offer. When BCE Development trading halted on June 23, JMB Realty thought BCE was going to announce its purchase of the U.S. properties, so it was flabbergasted when BCE announced instead that it had agreed to tender its 67% interest in BCE Development to a new offer from Olympia & York.

Meanwhile, Paul Reichmann's reputation as a finance savant peaked that year with a Japanese yen swap by Olympia & York. Reichmann bet US$800 million on the direction of the yen against the U.S. dollar in a yen-dominated mortgage. Olympia & York made millions when the yen rose against the U.S. dollar. (Six years later, Barings PLC's trader Nicholas Leeson would not be as lucky as Reichmann in the Japanese arbitrage game: Leeson lost his US$1 billion bet on the direction of the Nikkei index, bringing down his employer, a 233-year-old merchant bank.)

The global banks still fought to lend money to Olympia & York. For example, on Thursday, June 8, 1989, four banks — Canadian

Imperial Bank of Commerce, Royal Bank of Canada, Bank of Nova Scotia and National Bank of Canada — agreed to lend £400 million to O&Y subsidiary O&Y Realty Credit Corp., to help fund construction of Canary Wharf. Five days later, on Tuesday, June 13, 1989, a Citibank Canada-led syndicate of six Japanese banks agreed to lend an O&Y subsidiary US$500 million. The collateral for the Citibank Canada loan was Olympia & York's shares in Carena Properties, which in turn controlled Trizec. The Citibank Canada syndicate was also assigned O&Y's rights in Carena Properties under its shareholders' agreement with the Edper Group.

But the Reichmann mystique was about to end. The situation at Campeau Corp. was deteriorating. Retail operating results and sales were nowhere near projections. Ten days before Campeau Corp.'s annual shareholders' meeting, Campeau hired investment bank Hellman & Friedman of San Francisco to study the situation. The shareholders' meeting was held in Toronto at the Royal York Hotel, on Thursday, July 20, 1989, the same day as the nearby Enfield annual meeting. When open warfare erupted at the Enfield meeting, that became the lead story in the next-day business papers, bumping Campeau coverage in Canada.

At the Campeau Corp. meeting, Robert Campeau was ridiculously upbeat, holding up that morning's copy of *The Wall Street Journal*, which suggested Federated and Allied were in trouble and questioned whether they could continue to service their debt. "We've been tried, we've been hung and given reprieves so many times from all the newspapers in the country that it's just amazing we're still around," roared Campeau, calling his retail holdings second to none. "No one can stop us but ourselves," he told shareholders. Campeau's executives announced that US$1.2 billion of mortgage financing would be in place within 30 days.

Evelyn Davis, an annoying American who made it her mission to prowl the annual-meeting circuit of large U.S. companies, pulling stunts and asking inane questions of the CEOs, commented on the absence of Campeau director Albert Reichmann. She warned Campeau that Reichmann might be planning a "coup d'etat while you are away on vacation, basking in the sun." In fact, the Reichmanns had learned from their private investigator what everyone else seemed to suspect: Campeau's Federated and Allied Stores could not generate enough cash to pay their bills or the interest on their massive debt.

When Campeau's liquidity crisis became public about six weeks later, money manager Ira Gluskin wrote in the *Financial Times of Canada*, "Perhaps you have read in the paper that Campeau Corp. suddenly had a shortfall of working capital. Don't you think that analysts have been asking management questions about the company's working capital adequacy for months? The company did not suddenly run out of money. This is the last straw for me: Bob, you can go right down the drain as far as I'm concerned."

By August, even Citibank NA had turned its back on Robert Campeau. It refused to do the US$1.2 billion of straight mortgage financing it had offered in November. It was a vicious circle: There would be no mortgage financing until the liquidity problems were solved, and no working capital until the mortgage financing was in place. What was Campeau to do? Since he had long admired Paul Reichmann's financial exploits and even referred to him as a brother, Campeau expected Reichmann to come to his rescue with financial assistance. He jetted to Switzerland, where the Reichmanns were on their annual walking holiday at a kosher resort for Orthodox Jews in the Alps. Paul Reichmann reportedly did not want to be disturbed, but he agreed to meet Campeau in the chalet. Campeau told Reichmann that the U.S. retail units needed another US$250 million in working capital to survive the fall season and to pay for Christmas merchandise. Reichmann reportedly told Campeau he had concluded that Campeau was fighting a lost cause and would be better off filing for bankruptcy protection. And if Reichmann did put in more money, all of Campeau's remaining real estate would have to be offered up as collateral. Did Campeau want to risk everything? Perhaps he should go home and think it over.

By mid-August, the Reichmanns also had come across a confidential consulting report which detailed BCE Development's enormous problems in the U.S., where the developer was reportedly embroiled in a legal dispute and its cash flow was nowhere near projections. A Burns Fry fairness opinion on the Reichmann Two offer, prepared for the independent committee of BCE Development directors, said a major writedown in property values was necessary.

It was a tricky situation: How could the Reichmanns jet away from their second bid for BCE Development? But if the deal went through, Olympia & York might have to sue BCE for incomplete information. On the eve of the bid's expiry, Paul Reichmann summoned four BCE Development senior executives to his Toronto office at 9:30 p.m. and grilled them for information about the U.S. operations. "He should have been asking those sorts of questions eight months ago," one of the executives told John Stackhouse for *Report on Business Magazine.*

At 10:30 p.m., only an hour and a half before the midnight deadline, the four men were sent back to their offices to wait, as the trustees counted the shares coming in from across the country. Fortunately for the Reichmanns, only 88% of BCE Development's common shares tendered to Olympia & York's bid, narrowly missing the minimum 90% target. More than a third of the 7,000 small investors who owned BCE Development stock had refused to sell their shares. They thought Olympia & York's bid was too low, particularly since no one had bothered to explain to them why it was 25% less than the earlier $3.50-a-share joint-venture offer, so they rejected the bid, expecting that a better offer would be forthcoming. Sadly, they were wrong. At 2:30 a.m., Paul Reichmann called Raymond Cyr at BCE headquarters in Montreal to tell him that Olympia & York would not extend its offer. The deal was off. Reichmann reportedly "did not explain, nor did he apologize."

A bitter Raymond Cyr later accused Paul Reichmann of spending the summer flying around the globe in his private jet, putting out fires in his empire. There was merit to his accusation. While in Chicago for meetings about Santa Fe Southern Pacific, Paul Reichmann had even bid on the Sears Tower, the tallest office tower in the world and the ultimate trophy property. Meanwhile, the

Reichmanns were refusing to speed up the restructuring at Santa Fe Southern Pacific, much to Sam Zell's frustration. The brothers said they were concerned about the company's mountainous debt. When Santa Fe finally spun off its real-estate and energy divisions in December 1990, Zell sold off all of Itel's interests in Sante Fe except for the investment in Santa Fe Energy Resources.

Over in London, where the miraculous summer of 1989 had turned the city's central parks into green beaches strewn with sunbathers, Olympia & York was having difficulty rounding up tenants for Canary Wharf. As Chuck Young, who'd left Citibank to help manage the Canary Wharf project, later half-joked to *Canadian Business*'s Ross Fisher, "I am a prisoner...and Paul Reichmann says he won't release me until I lease Canary Wharf." British firms refused to leave their warren of pubs and clubs in central London for the development they had dubbed Wall-Street-on-Thames. And there was no longer a shortage of office space in the Square Mile, since the City of London had changed planning restrictions to allow more construction. The availability of several million square feet of new space caused rent levels to slide to half their peak levels.

At Canary Wharf, construction activity peaked in the second half of 1989. But an eight-week unofficial strike by the steel erectors, followed by a work to rule and other problems, put construction six months behind schedule, limiting progress on the tower to 12 storeys by year-end.

As if the problems at Canary Wharf weren't enough trouble for one summer, Robert Campeau was back. In late August he met with Paul Reichmann in London, where they hammered out a deal. Olympia & York would guarantee a US$250 million line of credit so that Federated and Allied could stock their shelves for Christmas. In turn, Olympia & York got another US$250 million of convertible debentures, backed by essentially all of Campeau Corp.'s unpledged real-estate assets, as the Reichmanns positioned themselves to "scoop up as many pieces" as they could if Campeau defaulted. Olympia & York also purchased warrants, giving them 38.4% of

Campeau Corp. shares, fully diluted. Campeau's personal stake was reduced from 54% to 43.2%, fully diluted. But the Reichmanns were calling the shots. They wanted to dismember the Campeau Corp. board, slashing it to 10 seats from 21. Two-thirds of the old guard would be dismissed and three Reichmann picks installed. In addition, Hollinger chairman Conrad Black, whose own board of directors then included both Paul Reichmann and Robert Campeau, was asked to represent Campeau's minority shareholders on the new Campeau board. And a special four-man committee of Campeau directors, headed by Olympia & York's Lionel Dodd, would oversee a restructuring of Campeau Corp.'s reeling U.S. retail divisions.

The changes were calculated to isolate Campeau from his failing U.S. operations and to give the Reichmanns control of the outcome. The committee planned to hire Merrill Lynch & Co. as advisers on the restructuring, replacing First Boston, and management consultants McKinsey & Co. to do a study of the U.S. retail divisions. The Reichmanns also agreed to help arrange and possibly participate in a new US$800 million bridge loan for Campeau Corp. on two conditions: The 17-store Bloomingdales chain had to be sold for a good price, and Campeau Corp. had to buy back at least 75% of Federated and Allied's junk bonds at prices no higher than where they traded on September 15, 1989 — a steep discount to their par value.

On Friday, September 8, 1989, Robert Campeau publicly admitted Campeau Corp.'s liquidity crisis and revealed that he had asked the Reichmanns to bail him out. On the following Tuesday, September 12, the Campeau Corp. board met for three hours in the company's Toronto headquarters on the 58th floor of Scotia Plaza, at the corner of Bay and King Streets, while reporters, photographers and television news crews waited outside the building to ambush the directors as they came out.

The board approved the Reichmann restructuring plan, but negotiations with creditors lasted another week, often going through the night in Toronto, as Campeau Corp. gathered layers of consents from a US$4 billion banking syndicate led by Citibank NA and co-managed by Osaka's Sumitomo Bank, with 13 other Japanese banks in the syndicate; from Bank of Nova Scotia, holders of property loans with Campeau's real estate as collateral; and from Edward DeBartolo, who had provided a US$480 million loan for the Federated takeover. Paul Reichmann reportedly negotiated directly with Citibank and Sumitomo and a Campeau envoy flew to see DeBartolo at his Ohio headquarters.

On Wednesday, September 13, panicked shareholders drove down Campeau stock to $3 3/8 from $13 1/2 on the Toronto Stock Exchange. Trading halted just after noon. TSE officials pressed Campeau Corp. to make an announcement.

A week after the board had approved the deal, all the creditors had come into line, and the stock resumed trading. The deadline for the Citibank loan had been pushed back to April 30, 1990. The new board's first action was to stop dividend payments on several series of preferred stock and common shares.

A month later, on Tuesday, October 17, 1989, Robert and Ilse Campeau hosted the opening gala for Scotia Plaza. The arriving 720 guests entered the cavernous, red-granite foyer to the melodious sounds of a 14-piece orchestra, sipped Moet et Chandon champagne and supped on fresh oysters and caviar, before taking elevators up to the 68th floor for dinner and dancing, as well as entertainment by comedian Jay Leno and singer Dionne Warwick. Paul Reichmann was one of the committee members, and Conrad Black was one of the two co-chairmen of the gala, which raised $800,000 for Covenant House, a shelter for street kids and children with AIDS. The gala was Campeau's first public appearance since early September.

Meanwhile, Campeau's September crisis had sparked a panic in the U.S. junk-bond market and contributed to a downturn in stock markets worldwide. The Roaring '80s ended on Friday, October 13, 1989, when the Dow Jones Industrial Average plummeted almost 200 points following news of the busted takeover deal for the parent of United Airlines. Then Federated and Allied junk bonds plunged in price on Monday, October 26, as word hit Wall Street that the Campeau restructuring was floundering. Campeau stock was dropping like a stone. As of November 15, 1989, almost two million

Campeau shares had been sold short. (Short sellers borrowed shares and sold them, betting that the price would fall and allow them to replace those shares at a cheaper price and reap a profit before returning them to the lender.) With Campeau shares trading at around $4 on the Toronto Stock Exchange, Robert Campeau's personal fortune of $550 million had almost evaporated.

And the Reichmanns had received a nasty shock. Robert Campeau had not told them that Edward DeBartolo Corp.'s US$480 million loan was guaranteed by Campeau Corp. In other words, the loan was secured by the Canadian assets as well as the U.S. assets. A DeBartolo claim on Campeau's Canadian properties might even rank ahead of a Reichmann claim. Olympia & York wasn't well secured after all. Then DeBartolo decided not to extend its US$480 million loan agreement to Campeau, a move that also terminated Olympia & York's US$260 million loan agreement. At the same time, Robert Campeau was badmouthing the Reichmanns, blaming them for a "half-hearted" rescue. Campeau Corp. had drawn down only US$150 million of Olympia & York's US$250 million line of credit, and had already paid back US$25 million.

By early December it was clear that the survival plan for Federated and Allied wasn't working. The Bloomingdales chain had attracted only rock-bottom bids, and the junk-bond holders refused to redeem their bonds at a steep discount. Creditors were bickering over the new financing plans, and nervous suppliers began halting deliveries to the stores. On December 6, 1989, Dun & Bradstreet Corp. advised clients not to ship goods to Federated and Allied. On December 12, Campeau reported a nine-month loss of almost US$300 million. And in a December 13 filing, Campeau Corp. mentioned the possibility of bankruptcy at Federated and Allied.

Senior officials of Citibank NA met twice with Paul and Albert Reichmann in mid-December, asking them to inject more money into Campeau Corp. or guarantee new debt for the U.S. retail divisions. Citibank NA and Sumitomo Bank were reportedly bitter when the Reichmanns refused. The bankers claimed that the Reichmann intervention had encouraged them not to take any action on Campeau loans that were technically in default. On December 21, 1989, Citibank NA sent letters to the head offices of Federated and Allied that said the retailers had failed to comply with covenants to their loans requiring them to prove their solvency. Citibank NA threatened to call US$2.34 billion of a working capital and receivables facility if Federated and Allied could not prove they were solvent by New Year's Eve.

The Reichmanns couldn't afford to fight with bankers, especially the Japanese, with their well-known aversion to bankruptcy matters, because they needed to arrange more financing for Canary Wharf. Paul Reichmann's agreement to become involved in a restructuring of Campeau Corp. and its retail subsidiaries had backfired. Since Olympia & York needed cash, but couldn't acknowledge it, Paul Reichmann considered selling Olympia & York's 35% stake in Carena Properties, whose Trizec shares were carried on Olympia & York's books at $2.16 a share. (An analyst had recently valued Trizec at $40 a share pretax.) But the Carena Property investment was already pledged as security for a US$500 million loan from Citibank Canada and six Japanese banks, so the Reichmanns secretly approached Edper's Carena Developments, their partner in Carena Properties and their replacement in the abandoned joint venture with BCE in BCE Development.

After Paul Reichmann jetted away from BCE Development for the second time in August 1989, there was a crisis of confidence at the company. Development work stalled on core properties, like BCE Place, which were essential if the company was to have any future at all; prospective tenants moved elsewhere; construction workers threatened to walk off the sites; and there was no cash to pay almost $350 million of loans coming due.

BCE had to prevail on Royal Bank of Canada to extend a $100 million emergency line of credit to BCE Development in September, so that the developer could pay its bills. In the weeks of crisis, Raymond Cyr reverted to Plan B: a sale of BCE Development's U.S. properties. BCE hired New York City investment banker Goldman

Sachs to deal with prospective buyers of the U.S. assets. As the vulture investors circled above BCE Development, JMB Realty came back with an offer to buy all of the company. But among the dozens of proposals that Raymond Cyr received, the one that sounded the most promising was from Gordon Arnell, a former executive with Don Love's Oxford Development Group, and one who was intimately acquainted with BCE Development's U.S. properties. For the past six months, Arnell had been president and CEO of Edper's Carena Developments, which was run out of the same offices as Hees.

Carena, formerly Canadian Arena Co., was looking for workout candidates, so that it could become more than a holding company for Trizec. Among its earlier workouts, Carena could count residential and commercial group Coscan Development Corp. and Western Canadian land development firm Consolidated Carma Corp.

In early September 1989, Gordon Arnell had flown to Montreal to meet with BCE's Raymond Cyr, and over the next month the two men worked out a deal, reportedly producing a simple seven-page agreement with no involvement from outside lawyers or financial advisers. BCE and Carena would inject $415 million into BCE Development through a joint venture company owned 50.1% by BCE and 49.9% by Carena Developments. Jack Cockwell, Bill L'Heureux, Arnell and one other Edper Group representative would be appointed to a new 11-member BCE Development board, and Carena would run the company. BCE Development would not sell off its U.S. properties, but the assets would be written down, as anticipated in the earlier Burns Fry fairness opinion. A September valuation by Goldman Sachs had pegged the value of the U.S. assets at $1.75 billion, or about $500 million less than their carrying value in the 1988 financial statements, representing a loss of about $3 a share on a stock then trading in the $1.70-a-share range.

The BCE Development bailout agreement was signed on Friday, October 6, 1989. Carena Developments immediately seconded a four-man team led by Gordon Arnell that could be parachuted into BCE Development to form the nucleus of a new management group. On the Tuesday after the Thanksgiving weekend, October 10, the workout team — Arnell, David Ferguson, Grant Sardachuk and Lawrence Herbert — moved into BCE Development's head offices on the 38th floor of the Toronto-Dominion Bank Tower and began a six-week stretch of toiling up to 18 hours a day, seven days a week, to develop a survival plan. Their assignment was to understand the company as quickly as possible, while maintaining communication with constituents — such as shareholders and lenders — through weekly meetings. Already a group of preferred shareholders, whose shares issued at $25 each were now worth only a dollar or two, was seeking to prove that BCE had abused their rights when it struck a partnership with Carena to restructure BCE Development.

Gordon Arnell, a Calgary-bred lawyer who regularly commuted home to his wife and his quarterhorse, Playboy, at his Alberta ranch in the foothills of the Rocky Mountains, met with irate BCE Development shareholders and creditors, flying from one BCE Development project to another, taking commercial flights, not a corporate jet. "They send the wrong signal," said Arnell, spouting the philosophy of a converted Edper man.

Accompanying Arnell in his travels was the bone-thin David Ferguson, 32, a University of British Columbia graduate in finance. Ferguson had been hired in 1987 from the real-estate division of Citibank Canada in Calgary as Carena's vice-president of corporate development. At BCE Development, Ferguson's assignment was to get up to speed on the real-estate assets, located in four North American centres.

To analyze the 80 properties, 500 leases and the market conditions in each city, he travelled every second week. Ferguson had been introduced to the Edper Group by Grant Sardachuk, son of Arnell's Trizec colleague Edmund Sardachuk. A former marathon runner with an MBA, the young Sardachuk had worked in the oil-and-gas division at Citibank Canada in Calgary. At BCE Development, Sardachuk's assignment was to learn the particulars of each corporate loan and categorize each debt category. "Our job is not to go in and change locks, throw people out and snatch assets," said the unpretentious Sardachuk, who lived in Oakville with his wife and drove a mini-van. "We don't have a liquidation perspective. There is a viable business [at BCE Development] and we are here to revive it."

The fourth team member, the tall, blond, square-shouldered Lawrence Herbert, a senior vice-president of corporate development at Coscan, later told shareholders that the "analysis of the situation at [BCE Development] and the declining [real-estate] markets soon made it evident that [BCE Development]'s condition was even weaker than had been supposed."

The plan was to sell some money-losing properties in the U.S. and focus resources on BCE Place in Toronto. Showing off a large model of the twin-towered complex, Arnell boasted, "It's the best commercial development in North America." But the team would have to drum up the $1.5 billion of financing needed to complete BCE Place, as well as other projects in Chicago; Minneapolis; Orange County, California; and Montreal. None of the financing had been arranged. Arnell said the turnaround would take "a lot of capital and a lot of patience" because BCE Development was in great financial difficulty. He then estimated it could take up to ten years for the developer to get back on its feet.

That December, Carena Developments got a distress call from Paul Reichmann. Olympia & York would write off $413 million on the carrying value of its Campeau investment in its fiscal year ended January 31, 1991. And it desperately needed more financing for Canary Wharf. Since hostilities had broken out over the Campeau restructuring, Reichmann couldn't go to the American, Japanese or Canadian banks, his usual sources of financing, so he suggested a private arrangement with Carena that would result in the merchant bank getting paid back with Olympia & York's Trizec shares. Thus the deal was designed to ultimately transfer Olympia & York's stake in Trizec to the Edper Group.

But first Reichmann offered Carena a minority interest in partnerships that owned three towers of the World Financial Center, Olympia & York's flagship American project. (American Express owned its own tower.) It was supposed to be a quick flip. Reichmann said he had been negotiating with another purchaser who was expected to buy the minority interest in the World Financial Center from Carena within three to six months. Carena said it decided to proceed with this investment because, among other reasons, Carena considered the World Financial Center a premier property and Reichmann had advised that Carena could realize a substantial profit upon a short-term resale. Carena also said it expected "the transaction would facilitate the restructuring of the ownership structure of the control position of Trizec."

On December 29, 1989, in a secret deal, Olympia & York Developments sold a 35% stake in three of the four towers of the World Financial Center for US$309.4 million in cash to Battery Park Holdings, a private company 100%-owned by Carena Developments, registered in Delaware earlier that month. Hees provided almost all of the financing, with Carena investing only a small amount of money. Despite all the financial drama surrounding Campeau Corp., both Battery Park Holdings and Carena later claimed that they "were not aware of, nor were they informed…of any financial problems experienced by the Reichmann family" or Olympia & York at the time of the transaction, which was supposed to be a temporary measure.

PART THREE

The Fall

Chapter 11

The "R" Word

Robert Campeau became notorious in North America as the man who had brought the economic boom of the 1980s to a crashing halt. The stock-market crash of October 1987 had sounded the alarm on the North American economy, but the collapse of the U.S. junk-bond market two years later was the final bell. The fall of Campeau Corp. marked the beginning of the recession.

"Campeau: Chapter 11 closes the book in U.S.," read *The Financial Post* headline on Saturday, January, 13, 1990. A Campeau Corp. director had tipped the newspaper the day before that Federated and Allied would file for court protection on Monday under Chapter 11 of the U.S. bankruptcy code.

The decision to file followed four full days of board meetings at Campeau Corp.'s Toronto headquarters in Scotia Plaza. The meeting on Monday, January 8, 1990, had lasted all day. The directors had hoped to conclude the meeting that night, but they did not have a plan to present to Citibank NA, which had been pressuring Olympia & York to decide how it was going to proceed in the restructuring. At the beginning of the year, Citibank NA had given Federated and Allied a two-week reprieve, until January 15, to prove their solvency, but had taken the precaution of extracting a US$250 million prepayment from Federated on a loan due April 30. Citibank NA also got Allied to promise to use "its best efforts" to arrange a meeting between Citibank and the four-member restructuring committee headed by Olympia & York's Lionel Dodd.

That Monday, Campeau directors considered the committee's plan to swap shares in a new company made up of a merged Federated and Allied for the Federated and Allied junk bonds — the new shares would be issued at the equivalent of about 40 cents for every dollar of junk debt. If the junk-bond holders agreed, there would be no need for the US$800 million bridge loan that Olympia & York had promised to arrange on the condition that at least three-quarters of the US$2.25 billion of junk bonds were repurchased at steep discounts. Negotiations between financial adviser Merrill Lynch and seven of the largest holders of Federated and Allied junk bonds had been under way in New York City since December.

The following day, Tuesday, January 9, 1990, Campeau Corp. agreed to name two representatives from the National Bank of Canada to the board. Four days earlier, National Bank had seized more than half of Robert Campeau's shares in Campeau Corp. when he defaulted on a $150 million loan made in December 1987 to finance his repurchase of Campeau subordinated debentures. That move stripped Robert Campeau of control, slashing his personal stake in Campeau Corp. from 43% to about 8%. National Bank, with a 35% interest in Campeau Corp., now ranked second only to Olympia & York, which had 38.4%.

On Wednesday, January 10, Federated and Allied junk-bond holders rejected the debt-for-equity swap. Meanwhile, cheques for merchandise shipped to Federated and Allied in the four weeks before Christmas went out in the mail.

By Thursday, January 11, 1990, Campeau Corp. directors had decided that Robert Campeau would surrender voting control of the U.S. division to a group of trustees to be appointed by the four independent members of the board, as a prelude to filing for bankruptcy protection. The aim was to remove Robert Campeau and his executives, vilified in the U.S., from the restructuring efforts and to distance the Reichmanns from the taint of bankruptcy proceedings. The four-member restructuring committee, led by Lionel

Dodd, would be dissolved. That day Campeau Corp. shares closed at $2.70 on the Toronto Stock Exchange.

The next day, Friday, January 12, 1990, Campeau Corp. shares bounded around in the $2.50 to $2.95 range, as bankruptcy lawyers in Federated's Cincinnati offices prepared for a filing. Citibank NA was expected to supply the so-called debtor-in-possession financing to Federated and Allied, which would kick in after a bankrupty filing to ensure that bills were paid, so that the stores could keep ringing up sales. But the Citibank syndicate balked because the Japanese banks, anxious about U.S. bankruptcy law, were unwilling to participate. Instead, Chemical Bank provided the necessary credit line.

Still, Robert Campeau wasn't willing to concede defeat. He made one last solo attempt to avert the proceedings by negotiating directly with Citibank NA on Sunday, January 14, 1990, in defiance of the Reichmanns. He won a four-day reprieve, but it was too late.

Federated and Allied filed for court protection on Monday, January 15, 1990, under Chapter 11 of the U.S. bankruptcy code. Ultimately, Campeau Corp.'s U.S. operations were renamed Federated Stores Inc., and all four planes in the Federated air force were sold, although separating Robert Campeau from his favourite jet wasn't easy. He reportedly ordered the pilot to bring it up to Canada, but the Gulfstream had been locked in its Cincinnati hangar to prevent such an abduction.

Campeau's net worth was now less than zero. His phone was disconnected and the gates shut at his four-acre Bridle Path mansion in Toronto. The mansion, held in his wife Ilse's name, was put up for sale, overpriced at $8.2 million. Campeau's 14.5-acre lakefront estate in Austria was safe from creditors, because the property was owned by a Liechtenstein foundation. For most of 1990, Campeau stayed in Toronto, even after the Campeau Corp. board of directors, led by the Reichmanns, ousted him as chairman and CEO at the August annual meeting. That had been coming since early 1990 "when Bob rejected the compromise that I extracted with difficulty from his directors, that he stay as non-executive chairman but retire as chief executive, and...became chiefly preoccupied with trying to launch spurious lawsuits against the Reichmanns," Campeau director Conrad Black wrote in his memoirs. In 1991, Campeau was more frequently found in Austria, except for the occasional public sighting in Toronto, such as the Saturday, December 14, 1991, fundraising performance of "12 Angry Men *and Women*" at the Bluma Appel Theatre, with lawyer Julian Porter playing one of the celebrity leads. Campeau was in the audience, in one of the $100 seats.

U.S. short sellers had made outrageous fortunes from the fall of real-estate developer Campeau Corp., so after Federated and Allied Stores filed for Chapter 11 bankruptcy they sniffed around Canada for other good short plays in the bloodied real-estate sector.

In early 1990, Yale-educated James Chanos of Kynikos Associates in New York City targeted Edper's Trizec and Bramalea as potential carrion, because of their high debt levels. Trizec's consolidated long-term debt for its 1989 year-end was $7.6 billion, with subsidiary Bramalea contributing more than half of the total.

One money manager called short sellers "an important part of the investment ecology, like hyenas and vultures that kill off the weak and devour the dead." Short seller Joseph Feshbach argued that they are hype detectives. "Cash-flow analysis is important because if a company is reporting big earnings and burning cash and not building real value, then obviously it has confused public relations with financial solvency," he said.

Hailed as the short-selling kings during the 1980s, Joseph Feshbach and his two brothers sold stocks short from cluttered offices in Palo Alto, California, but lived flamboyantly, spending a reported US$11 million to buy their own private jet in December 1990. They specialized in shorting small companies which they believed had hyped their stories or even cooked their books. For example, in 1985, Toronto stockbroker Pierre Panet-Raymond had taken his suspicions about National Business Systems and its CEO Clive Raymond to the Feshbachs, and later shorted the stock for them. By the time he was proved right in early 1988, Panet-Raymond was an established Canadian short seller with about 150 small clients, and the Feshbach brothers had almost US$1 billion under management from a diverse group of big clients, including Microsoft billionaire Bill Gates.

In contrast to the Feshbachs, James Chanos typically shorted big companies. Chanos worked out of plush offices on Fifth Avenue in Manhattan, but took the subway to work and spent his lunch hour shooting baskets at a nearby court. He had reportedly named his company Kynikos after the Greek school of Cynics famed for their independent thought, and his short-selling fund Ursus, the Latin word for bear. Chanos couldn't short Olympia & York, which was most vulnerable to Campeau's domino effect, because all the shares were held by the Reichmann family.

Instead, Chanos went after developers Trizec and Bramalea, controlled by the Edper Group and Olympia & York. For Canadian analysis, Chanos turned to Alex Winch, an independent analyst who ran Grafton Capital, his private research company, out of his Toronto home. Winch produced a series of reports, applying his standard set of formulas to Trizec and Bramalea. Some said that Chanos circulated the reports to other short sellers and to contacts in the Toronto media, to put the heat on Trizec. But Winch later claimed in an interview with me that the reports were never circulated beyond Kynikos & Associates. And when I asked if the Edper Group had caused him any trouble when they discovered his role in the short selling of the group's stocks, Winch quipped that he had had "very satisfactory dealings with [the Edper Group]...*very* satisfactory."

Short selling tended to be a self-fulfilling prophecy, because short sellers usually did not jump on the bandwagon until there was negative momentum. And Bramalea's shares had been in a freefall since December 1989. Other companies in the Edper Group soon followed Bramalea in a downward spiral, with most of the group's publicly traded shares in steady decline throughout the first two-thirds of 1990, before gathering speed in September.

There was little hint of trouble at Bramalea's annual meeting in February, but four months later Trizec appointed Texas workout specialist Marvin Marshall as CEO of Bramalea, to replace Ben Swirsky.

Bramalea, Marvin Marshall said, "hadn't grasped the difficulty that the real estate business was going to experience, because the good times had gone on so long in Toronto." Marshall's survival strategy for Bramalea was to immediately cancel several projects: Among them were the joint-venture US$400 million downtown Chicago office tower; the $100 million refurbishment of the Hudson's Bay Co. Tower in Toronto; and the hotel/condominium block within the new CBC Broadcast Centre in downtown Toronto. He also put the retail/condominium redevelopment of the old post office site at 40 Bay St. — a joint project with Trizec — on hold. To reduce debt, Marshall put several properties on the selling block, including two of the company's four hotels, several shopping centres in the U.S., and much of Bramalea's land bank in Ontario and southern California. To slash costs, Marshall dumped about 350 employees, mostly in middle management.

By August 1990, Trizec was one of the largest holdings in the Kynikos fund, James Chanos wrote in his third-quarter letter to his limited partners. Trizec and Bramalea were a "short seller's dream," he wrote. "We believe that a strong case can be made that the common equity in Trizec is worthless." Other powerful short sellers, such as New York's Tiger Fund, also began shorting the stocks.

The hype detectives had also targeted Royal Trustco, which was scrambling to put a positive spin on its forays into the scandal-ridden savings and loan industry. By the end of the 1980s more than 600 savings and loans were insolvent, costing U.S. taxpayers several hundred billion dollars. Early in 1990, Royal Trustco stopped lending to commercial real estate in Britain, and replaced its management in London.

In February, Royal Trustco seconded its chief financial officer, Barry Henstock, to work with the Pacific First management team as vice-chairman. When Pacific First chairman Jerry Pohlman complained about the lack of clarity about who was in charge, he was told in a memo from Royal Trustco CEO Michael Cornelissen that "if Barry [Henstock] has involvement with [Pacific First Financial] operations, has questions or suggestions, he does so as the representative of the shareholders…[and that] to disagree with Barry or to have friction with Barry is to disagree with the shareholders."

Royal Trustco's managing partner of public affairs, Sheila Robb, had the job of selling Pacific First to the Royal Trustco shareholders. She started with the annual report, or what she called the "foremost investor relations document produced by a company," on average taking six months to prepare, involving five people working an average 52 hours a week, and costing around $350,000. "Use it as an investor relations tool, use it as a corporate marketing tool," Robb later recommended at a 1990 conference on annual reports.

In a break from tradition, Royal Trustco split its 1989 annual report into two sections: an editorial section for the shareholders and a detailed financial section for the analysts. A U.S. study had found that shareholders read only 3.5% of an annual report, so Royal Trustco decided to make its 1989 report reader-friendly. Robb started with an editorial lineup — a skeleton of story ideas. "We had just acquired a healthy savings and loan institution in the Pacific Northwest of the United States. The media was concentrating its fire power on the failing thrifts and we needed to explain why we were making this apparently radical move. This, we judged, was our most important corporate story. So we made it our cover story and gave straightforward business reasons for our decision." It worked in the short term — 90% of shareholders read all, most or some of Royal Trustco's 1989 annual report, which resembled a glossy magazine. It also cemented Robb's reputation for running one of the flashiest public affairs departments in the business.

At the Royal Trustco annual meeting on Thursday, March 29, 1990, Michael Cornelissen expanded on the theme, arguing that the Pacific First deal was the "single most important strategic move Royal Trustco [had] made in its 90 years of existence." These were words that would come back to haunt him. "The United States can present stupendous potential," Cornelissen told the shareholders gathered in Roy Thomson Hall. "You remember when, in 1977, economists were predicting the demise of New York City? That's when Olympia & York bought eight Manhattan office buildings for $575 million. Today that same real estate is worth more than $3.5 billion. Now there's a contrarian move that paid off. Royal Trust's contrarian move comes after a period of consolidation in Canada and international growth. So our timing was right." Cornelissen disputed the idea that Royal Trustco would join the "Canadian Business Hall of Infamy — the museum of Canadian firms who entered the United States and have failed." In response to concerns about Royal Trustco's falling share price, Cornelissen reminded shareholders that Royal Trustco's management owned $75 million in stock. "I am confident that we will continue to provide long-term growth and that our share price will reflect this."

Yet, behind the scenes, Michael Cornelissen was busy putting out fires. In May 1990, Cornelissen quietly dispatched senior executive Laurent Joly over to London to clean up the mess at Royal Trustco's European division. Joly, a handsome, gold medal-winning CA from Touche Ross in Montreal, had joined Royal Trustco at the beginning of 1986, where he was mainly responsible for raising capital and managing the company's corporate investments. In London, Joly, 36, installed a collection team for the high-risk British loan portfolio. Joly also replaced management at Royal Trustco's Swiss bank, which was riddled with problems, not the least of which was a mini-insider trading scandal involving the unit's former president and vice-president and a local garage owner. The Swiss government alleged the unit's former president had sold Royal Trustco shares in 1988 on rumours that the company would report poor results and so avoided a market loss of 3,500 Swiss francs ($3,300). The government also charged that one of the unit's former vice-presidents had informed a garage owner about Royal Trustco's finances, and the man earned 3,800 francs speculating in the company's shares. However, Switzerland's one-year-old insider trading law did not cover information on a company's poor performance. Later, in 1990, the three defendants were acquitted in Switzerland's first insider trading trial.

Michael Cornelissen was consistently bullish about what shape Royal Trustco was in. Of course, he and his colleagues had a vested interest in selling a positive story. For example, Sheila Robb was one of the 150 Royal Trustco executives worldwide whose compensation was dramatically affected by movements in the price of Royal Trustco stock. Robb owed $1.6 million under the Royal Trustco management share-purchase plan. She had paid an average $14 a share for her 115,000 shares.

Royal Trustco had even brought six senior executives from Pacific First into the Royal Trustco plan, although some adjustments had to be made because of differences in the U.S. tax system. In Canada, the stock-loans were deemed a taxable benefit, but there was an offsetting deduction for investment interest expense which was not available in the U.S. Royal Trustco set up a put-call arrangement for Pacific First that paralleled the Canadian plan. For example, Pacific First could put $1 million of stock back to the executive and force him or her to buy it. It was the same dynamic as having to repay a $1 million loan.

There was another feature to the plan: Pacific First stock wasn't publicly traded because Royal Trustco owned 100% of the shares, so Royal Trustco had to manufacture a price/earnings multiple for Pacific First. The manufactured multiple was based 70% on the multiples of a comparative group of U.S. thrifts and 30% of Royal Trustco's stock, but not to the same degree as that of other executives worldwide. Critics said Royal Trustco had grown fanatical in its implementation of the Edper pay-for-performance plan.

And Royal Trustco continued to expand in the U.S. In June 1990, it added to its investment in the savings and loan industry when Pacific First purchased certain assets and assumed certain deposit liabilities of American Savings and Loan Association in Oregon from Resolution Trust Corp., the U.S. government's liquidation clearing house for troubled thrifts, for US$30 million. The transaction added 45 branches and US$1.2 billion in deposits to Pacific First's existing franchise in Oregon. Also in June, Trilon Financial CEO Ken Clarke was appointed to the Royal Trustco board, as the company sold its fee-based operations in Luxembourg, Hong Kong and Singapore. The following month, Pacific First sold 17 Utah branches.

Then, in July 1990, reliable Royal Trustco, which had posted annual growth of 13% to 15% in earnings per share for the previous seven years, surprised Bay Street by reporting a second-quarter earnings drop of 17.4% to 38 cents a share at the end of June from 46 cents a year earlier. Although a larger float of shares was partly responsible, the decline fed into fears about Royal Trustco's new thrust into the savings and loan industry and created negative momentum for the stock.

The falling share price put Royal Trustco managers in a bind, so the board decided to ease the terms of the share-loans to its senior managers. Instead of five years, they would have 10 years to pay off the debt from their management share-purchase plans. Without the extension, $2.46 million in loans to eight senior people would have come due before the end of 1990. Altogether, 26 officers and directors owed $26.9 million under Royal Trustco's management share-purchase plan, with chairman Hartland MacDougall on the hook for $2.4 million and CEO Michael Cornelissen for $2.3 million.

Michael Cornelissen was in no position to pay back his loan. His personal life was a shambles. He had paid a heavy price for his sexual follies when his aerobics instructor slapped him with a paternity suit and his wife kicked him out of their family home in Oakville. These midlife antics might not have mattered if Cornelissen had been in a different industry. But financial services was an industry based entirely on confidence, and it was easy to shake that confidence.

Trevor Eyton, as deputy chairman of Royal Trustco and the most senior Edper Group representative on the Royal Trustco board, was the logical person to call Cornelissen on his behaviour.

Even his replacement, James Miller, later characterized Michael Cornelissen as a "wonderful person" but also someone who "was sick, longer than he realizes, before his divorce." Still, Cornelissen's sexual escapades were not yet common knowledge outside the Bay Street village, and he was a tireless worker at Royal Trustco.

In late August 1990, Cornelissen invited columnists Barry Critchley and me and two editorial-page editors, all from *The*

Financial Post, to lunch in Royal Trustco's executive boardroom. Earlier that month, I had written an Off-the-Record column entitled "Royal Trustco mum after earnings drop," detailing an unnamed analyst's claim that he was being stonewalled by Royal Trustco: "[There is a] general reluctance to speak....I've had a tough time getting information from the company ever since the second-quarter numbers came out." Royal Trustco's meetings with analysts had been on an ad hoc basis, with one after year-end and another sometime during the year, but that had changed in 1989 when Royal Trustco told analysts it wanted to schedule regular quarterly meetings. There was a meeting soon after the first-quarter results were reported, but not after the second-quarter results. Cornelissen said Royal Trustco had simply postponed its second-quarter meeting until September, because "too many people are away in the summer." How could anyone claim that he had been shut out, Cornelissen asked me. After lunch, Barry Henstock presented a slide show trumpeting Pacific First as a good investment and answered questions about the U.S. savings and loan industry.

Meanwhile, Royal Trustco stock had dropped to $14, and my unnamed analyst source — Alain Tuchmaeir of McLean McCarthy Ltd., a subsidiary of the Deutsche Bank — had recommended selling the shares. It was the first in a series of Royal Trustco sell recommendations from Bay Street.

Over the previous 10 months, Royal Trustco stock had fallen from almost $19 to the $13 1/2 range. Short sellers took some profits in the first half of August — Royal Trustco's short position on the Toronto Stock Exchange shrank from almost 600,000 shares at the end of July to about 41,000 shares by mid-August — but they would be back.

That didn't stop Royal Trustco's U.S. expansion. In September 1990, Pacific First purchased certain assets and assumed certain deposit liabilities of the Williamsburg Federal Savings and Loan Association from Resolution Trust Corp. for US$3.3 million. The transaction added US$121 million more in deposits to Pacific First's existing franchise in Oregon.

"Royal Trustco was pretty cocky in the up years," James Miller later said. "Who would have thought inflation would come under control and real estate would get killed?"

Hees was also on the short sellers' hype list in early 1990. As one analyst put it, "They think their shit doesn't stink."

For example, Hees's rights offerings were controversial. (In a rights issue, shareholders get the right to buy new shares in proportion to what they already hold. Hees backstopped these offerings, picking up and using any rights that were not exercised by others.)

Unicorp. In January 1990, BrasPower Ltd. (a joint venture of Hees and Brascan) backstopped a $53.7 million Unicorp rights offering, picking up a 22% stake in the company. The previous autumn, Unicorp had written off US$138 million of its U.S. assets. Shareholders in the U.S. subsidiary launched a class-action suit, alleging that a deal between Unicorp and Hees affiliate Coscan Development Corp., where Coscan would buy and operate the real-estate assets of the U.S. subsidiary, was not at arm's length.

The next step in the plan to transfer Unicorp's gas utility to BrasPower was to sell Unicorp's interest in Lincoln Savings Bank, by selling either its parent, Unicorp American, or the thrift itself. Unicorp couldn't get satisfactory offers, so it decided to distribute the common shares of Unicorp American to Unicorp Canada shareholders. But the U.S. Office of Thrift Supervision put a wrinkle in that plan because of its rule that only one arm of a corporate group could invest in the thrift industry. The Edper Group already had an investment in Pacific First, through Royal Trustco. BrasPower decided not to take part in the share dividend, thus making George Mann the major owner of Unicorp American and the U.S. thrift. But the regulators weren't convinced that Mann was at arm's length from the Edper Group. And there were several other problems with the dividending-out plan.

Matters came to a head in early 1992, when Unicorp Energy (the renamed Unicorp Canada) sold its 60% holding in Union

Energy, which owned Union Gas, in order to meet a financial crunch from the almost $200 million of preferred shares that Unicorp had to redeem or refinance that March 31 and a $120 million line of credit from the National Bank of Canada that also needed to be refinanced. As a result, the Edper Group lost the gas utility it had coveted since the early 1980s.

Pagurian. On May 2, 1990, Christopher Ondaatje stepped down as vice-chairman of Hees and chairman of Pagurian, but not without a few parting shots at Hees. Ondaatje said Hees had had no right to take operational control of Canadian Express and install its own executives. Pagurian had owned convertible preferred shares of Canadian Express, not common shares, Ondaatje argued. Relieved to see the back of Ondaatje, one Hees manager retorted, "We're hardworking beavers; [Ondaatje's] more like a flamboyant peacock."

Canadian Express. By January 1990, Hees had upped its interest in Canadian Express to 25% through a year-end rights offering of 41.6 million common shares at 70 cents a share. Three months later, Hees said it wanted to buy another 40 million common shares at 40 cents a share, through a formal tender offer. Canadian Express director David Hennigar, a member of the three-man committee of independent directors formed to evaluate the offer, kicked up a fuss. Hennigar, who represented minority shareholder Crownx Inc. on the board, complained to the Ontario Securities Commission that in its information circular Hees had not disclosed a spring 1989 Wood Gundy Inc. valuation of Canadian Express at $1.35 a share, mainly on the basis of Canadian Express's stake in Enfield. Hees argued that the valuation was no longer relevant because of the steep drop in the price of Enfield stock. But the commission halted the bid. Canadian Express eliminated its common-share dividend and delayed its annual meeting, while Hees prepared a new information circular.

Meanwhile, Hees had sent a letter to Crownx complaining that David Hennigar was disruptive. "We will not tolerate war in the boardroom," Bill L'Heureux said.

In early September 1990, the Ontario Securities Commission said Hees could go ahead with its bid. A few weeks later Hees renewed its offer, and a new independent committee, including David Hennigar, was formed. The committee hired BBN James Capel as its financial adviser to produce a fairness opinion on the offer.

On October 15, BBN James Capel submitted its final amended opinion to the independent committee, valuing Canadian Express shares between 16 cents and 59 cents. Hennigar was angered by the valuation — first, it was less than the Hees offer and second, the wide range of values made it "virtually useless," he said. Hennigar presented a minority dissenting report which was attached to the BBN James Capel opinion and the committee's recommendation that shareholders tender their shares to Hees's offer. On October 18, Hees brought its stake in Canadian Express up from 25% to 41%, and Canadian Express announced it would hold its annual meeting on December 13. Not long after, small Canadian Express shareholders, who had tendered a pro-rated 27% of their holders to Hees's offer of 65 cents a share, watched the rest of their holdings drop to around 15 cents a share.

Enfield. In mid-May 1990, Enfield president Bill L'Heureux announced a rights offering to existing shareholders at $2.50 a share (far below Enfield's high of $9.50 a share at the height of the previous year's takeover battle). Blair's Algonquin sent a letter to Enfield dated June 14, the last business day before the rights offering expired and one month after Algonquin had received notice of the rights issue. In the letter, Algonquin alleged that Enfield's financial reports from September 30, 1989, to May 9, 1990, contained deficiencies. Blair alleged that Hees had adopted an aggressive accounting approach (by taking huge writedowns on Enfield's investments in Consumers Packaging and Federal Pioneer) that presented Enfield in the worst possible light at the time of a rights issue. He had hired the accounting firm Coopers & Lybrand to do a forensic analysis. Manfred Walt phoned the Ontario Securities Commission to advise them that Enfield would respond to the allegations by noon on

Monday, June 18. Walt also phoned the Toronto Stock Exchange to request that no action be taken.

In his June 18 affidavit, Manfred Walt said that Enfield's auditors, Deloitte & Touche, had reviewed all of the matters raised in the Coopers & Lybrand letter and had confirmed that Enfield's financial statements for the year ended December 31, 1989, were "presented fairly in accordance with GAAP [generally accepted accounting principles] and that there [was] no need for management to revise [the] financial statements."

Walt also argued that Michael Blair had "been engaged in a highly publicized 'war' in the courts and through the press against" Hees since early 1989. Walt summarized all their battles to date, and provided a list of the lawsuits that Blair had filed so far. Walt then concluded, "In the meantime [there is an] overhang [in the market] of approximately 2 million [Enfield] shares held illegally by the pension plans of Enfield and its subsidiaries. The circumstances of such illegal purchase on [August 11, 1989] are the subject of an ongoing investigation by the Ontario Pension Commission and it is possible that such authority may implicate certain of the then officers of Enfield, including Mr. Blair. Again, it is in Mr. Blair's interest to allege other reasons for Enfield's current trading price in order that attention not be focused on this possible contributing factor."

That trading offence had come to the notice of the Ontario Pension Commission on October 1, 1989. Within a week, the commission appointed an investigator, who tape-recorded witnesses in the final months of 1989. The investigation was concluded in January 1990. Seven months later, on August 22, 1990, Michael Blair, Carole Penhale, Ben Webster and Jacques Lavergne were charged in connection with the controversial Enfield trade.

Almost a year later, on September 23, 1991, the hearings began in a courtroom in Old City Hall, where Michael Blair spent much of the opening argument working on a crossword puzzle. Ultimately Penhale was fined $25,000 for failing to fulfil her fiduciary duty under the Pension Benefits Act, but the commission was unable to prove that Blair, Webster or Lavergne had been aware of Penhale's actions.

Two years later, in October 1993, Michael Blair won a victory against Hees in the Ontario Court of Appeal, when it ruled that Blair had acted "honestly and in good faith" as chairman of the Enfield shareholders' meeting on July 20, 1989. But Hees won the right to appeal that decision to the Supreme Court of Canada.

In the final months of 1993, Blair and his long-time foes (including Jack Cockwell and Trevor Eyton) were back in an Ontario court, on a different matter. Five months later, on April 27, Blair won the right to have an independent auditor, Arthur Andersen & Co., examine accounting practices and related-party dealings at Enfield since 1989. Blair had alleged that the Hees and other Edper Group companies used Enfield to deal in group securities for their own ends. He claimed that the dealings had contributed to a $63 million drop in the value of his Enfield stock.

A year earlier, the Edper Group's preferred-share specialist, George Myhal, had spoken about one of these related-party transactions in a round-table discussion with *The Financial Post*: "[Enfield subsidiary] Federal Pioneer...through the chief financial officer, Jacques Lavergne, approached me, and they had been, in their right, significant investors in the preferred-share market before any involvement with Hees....After some discussions, we agreed...they would become one of our clients....We would manage their preferred-share portfolio."

Myhal said he suggested that Federal Pioneer make an investment in Varitech. "The nature of the [Varitech] shares are that the holder can retract them at any time so they're, in effect, a proxy for a money market instrument." Another Edper affiliate, North Canadian Investments, was looking to sell its Varitech shares, so Myhal acted as the agent. But he also acted on behalf of North Canadian Investments. "I didn't charge a commission," Myhal recalled. "I had no role to play other than to facilitate the transaction, to help one client sell shares to another client who wanted to buy the shares." The Federal Pioneer purchase was authorized by Lavergne. Then the "Michael Blair thing erupted and I know that particular transaction has come up repeatedly in court documents and elsewhere as an example of us being in conflict," Myhal later recalled. "The thing I have to keep underscoring is that there was no conflict because I, as the president of Varitech, had nothing to gain from the transaction. We...Hees had nothing to gain."

By the end of 1994, Arthur Andersen had not submitted its report yet, but one thing was clear — Blair's war with Hees was a fight to the death. Blair was still convinced he could prove his allegations that Hees had colluded with Gordon Capital, Conrad Black's Ravelston, Andrew Sarlos & Associates and other parties in the Enfield takeover battle. By then, Blair had run up legal bills of more than $1 million and was acting as his own lawyer. But if Blair's legal actions were ever successful, Hees would have to pay him millions of dollars.

BCE Development/BF Realty/Brookfield. In January 1990, BCE Development wrote down $550 million of assets, mainly in the U.S., and recorded a $61 million loss on currency translations, leaving a negative shareholders' equity of $72 million.

The new management team from Carena chose BCE Development subsidiary Brookfield, which owned BCE Place, as its principal operating subsidiary, transferring BCE Development's other viable properties to Brookfield to create a "financial entity," in the words of Carena team member Lawrence Herbert, who would later become president of BF Realty.

Thus BCE and Carena provided their $500 million of financing to Brookfield, not to BCE Development. The plan was to convert Brookfield's credit facility from debt to equity through a rights offering for BCE Development's existing shareholders.

On Thursday, June 28, 1990, outraged shareholders yelled and screamed for two and a half hours at the annual meeting of BCE Development. What had happened to the value of their shares?

For Ed Nordholm, the Edper Group's latest recruit from law firm Tory Tory DesLauriers & Binnington, it was a trial by fire.

The shell-shocked Nordholm missed the wedding of his former Osgoode Hall Law School classmate Loudon Owen at Timothy Eaton Church that Thursday evening, but he and his wife, Gwyn, made it to the reception. Not long after, Owen was named to the board of BF Realty (the renamed BCE Development).

Meanwhile, at Brookfield, BCE and Carena had to hike up their financing commitments to $700 million in 1991. By mid-year, it was clear that the planned BF Realty rights offering would have to be postponed, and BCE and Carena agreed to extend the maturities of their loans until April 1993. But by then BF Realty still had no net asset value.

A year later, in April 1994, Loudon Owen's merchant bank, the McLean Watson Group, bought control of BF Realty for $1. Owen spent several months working on a restructuring plan, but in early 1995 he concluded that there was no intrinsic value in BF Realty, and the company filed for bankruptcy.

National Business Systems. Plagued by class-action suits from National Business Systems' U.S. shareholders, Tim Casgrain finally got the company's $40 million financial plan approved by NBS creditors in April 1990. It was a long haul, but NBS was successfully restructured and sold in late 1994.

Meanwhile, in June 1990, the Ontario Securities Commission had unveiled Draft Policy 9.1, a new policy statement aimed at protecting minority shareholders in related-party deals. Bay Street dubbed it the Hees Directive. Garfield Emerson, the former takeover specialist for the Reichmanns, whose law firm, Davies Ward & Beck, had been involved in five major Olympia & York acquisitions, including Gulf and Hiram Walker, added some levity to the debate several months later, when he recited his ode to the policy at a conference in Toronto. It began:

From a little Edper grew a mighty Hees,
Trevor and Jack accumulated Trizec, Brascan, Noranda,
Royal Trust and others with sophisticated ease.
Then along came Enfield and Canadian Express,
And a little corporate brouhaha savoured by the press.

Hees denied that Policy 9.1 was aimed primarily at the Edper Group.

By then, Toronto short seller Pierre Panet-Raymond had gone public with his own criticism of Hee's accounting practices. In late August, one institutional investor of Hees sold a block of 1.6 million shares, sparking a sharp drop in Hees's share price.

During the third week of January 1990, when Campeau Corp.'s Federated and Allied Stores had filed for bankruptcy, Campeau director Albert Reichmann was far away, in Hungary.

Reichmann's was one of three private jets at the Budapest airport belonging to the financial backers of Central European Development Corp., a private company that planned to invest more than US$50 million in the restructuring economies of Hungary and Czechoslovakia. Mining millionaire Peter Munk, another financial backer, was in Klosters, Switzerland, at his ski chalet, but kept abreast of events in Budapest and Prague by phone.

Albert Reichmann was a long-time benefactor of Central Europe, his philanthropy rivalled only by that of his fellow Austro-Hungarian George Soros, the New York-based manager of one of the world's best-performing investment pools, the Quantum Fund. But where Reichmann was involved in projects supporting Jewish faith and Jewish education, Soros avoided Jewish causes. Soros's foundations supported education that would encourage the development of Western-style democracies and market economies in Central Europe.

George Soros was descended from a Jewish family called Schwartz which had fled persecution in Czarist Russia. Born in Budapest in 1930, Soros enjoyed an upper-middle-class lifestyle until World War II erupted. His lawyer father paid for Soros to pose, using false identity papers, as the godson of an official of the

Hungarian Agriculture Ministry responsible for confiscation of Jewish property. At the age of 14, Soros personally delivered notices to Jews headed for the gas chambers.

In late 1988, Soros teamed up with Andrew Sarlos, a Toronto-based hedge-fund manager and fellow Hungarian, to work on a Hungarian investment fund. On the heels of the collapse of the Berlin Wall in November 1989, the pair launched the US$80 million First Hungary Fund. Not long after, Soros and Sarlos had a falling out, when Soros withdrew from the Hungarian fund. Soros said it conflicted with his philanthropic activities.

Thus it was Sarlos who was approached twice by Ron Lauder (son of Hungarian-born cosmetics empress Estée Lauder) about establishing the Central European Development Corp. Sarlos formed the fund in partnership with Lauder and another American, Mark Holtzman, and with financial backing from Albert Reichmann, developer Joe Lebovic (a long-time friend of Sarlos's and a major Trizec investor), U.S. shopping-centre magnate Melvin Simon, U.S. vulture investor Sam Zell and Peter Munk, among others. "Andy pushed it," Munk recalled. "Those were all lovely guys, but I hate losing money. It's like skiing badly, it undermines your confidence." Ultimately, Munk lost about $2 million in the venture.

Of all the fund's investors, Peter Milkos Munk had come from the most privileged background. He was born in Budapest in 1927, the scion of a Jewish banking dynasty, then one of the richest families in Hungary, but his aristocratic lifestyle had come to an abrupt halt with the Second World War. After spending six weeks in the notorious Bergen-Belsen concentration camp, the Munk family traded much of their fortune to the Nazis in exchange for their lives, fleeing to the relative safety of Switzerland.

After failing a Swiss technical exam, the teenage Peter Munk left Europe in 1948 for Toronto, where an uncle was already living. Munk finished high school and then studied electrical engineering at the University of Toronto, where he ended up sharing a house in Rosedale with upper-crust David Gilmour, the son of a Bay Street investment executive. In 1958, the two friends pooled their talents in a start-up venture called Clairtone Sound Corp., manufacturing high-fidelity stereos. In 1960, Clairtone went public. By the mid-1960s, sales were booming, so Munk and Gilmour decided to expand their product line into colour television sets. The Nova Scotia government provided some financing for their new venture, after Clairtone agreed to locate its manufacturing plant in that province. But Clairtone was soon put out of business by the Japanese consumer electronics juggernaut. In 1967, Munk and Gilmour were ousted from the company. Four years later, the Nova Scotia government shut down the plant.

Peter Munk had lost both his business and his reputation. His humiliation was complete when his lawyer, John Tory of Tory Tory DesLauriers & Binnington, invited him to lunch at the Royal York Hotel. Tory brought along a "geek with big glasses" to meet Munk, and explained that he was turning over Munk's file to this other lawyer from the firm, Trevor Eyton — a nobody. Munk felt he had been "kicked downstairs…relegated to third class."

But Peter Munk bounced back, finding another prominent Toronto lawyer — Howard Beck of Davies Ward & Beck — to handle his deals. Munk saw a strategic opportunity in the burgeoning Japanese tourist trade. He and David Gilmour put down money, sight unseen, on property on the rainy side of Fiji, where they built the Beachcomber. It was the first in a string of more than 50 luxury hotels in the Pacific, incorporated in 1969 as South Pacific Properties Ltd., with financial backing from British investors. Munk and Gilmour operated out of London, where Munk met his second, much younger, wife Melanie, whose wealthy family hailed from nearby Horsham.

When a global recession hit the tourist industry in the mid-1970s, David Gilmour recruited a new investor, Saudi financier and arms dealer Adnan Khashoggi, whom Gilmour had met at a London dinner party. Then, with Khashoggi's help, Gilmour wangled an invitation from the Egyptian government for South Pacific Properties to build a $400 million joint-venture resort near the pyramids. In 1978, the Egyptian government cancelled the project.

Peter Munk was embarrassed by the aborted deal. In 1979, he decided to move his corporate headquarters to Toronto. He said he wanted to educate his four children — Anthony and Nina from his first marriage and Natalie and Cheyne from his second — in Canada. By then Trevor Eyton, the "geek" lawyer, had become a somebody, a "Mr. Big Shot, Mr. Toronto, Mr. Canada," Munk recalled. (That was the year Trevor Eyton helped orchestrate back-to-back deals for Edward and Peter Bronfman: Edper's partnership with the Reichmanns in Trizec and the hostile takeover of Brascan.)

By contrast, Peter Munk's name was still synonymous with Clairtone in Canada, despite his great success overseas. In 1981, Munk and Gilmour rolled some of their profits from the sale of South Pacific Properties for US$128 million into a small oil-and-gas company called Barrick Petroleum Corp. A year later, Barrick Petroleum picked up John Bitove Sr.'s junior oil-and-gas interests in a reverse takeover. Not long after that, the price of oil plummeted. Munk rolled Barrick's losses into his private holding company.

It was time to change course. Munk identified a new strategic opportunity in the gold industry. Anticipating a shift in investment patterns, when European investors would look for a politically correct alternative to South Africa for their gold allocations, Munk decided to assemble a large North American gold producer.

Since Barrick couldn't afford to buy a big producer, it went bargain-hunting. Munk picked up an experienced mining management team headed by Robert Smith, when Barrick went after financially distressed Quebec gold company Camflo Mines Ltd. in 1983. Many small acquisitions later, the patched-together American Barrick targeted Britain's giant Consolidated Gold Fields PLC in a failed, but audacious, takeover attempt.

Then, in 1987, American Barrick unexpectedly emerged as a major player when it hit the motherlode at its Goldstrike mine in Nevada. The Carlin Trend, northeast of Reno, was said to be the world's richest gold discovery since South Africa's Witwatersrand.

Peter Munk decided to use this new wealth from gold to expand into other potential turnaround situations. In 1987 Horsham Corp., the private holding company which owned the controlling 20% stake in American Barrick, went public. A year later, Horsham acquired 60% of bankrupt Clark Refining and Marketing Corp. of St. Louis for US$454 million, teaming up with vulture investor Sam Zell to do a workout of the private oil refiner. In 1989, Zell was named to the Horsham board.

Thus, at the end of the 1980s, Peter Munk was back on top of his game and could well afford to invest in Hungary, the homeland he had fled more than three decades earlier.

In the fourth week of January 1990, some of Central European Development Corp.'s financial backers left Budapest for Prague, where they met newly elected president Vaclav Havel, a long-time dissident imprisoned by the Communist regime. Andrew Sarlos himself had been locked up in a Hungarian prison for his political views three years before the 1956 uprising. Meanwhile, financial backer Albert Reichmann, the founder-chairman of the USSR-Canada Trade and Business Council, had flown on to Moscow with a group of Canadian businessmen.

While his brother Albert was overseas in early 1990, Paul Reichmann was forced out of seclusion. He set up interviews with prominent U.S. publications in an effort to rehabilitate Olympia & York's image in the aftermath of the Campeau debacle.

Olympia & York's withdrawal from Campeau Corp. was the first public clue that its financial resources were limited. In retrospect, another public clue came on Tuesday, January 30, 1990, when Olympia & York announced plans to acquire the public's 11% interest in GW Utilities, but did not go ahead with the transaction. "Even though the cash required was [relatively] small, they obviously didn't have the [$144 million]," an Olympia & York official said later. GW Utilities eventually unloaded its subsidiaries, but the company itself was not taken private.

During 1990, Olympia & York also quietly shopped its controlling stakes in Gulf Canada and Abitibi-Price. But there were no takers. Gulf's earnings were weakening, and Abitibi-Price was losing money. Olympia & York also privately attempted to merge

Abitibi-Price with forestry company Stone Container Corp. of Chicago, but the deal fell apart.

Meanwhile, it was still a peak construction period for Canary Wharf — the locals had nicknamed the construction site Legoland. But by mid-June, only half of the 4.3 million square feet of office space in the first phase of Canary Wharf was spoken for, despite bargain-basement leasing terms.

That same month, Paul Reichmann had overseen negotiations with American Express executives in New York about a deal to move their London employees into 300,000 square feet of office space at Canary Wharf. In return, Olympia & York agreed to take over some of Amex's existing leases in London and to provide $50 million for moving and construction expenses.

Paul Reichmann also persuaded Conrad Black to move the Telegraph Group into 125,000 square feet of office space in Canary Wharf Tower. But Olympia & York had to buy the Telegraph's building in nearby South Quay Plaza, which Black had acquired just three years earlier. Black later claimed that the Telegraph Group made a profit of £27 million on the deal.

Later that summer, actor Michael Caine sat one lady away from Paul Reichmann at a private dinner at 10 Downing Street in London, hosted by British Prime Minister Margaret Thatcher for her Canadian counterpart, Brian Mulroney. Reichmann had brought his own paper bag of kosher food to the table. Spotting the *yarmulke*, Caine assumed Reichmann was the Chief Rabbi of England, until Reichmann informed him that he was the Canadian real-estate developer building Canary Wharf.

Even as Canary Wharf floundered, Paul Reichmann concocted grandiose plans. (At least he had finally backed out of his on-again-off-again bid for Chicago's Sears Tower, citing tax complications with the deal.) In mid-1990, Olympia & York said it would construct three office towers, valued at about US$250 million, at San Francisco's Yerba Buena site. Olympia & York also pressed ahead with a plan to participate in a project to construct a US$30 billion financial centre on landfill in the Tokyo bay. If that dream had materialized, Olympia & York could have laid claim to office cities in all three of the world's financial capitals: Tokyo, New York City and London.

At the same time, Olympia & York was looking at property in Berlin, to hedge its bets in case London did not turn out to be the financial capital of Europe. (Indeed, Peter Munk's Horsham Corp. beat the Reichmanns to Berlin, founding Horsham Properties GmbH in 1990 to develop commercial properties in Germany. Its first project was a 600-acre office and industrial park south of Berlin.)

Meanwhile, Albert Reichmann had come back from his travels with commitments to build a $100 million, nine-story office building in Budapest and a US$250 million, 60-storey office building in Moscow. He had also set up a possible joint venture for Gulf Canada in the Soviet Union.

But how would all these projects be financed? Even the Edper Group was turning its back on the Reichmanns.

Edper's Carena sent a letter to the Reichmanns on Thursday, August 23, 1990, giving notice that "for various corporate and business reasons, we have now concluded that we wish to dispose of our partnership interests in the World Financial Center project."

Through the letter, Battery Park Holdings Inc. offered the Reichmanns the opportunity to purchase Battery Park Holdings' stake in "an all cash transaction at a price of around US$280 to US$300 million." Carena further advised that, if the Reichmanns declined the opportunity, Carena "would then be free to sell [its] interests to a third party during the following 12 months, upon similar terms."

The smell of blood at the Edper Group had unleashed the pack-running aggressions of Bay Street. "The magic is gone — love turns to hate very quickly," said one analyst. At the height of the crisis, Bill L'Heureux phoned me at *The Financial Post*, irate because I had used the word "imploding" in a story about the group in that morning's paper. "You can kick us when we're down, but we'll be back, and we won't forget," he warned. The

Hees managers felt besieged. They also complained to *The Globe and Mail*, accusing reporters of being in league with the short sellers for profit, as rumours whipped up and down Bay Street.

Companies targeted by short sellers often blamed them for all sorts of base tactics such as spreading rumours about the CEO being a drunk, terminally ill or even dead. In fact, a source phoned me to say he'd just heard that Hees managing partner Manfred Walt had been carried out of Commerce Court West on a stretcher. When I phoned Hees vice-president of investor relations Deirdre McMurdy (hired away from the *Globe* on September 1, 1990, to head Hees's new public relations effort) to check the story, she was amazed; there was no truth to it whatsover. And why a rumour about Walt? If someone wanted to cause an investor panic, why not say that Jack Cockwell had been carried out on a stretcher? By then, umpteen versions of the story were trickling back to Hees — Walt had had a complete breakdown and left the offices in a strait-jacket; Walt had had a heart attack and was now undergoing bypass surgery; Walt was terminally ill from cancer or a brain tumour.

Short sellers were having a party. In the U.S., the third quarter of 1990 was a bonanza for short sellers, with average returns of 35% — almost as good as the average returns of 40% in the fourth quarter of 1987. Toronto Stock Exchange figures for the first half of September showed the number of Trizec A shares sold short tripled to 31,900 and Bramalea common shares sold short rose 230% to 340,500. The short position on Hees common shares jumped 126% to 64,200 shares; on Royal Trustco common shares, it grew 79% to 57,500 shares. The growing short positions on those companies bucked a market trend on the TSE. Short positions overall fell 10% in the first half of September from the last half of August, the TSE said.

Then, on Wednesday, September 19, 1990, the Reichmanns announced they had hired investment bankers Lazard Frères to sell their 20% direct interest in Olympia & York (USA). They hoped to raise about US$700 million from the sale.

Hong Kong investors checked out the properties, but decided the price was too high — the plummeting New York real-estate market had not touched bottom yet. Around the same time, a US$550 million mortgage on a lower Manhattan property came due to Sanwa Bank. Olympia & York agreed to pay Sanwa US$200 million in exchange for time to refinance the rest of the mortgage.

The same day, Trevor Eyton had got a call from his friend Prime Minister Brian Mulroney inviting him to become a member of the Canadian Senate. Eyton had long lusted after after a seat in the Upper House.

The next day, Thursday, September 20, 1990, a broad-based plunge in Edper Group stocks prompted the Toronto Stock Exchange to request an explanation from the group, which later issued a press release stating that it had "no knowledge of any corporate development within Edper or any of its principal affiliates which would adversely affect the value of the shares in any of these companies." The release added that Edper was "confident that each of these companies [was] in sound financial condition" — referring specifically to Edper, Hees, Carena and Brascan. "The Reichmann news added fuel to the flames of the market," Deirdre McMurdy told the press.

By then, a four-man Edper team — Jack Cockwell, Bill L'Heureux, Manfred Walt and George Myhal — had decided to hold several information meetings to reassure institutional investors and retail brokers that all was well within the group. McMurdy had set up the first meeting for the following day, September 21, at the offices of RBC Dominion Securities in Commerce Court South.

But Jack Cockwell and Bill L'Heureux arrived late for the meeting, leaving 75 major institutional clients and retail brokers cooling their heels. Cockwell and L'Heureux had been delayed by internal meetings with Trevor Eyton, who had decided to accept the Senate appointment. It was an inauspicious opening for the Edper road show. A combative Cockwell did most of the talking, discussing a wide range of issues, including: Were there cash deficiencies in the group's corporate structure? How did the partners view the fall in stock values? How did the fall in stock prices affect partners personally? Would there be dividend cuts and asset sales? Cockwell argued that cash flow-deficient companies such as Edper and Brascan were offset by liquid companies such as Pargurian and Hees, so there were no cash deficiencies in the group, the fall in stock prices was a market judgment and not an impairment of value, and the average cost of shares for partners was much less than reported in the financial press. For example, L'Heureux had an average cost of $8.33 on his Hees shares. The shares had closed at $16 1/2 that Friday. Cockwell also said, "We tend to view dividends as a cost of doing business. Cutting dividends [was] a cop-out."

Cockwell was reportedly enraged when an RBC Dominion Securities broker challenged one of his answers. Edper and Pagurian (which Cockwell had said were the locus for the Bronfman and management stakes) and Brascan and Hees (which Cockwell had said were holding companies designed for public participation) were all separate legal entities, the broker said. They could not trade liquidity back and forth.

On the subject of Bramalea, the four Edper men said they had done a thorough review of the developer's assets and "had found no fundamental change in values, no permanent impairment in values." Five days later, Bramalea would announce a $115.2 million third-quarter writedown. That Friday, the Edper team also denied knowledge of heavy losses at Royal Trustco. Four months later, Royal Trustco would shock Bay Street with a staggering $251 million fourth-quarter loss.

The following week, the Edper road show stopped at Wood Gundy in the Royal Trust Tower, where the presentation went a bit more smoothly. Similar meetings were held at Burns Fry in First Canadian Place and at Gordon Capital in the Toronto-Dominion Bank Tower.

Short sellers were delighted on Wednesday, September 26, 1990, when Bramalea CEO Marvin Marshall announced the $115.2 million third-quarter writedown, reflecting a deterioration in land

values in Ontario and southern California. Pretax, the writedown to-
talled $223 million. On the plus side, Marshall managed to sell $570
million worth of properties during fiscal 1990.

The same day, Trevor Eyton held an afternoon press conference
at the Sutton Place Hotel, the site of many Eyton family celebrations,
to announce his Senate appointment.

Later that afternoon, in an interview at his offices at Gordon
Capital, financier Andrew Sarlos told me of his affection for Eyton,
revealing how Eyton, Sam Belzberg and Albert Reichmann had
stood by him when Sarlos was in financial trouble during the recession of 1981–82. But Sarlos thought the Senate appointment
was a mistake for Eyton because, in his opinion, Brian Mulroney was
simply rushing 10 warm bodies into the Upper Chamber who would
stand when told to in order to pass the legislation for the Goods
and Services Tax. In his memoirs, Sarlos said it demeaned Eyton to
"allow his talent and reputation to be enlisted in a politician's opportunistic and cynical adventures." Sarlos also revealed tension
within the Edper Group. Eyton and Jack Cockwell were estranged,
he said. "It wasn't Trevor's brain," Sarlos said, "it was his personality that was acceptable [to] Canadian institutions." Cockwell was
a "smart, financial man" but his "personality was not suitable."
And Bill L'Heureux was "not as good" as Eyton, Sarlos said.

Later that same Wednesday, the Edper road show stopped at
Midland Walwyn Capital Inc., where the four Edper executives
handed out a bulletin listing points of discussion. In a three-and-a-
half-hour session, the executives answered questions about the in-
terrelationship of preferred shares within the group, management
compensation schemes, structured partnerships and projected
earnings. When Jack Cockwell was asked what the group had
learned from the crisis, he replied, "to be more humble."

On the last trading day of the month, Friday, September 28,
1990, it was clear that the interlocking empires of the Edper
Bronfmans and the Reichmanns had come under pressure that year:
Trizec A shares were down 57% to $12.50 from their 52-week high
of $29; Bramalea shares had fallen 75% to $6 from their year high of

$23.63; Trilon Financial A shares were down by 37% to $14 from $22 1/8; Royal Trustco shares had plunged 46% to $10 from $18.50; and Royal LePage shares were down 52% to $6.75 from $14.

Among Edper's senior holding companies, Pagurian A shares were down 30% to $6 3/8 from their 52-week high of $9 1/8; Edper Enterprises had fallen 59% to $11.50 from $28; Hees shares were down 52% to $15 from $31.25; Carena shares had plunged 56% to $13.13 from $30; and Brascan A shares were down 51% to $15.25 from $31.38.

That October, Royal Trustco issued a nine-month report to shareholders. In it, Michael Cornelissen wrote that earnings in 1990 would be "lower than the previous year," citing problems in Europe. He disclosed that a fire-fighting team had been sent to Britain in mid-1990, but did not prepare shareholders for the magnitude of the losses. He did reassure them that the Royal Trustco common-share dividend was not in danger. Patricia Meredith, an analyst with Woody Gundy, was tracking the effect of the European problems, as well as the troubles at the California thrifts, through the second half of 1990. She later told me that one of the many factors in her Royal Trustco sell recommendation was Cornelissen. "A man with that many personal problems couldn't possibly have his eye on the ball," she said. There was no mention of the Cornelissen factor in her research report.

On Thursday, October 11, 1990, the Conference Board labelled the economic downturn the first "made-in-Canada" recession, sparked primarily by Bank of Canada Governor John Crow's policy of high interest rates. "Whether or not the current state of the economy is technically called a recession is not the key issue," retorted then-Finance Minister Michael Wilson. By December, Statistics Canada had stated the obvious, and Wilson had not only used the "R" word, he had conceded that the recession was going to last longer than expected.

Meanwhile, on Wednesday, October 31, 1990, the Reichmann family secretly bought 50% of Battery Park Holdings through a numbered company from Carena for $140 million, with a loan from

Hees. That gave the Reichmanns a direct interest in the World Financial Center, as well their indirect interest through Olympia & York. Hees's two loans to the joint partners of Battery Park Holdings — Carena and the Reichmanns — were secured by direct partnership interests in the World Financial Center and other security.

Chapter 12

Cracking Under Pressure

In the final months of 1990, the Edper Group had to bend some of its sacrosanct business principles to cope with the financial shocks battering the empire.

By then, the group managers had borrowed an eye-popping $250 million under their management share-purchase plans, to load up on group shares that had lost more than half of their market value over the previous year. At the end of 1990, the notorious stock-loan plans were abandoned in favour of management share-option plans. Group companies also introduced cash bonuses and began hiking up their below-market salary ranges to narrow the gap with industry standards.

At the same time, Partners Holdings, the elite group of senior Edper managers who had replaced Edward Bronfman at the top of the Edper empire in 1989, began searching for an outside partner for Pagurian. They had financed their own $200 million-plus investment in Pagurian with bank loans secured with their personal holdings of beleaguered group shares. Over the next year, they reportedly approached Conrad Black and Paul Desmarais, among others.

Still, the managers' main priority in late 1990 was the so-called Edper capital-recovery program, which involved raising additional common equity, refocusing businesses on core operations, selling

noncore assets and developing new sources of financing throughout the group. For example, that autumn Hees raised capital in
the U.S. for the first time, borrowing US$330 million from U.S.
insurance companies.

Meanwhile, Kimberley Noble was working on a series about the
Edper Group for *The Globe and Mail*. During the fourth week of
November 1990, she spoke to Jack Cockwell, on the condition that
she would not put him on the record about any of the Edper companies. He talked at length about general strategy, but referred specific questions to Bill L'Heureux and Manfred Walt. Although Walt
said he was too busy to see her, L'Heureux scheduled an interview
for the morning of Friday, November 25. Ahead of the interview,
Noble submitted a list of questions to Deirdre McMurdy, as requested.

The questions, which Noble later printed in *The Globe and
Mail*, indicated to the Hees partners that someone with access to
privileged information was talking to Noble. Hees suspected both
Michael Blair, a former member of Hees's audit committee, and
Christopher Ondaatje. Noble had asked several questions revealing
an inside knowledge of several private transactions, some involving
Jack's younger brother, Ian Cockwell. For example, she asked
whether privately held Waruda Holdings or Arteco Holdings were
connected to the Edper Group. She also wanted to know who owned
George Mann's private holding company, Townsview Investments
Ltd. She asked what was the size of the stake in Pagurian Corp.
now owned by group managers, including Jack Cockwell, and others who were not legally insiders of Pagurian. She also asked whether
Pagurian had provided additional financial support for private holding companies within the Edper Group since the spring of 1990.

When Noble arrived at the Hees offices for the interview on
November 25, Deirdre McMurdy told her that Bill L'Heureux refused
to see her. He would not come out of his office, prompting some on
Bay Street to imagine him cowering under his desk. Noble claimed
that McMurdy informed her that the Hees managers were planning to go directly to the publisher of *The Globe and Mail* to prevent any stories related to these questions from appearing in the

newspaper. Noble also claimed that McMurdy told her L'Heureux and other senior officials from Hees had decided that they would not agree to any interviews for at least six months. McMurdy disagreed with Noble's characterization of events. Later that afternoon, some answers to Noble's questions began to trickle in by fax and letters to *The Globe and Mail*.

Despite Hees's threats, the first instalment of Noble's eight-part series was published in *The Globe and Mail* on Monday, November 28, 1990. Noble opened with a front-page article in the Report on Business section, titled "Crisis of Confidence: Bronfmans keep investors in the dark." Noble used a stockbroker's analogy which compared investing in the Edper empire to watching a basketball game in the dark: "Shareholders-spectators know there's a game going on because they can hear the ball bouncing and feet scuffling on on the floor; they just can't see what's happening. But there is a big electronic board overhead that periodically flashes the score so spectators can see how their team is doing." Hitting on Bay Street's concern about managed earnings at the Edper Group, Noble pointed out that Cockwell & Co. told their shareholders ahead of time what the score would be. "They believe the audience should be satisfied as long as the numbers match up to what the managers promised." With the Edper Group stocks in freefall, this was no longer satisfactory. Investors are "much less willing to bet on the brains and connections of a deal-driven organization that won't tell outsiders how much money it has, where this is held, how it is moved among affiliates, to whom it is lent and how exactly it grows in value." As one Edper group manager told Noble, "We feel the taint. People are wary of doing business with us. It may not be justified but it's there." On the second page, Noble told the tale of her cancelled interview with Bill L'Heureux and published the list of questions that had prompted Hees to cancel the interview.

That week Deirdre McMurdy quit her three-month-old position at Hees, embarrassed and frustrated by Hees's inept handling of her former *Globe* colleague. She claimed that the Hees partners had ignored her recommendation to "be more open" with the press. The following month, Hees hired Tom Reid of Reid Management

Consultants in Toronto as a public relations adviser and set up meetings with senior editorial managers of *The Globe and Mail* to clarify "the misunderstandings." For public consumption, Reid said he had advised Hees that they hadn't done themselves any favours by evading Noble. "The first two or three times [Noble] tried to get the company to respond she got beat up," Reid told Jennifer Wells for the *Financial Times of Canada*. To Bud Jorgensen of *The Globe and Mail* he said, "It's been largely a problem of [Hees] not understanding the role of the media in a democratic society." Reid also said he had advised Jack Cockwell not to do any more off-the-record interviews with journalists. The group would designate one spokesman, Bill L'Heureux, who would be made available to all the press. Reid said he also suggested that Hees be "a bit more humble." But at the same time, Reid Management began to "audit" Noble's coverage, which her managers at the *Globe* thought was a basis for legal action against her. A former Report on Business managing editor, Timothy Pritchard, later claimed that Hees also fed innuendo about Noble's "unreasonable bias" into the Bay Street network.

The press mess at Hees wasn't helping the Edper Group. It was tainting the operating companies, already reeling from the effects of the recession and the real-estate bust. Although Hees's workout situations were a small percentage of the Edper Group's total corporate investments, they had generated enormous negative publicity, Bay Street's financial analysts said. They also had contributed to what one analyst described as an "investment boycott" of the group by some institutional and individual shareholders. "Most of the workout companies were headed for bankruptcy before Hees stepped in, but investors don't distinguish between the basket cases and other public companies in the group," he said. "Investors who've been caught with the short end of the stick in one Edper company wind up an enemy of the group."

Four companies under Hees's surgical knife were among the biggest losers on the Toronto Stock Exchange in 1990. On December 14, preliminary figures from the Exchange showed that shares of Consolidated Enfield, BCE Development, Unicorp Canada and

Canadian Express had lost more than 80% of their stock value during the year. With respect to Hees's biggest loser, Consolidated Enfield, one Bay Street analyst said, "In hindsight Hees should have sold Enfield to [Michael] Blair. Enfield is a disaster." Taking into account a five-for-one share consolidation, the Enfield stock had fallen from the equivalent of $26.88 a share to the $2.10 range. "You have to question the investment decisions that led Hees to make commitments to these basket cases," said another analyst. Bill L'Heureux responded, "Restructuring by its very nature is hard on common share prices. The market has been in decline for three years and 1990 has been particularly hard on share prices. The companies we're working with have to be looked at over the long term. For example, in the case of Brookfield Development Corp./BCE Development, five to seven years had always been the forecast for a turnaround." Analysts argued that Hees's management services business should be separated from other public companies in the Edper Group. Senior managers in the Edper group were spending too much time on the workout companies, one analyst said. "They've taken their eyes off the ball."

Jack Cockwell addressed the concerns five months later at the Brascan annual meeting when he tried to clear up some of the misconceptions about the Edper Group: "We recognize that we need to do a better job at explaining the distinction between a strategic acquisition and a workout assignment when we are called in to help a troubled company in the future." He pointed out that the group had made no major strategic acquisitions since 1986, other than Falconbridge in 1989. He then defined workouts as "when one of our affiliates is called in by the owners or bankers to produce a soft landing for a company in financial trouble with the objective of nursing it back to health, and there have been many of these" in the previous five years. He did concede that, from these workout assignments, the Edper Group "sometimes obtain a valuable business unit to meld with their other operations."

But there was more bad press when Hees shut down operations at literary publisher Lester & Orpen Dennys Ltd. on Wednesday,

January 9, 1991. Hees had put undisclosed money into the company to finance its fall 1990 publishing list, but had failed to find a buyer. "We had to do what we had to do," said Hees chairman Tim Price, after meeting with the publisher's 13 dismissed employees.

Less than a month later, on Thursday, January 31, 1991, Royal Trustco shocked Bay Street with its first-ever loss, providing a jaw-dropping $143 million for its British loans, $30 million for its restructuring in Europe and $84 million for a writedown of its U.S. investment portfolio for a total of $257 million in the final quarter of 1990. Among other things, Royal Trustco said it had run afoul of U.S. banking regulations which prohibited the same corporate group from owning more than one thrift. It had to sell half of its holdings in GlenFed at only 60% of the price it had paid in 1987.

The losses were "nonrecurring" and unrelated to operations in Canada and the U.S., said Michael Cornelissen, who had offered his resignation to the Royal Trustco board. It had been rejected, but the vote was not unanimous. Royal Trustco planned to replace its losses with new equity, tapping the market for $200 million in a rights offering.

On Wednesday, February 6, 1991, Dominion Bond Rating Services Ltd. downgraded all of Royal Trustco's credit ratings. "It was known that [Royal Trustco's] fourth-quarter earnings would likely be under pressure from one-time actions such as restructuring costs and writedowns on certain investments, but the magnitude of the problems greatly exceeded expectations," the rating agency said in its report.

Amazingly, Royal Trustco shares proved resilient that Wednesday, topping the most active list on the Toronto Stock Exchange and closing up 1/8 to $7 3/4. One analyst attributed the rise to the covering of positions by short sellers. In the two-month period from December 15, 1990, to February 15, 1991, Royal Trustco's short position on the Toronto Stock Exchange rose 545% to 394,450 shares. The analyst said there was also continued buying by retail investors. Indeed, of the 2.9 million Royal Trustco shares traded that Wednesday, there were few large blocks. Institutional investors had fled Royal Trustco stock. Only retail investors continued to believe in the Royal Trustco story.

Hees had released a preliminary financial statement about the impact of the Royal Trustco loss on its own earnings.

That Saturday, February 9, 1991, a five-part series on the Edper Group began in *The Financial Post*, called "Hees-Edper: Empire Under Pressure," written by senior editor Philip Mathias. The series had been researched and ready for publication since mid-December. Mathias had decided to use the moniker "Hees-Edper" because of Hees's linchpin position in the empire. Mathias's front-page article was titled "Questions are mounting for Hees-Edper." Inside, a second article raised concerns about possible cash-flow deficiencies in the empire.

On Tuesday, February 26, Mathias received a 19-page audit of his series, prepared by Tom Reid of Reid Management Ltd. Reid wrote, "Mr. Mathias is an able professional who confronted a massive undertaking trying to untangle Hees/Edper. His lack of intimate familiarity with the assorted companies and their transactions, and his innocence regarding balance-sheet issues, conventional financial reporting, and the architecture of financial strategies employed by Hees-related companies has resulted in several inaccuracies and misunderstandings about Hees/Edper and related transactions. As a result, Mr. Mathias' articles were harmful to the group's reputation in some notable areas. Our recommendation is that Mr. Mathias be invited to review this audit and broader issues with appropriate Hees partners."

Hees also took issue with Philip Mathias's hypothesis that the senior Edper managers were moving in the direction of control of the Edper Group. "The Peter Bronfman family controls the group; and has no plans or intention of giving up control," Reid wrote. (Four years later, in February 1995, Mathias was proved right when Peter Bronfman announced he was giving up legal control of Edper to the senior Edper managers.) But what Hees really objected to was the overall tone of Mathias's articles. As Reid put it, "Three general theses...are left with the reader: common shareholders of Hees-related companies are somehow treated unfairly; Hees abuses tax accommodations; Hees creates an illusion of larger assets and equity. All are wrong and the arguments leading to these conclusions are developed on the basis of the unsteady financial naivete referred to in the introduction."

But Mathias was by no means alone in his views. Most of Bay Street's analysts shared his concerns.

Meanwhile, the Edper capital-recovery program was under way. Shortly after the end of the six-week Gulf War, the group took advantage of a bullish market to issue a slew of equity offerings. For example, on March 6, 1991, Trizec raised $135.4 million selling shares and warrants. (Trizec shares had rebounded on the Toronto Stock Exchange, climbing 16% from the beginning of the year to trade in the $15 range.)

After watching Trizec stock fly out the door, Carena Developments tried its luck, but raised only $75 million. Bramalea and Coscan Developments also tapped the markets with $100 million and $51 million share and warrant offerings, respectively.

By then, Royal Trustco had completed its $200 million rights offering. Next up was London Insurance Group with a $126 million issue of straight common shares (no warrants). In June, Brascan raised $127.7 million from an offering of shares and warrants, followed by MacMillan Bloedel with a $151 million common-share offering, and Noranda Forest with a $166.4 million rights offering. Last, but not least, Edper Enterprises raised $82.3 million from a rights offering. Altogether Edper Group companies raised $1.4 billion in the equity markets in 1991, with $666 million of that purchased by outside investors. There was also $1.6 billion of long-term financings in the group that year.

The Edper Group was also selling assets: Noranda raised $424 million from the sale of Canada Wire & Cable; John Labatt picked up $600 million from the sale of JL Foods (after years of expansion into the food business, Labatt was refocusing on its brewing and entertainment businesses); Brascan netted $231 million from the sale of manufacturer M.A. Hanna; the real-estate companies raised $700 million from various asset sales; and the oil-and-gas companies raised $150 million from the sale of various natural gas assets. Altogether the Edper Group raised almost $2.1 billion from major asset sales in 1991.

Even at Royal Trustco, the worst seemed to be over. At the Royal Trustco annual meeting on April 4, 1991, Michael Cornelissen said, "We have a couple of black eyes, but no broken bones," as he took personal responsibility for Royal Trustco's losses. "We made conservative provisions and started 1991 with a clean slate." But had they?

Behind the scenes, there were serious problems in the U.S. operations. In early 1991, Royal Trustco had to quietly inject U.S.$150 million of capital into Pacific First. One month after the annual meeting, Royal Trustco's in-house lawyer Bill Inwood reportedly wrote a memo to Michael Cornelissen and other senior managers predicting that the Office of Thrift Supervision would give Pacific First a regulatory downgrade because the thrift was not setting aside adequate loan-loss provisions for its commercial real-estate portfolio, particularly in California. Cornelissen and other senior managers flew to Seattle and back to attend meetings of Pacific First's investment committee. Pacific First chairman Jerry Pohlman later claimed that Royal Trustco pressured him not to take the loss provisions. In a memo to his own files before he quit Pacific First in June 1991, Pohlman wrote, "We are in the position of repeatedly pushing back on Royal Trustco efforts to rewrite the evidence of credit deteriorations at [Pacific First Bank]. In my view, what they are attempting to do is very close [to] — if not in fact — a cover up of facts that would influence investors in the [May 1991] Trilon rights offering if they were known." In August 1991, the Office of Thrift Supervision issued a confidential report which ordered Pacific First to replace its senior management team. The report said Pacific First was "severely troubled" and that its level of capital was "only marginally adequate." The report also said Pacific First had pursued overly aggressive growth and concluded, "We consider Pacific First to be a problem institution." By then Royal Trustco had had to inject a further US$150 million into Pacific First (in the form of participation interests) to keep it from failing. Pohlman argued that the participation interests were another way for Royal Trustco to mask the deterioration in Pacific First's loan portfolio. Since holding companies were not subject to the same regulatory pressures to take loss provisions, private holding company RT Holdings, not Royal Trustco, purchased the US$150 million of participation interests in a portfolio of Pacific First loans. Pohlman argued that Royal Trustco management had misled investors in Canada about the true health of Pacific First. For example, Royal Trustco reported a $107 million profit in 1991, taking only US$7 million of loss provisions. Pohlman alleged that Royal Trustco should have taken at least US$100 million of loss provisions in the U.S., which would have put Royal Trustco in the red for the second consecutive year. Royal Trustco argued that Pohlman was a poor manager who would have been dismissed if he had not left in mid-1991.

On the lighter side, in late November 1991, overgrown schoolboys Senator Trevor Eyton, Peter Munk and Conrad Black played a prank on the Prince and Princess of Wales at a gala dinner at Toronto's Royal York Hotel. Charles and Diana had been presented with a book-shaped Cartier silver box, which was left unattended. When it was later discovered filled to the brim with Laura Secord chocolates, the Eyton-Munk-Black table, one of two next to the Royal tables, burst into guilty laughter. Not surprisingly, the Prince and Princess did not dance together. But the glitterati didn't notice. They were too busy speculating about the state of another marriage — where was Black's wife, Joanna?

Unofficially separated since mid-1991, Conrad Black was "profoundly in love" with London-based journalist Barbara Amiel. With his attentions elsewhere, Black and his wife, Joanna (who had changed her name from Shirley), had a "somewhat mean little holiday" that Christmas. They hosted their customary party at their Park Lane Circle mansion in Toronto and then travelled to Palm Beach as a couple, where they attended the annual party co-hosted by the Eytons and the Bitoves on a rented 150-foot yacht called *Popeye*. Peter and Melanie Munk also attended the party, and Munk reportedly wore a "flamboyant cape and fedora," befitting a man whose compensation in 1991 had exceeded $36 million.

In June of 1992, Black served his wife with divorce papers. Then on Tuesday, July 21, he married Amiel at the Chelsea Registry Office in London. It was Black's second marriage, her fourth. After the ceremony, the couple went directly to a party for the Queen Mother at Claridge's and then on to Annabel's for a post-wedding dinner for 20 guests, where Black reportedly sat between Margaret Thatcher and Fergie, the Duchess of York. When the wedding tour reached Toronto, a handful of friends and relatives were invited to dinner at the exclusive Founders Club restaurant at SkyDome. Among the favoured few were the Eytons and the Munks. Even Black's old foe, *The Globe and Mail*, which had been forced to publish an abject apology to Black in 1989, while lurching back to the right politically under editor William Thorsell, had splashed the wedding photograph across the front page. By then, the "forces of CanLit" (Canadian Literature), as Black had dubbed them, had a new enemy: the Edper Group.

Five months earlier, on Wednesday, January 22, 1992, Hees president Bill L'Heureux had faxed a letter to the president of publishing company Macmillan Canada indicating Hees might take legal action on a book about the Edper Group being written by Kimberley Noble. "While it is generally our desire to refrain from legal action, it is quite possible that defamatory material, containing erroneous and damaging statements, will be submitted to you by Ms. Noble....Our experience suggests that at least some portions of the manuscript will be actionable if published," L'Heureux wrote. "We have no desire to interfere with the publication of the book, but rather to caution you in view of our experience." Macmillan decided not to go ahead with the book. HarperCollins later published a pamphlet by Noble entitled *Bound and Gagged*, which recounted her experiences with libel chill.

In November 1990, Paul Reichmann successfully completed negotiations with a consortium of six European and five North American
banks for a £500 million construction loan for Canary Wharf.

"Financing is more difficult now than before because of two
factors — U.S. and Japanese banks made many mistakes and are still
worried about other parties," Paul Reichmann later told Diane
Francis for *The Financial Post*. "We did a £500 million deal [for
Canary Wharf] which was difficult to put together, involving 10
banks for interim financing."

Only two U.S. banks — Citibank NA and Manufacturers Hanover
— participated in the Construction Club loan. The other North
American banks involved were the Canadian Imperial Bank of
Commerce, Royal Bank of Canada and National Bank of Canada.
But Paul Reichmann needed to raise another £500 million of long-term
financing for Canary Wharf Tower, and the market was not receptive.

Olympia & York was running out of sources of financing. By
then the Reichmanns had abandoned the proposed sale of their
20% interest in the U.S. real-estate portfolio.

On December 14, 1990, GW Utilities completed the sale of its
82% stake in Consumers' Gas Co. to British Gas PLC for $891 mil-
lion. Olympia & York got its $351 million share of the proceeds
through a special $10-a-share dividend in early 1991.

By the end of January 1991, the Reichmanns had to secretly
pump their own cash into Olympia & York Developments to stave
off a financial crisis. A Reichmann-owned family company bought
four properties — 5140 Yonge Street and Queens Quay Terminal in
Toronto, Charlottetown Mall in Charlottetown and Place des Quatre
Bourgeois in Ste. Foy — from Olympia & York Developments on
January 31, for an aggregate sale price of $261 million, $114 million
of it in cash. Another Reichmann-owned family company bought
Olympia Floor & Wall Tile from Olympia & York Developments on
the same date for an aggregate sale price of $160 million, $143.6 million of it in cash. There were other, smaller, transactions for a total
infusion of almost $500 million.

On February 15, 1992, GW Utilities raised another $900 million in the block-trade sale of its 8.9% stake in Allied-Lyons. Olympia & York got its $421 million share of the proceeds through a special $12-a-share dividend.

Meanwhile, Olympia & York had come under pressure from Citibank Canada to provide security for the US$250 million remaining of a US$750 million loan made in 1987 to bankroll Olympia & York's purchase of Santa Fe Southern Pacific Corp. An internal Citibank study had reportedly forecast that Olympia & York had a 20% chance of going bankrupt in the first quarter of 1992 and an 80% chance of going bankrupt in the fourth quarter of 1992.

Then, in June 1991, rumours spread around the world that Olympia & York had defaulted on a loan to Citibank. Spokesmen for both Olympia & York and the bank said the rumours were "groundless." That same month, Olympia & York managed to close a US$160 million loan led by Bank of Montreal and JP Morgan to refinance some of the American property holdings.

In October 1991, Paul Reichmann managed to persuade Hong Kong billionaire Li Ka-shing to buy a mortgage on Olympia & York's 60 Broad St. property in Manhattan at a discounted US$57.5 million in return for a 49% stake in the building.

That same month, GW Utilities sold Interprovincial Pipe Line Ltd.'s U.S. assets for US$580 million. Olympia & York got its $175 million share of the proceeds through a special $5-a-share dividend in early 1992.

That October, Olympia & York took over the half of Scotia Plaza it did not own in return for assuming its debt. And in November, Campeau Corp. was restructured into a new company called Camdev Corp., with Olympia & York controlling two-thirds of the equity.

Meanwhile, Olympia & York was working around the clock to provide a breakdown of its consolidated cash flow and list of debts for four Canadian banks: Canadian Imperial Bank of Commerce, Royal Bank of Canada, Bank of Nova Scotia and National Bank of Canada. By then the rules had relaxed, out of necessity. The *goys* at Toronto headquarters were encouraged to stay after sundown on Friday nights and to work on Saturdays, recalled one non-Jewish manager. But the Reichmann brothers continued to observe the Jewish Sabbath. Then, one Friday night in late autumn, the same manager was shocked to find Albert Reichmann still working in his office, long after the sun had set. "That's when I knew how bad it was," he said. How could it have gone so wrong? As a young business graduate, the manager had once decorated his bachelor Christmas tree with balls emblazoned with photos of Paul, Albert and Ralph Reichmann — the Toronto equivalent of the "three wise men," he had joked.

Paul Reichmann had asked the four banks for a US$240 million credit line, knowing that Morgan Stanley had the right to sell its building at Canary Wharf, 25 Cabot Square, to Olympia & York for US$240 million sometime between December 12, 1991, and June 30, 1992. Unfortunately for Olympia & York, Morgan Stanley exercised that option on December 12 and demanded its money. Olympia & York disputed the timing of the sale-leaseback, arguing that it didn't have to pay until June 30.

Separately, Olympia & York had hired Morgan Stanley to raise US$200 million through a private placement to Japanese investors. The placement failed. "But they didn't tell us until the very last second," complained one irate Olympia & York executive to *The Financial Post*. By that point, the usually soft-spoken Paul Reichmann was losing his composure in meetings, lashing out at subordinates.

That December, Olympia & York quietly put four towers in Toronto up for sale: First Canadian Place, the Exchange Tower, Scotia Plaza and the Aetna Centre. Li Ka-shing and fellow Hong Kong billionaire Cheng Yu-Tung looked at the flagship First Canadian Place, but were put off by its complicated leaseholds. The two Hong Kong billionaires and other investors also questioned the debt-to-equity ratios on the four towers.

Then just as Paul Reichmann reached an agreement with the four Canadian banks on the US$240 million credit facility, the banks discovered that Olympia & York had recently pledged additional security to Citibank Canada (Olympia & York's 66% stake in Camdev Corp. and mortgage receivables, as well as a second mortgage on 555 Yonge Street and assignment of rentals) for a pre-existing US$250 million loan, in return for an additional US$55 million in loans. The four Canadian banks demanded the same treatment. They wanted additional collateral for their pre-existing £400 million loan to Canary Wharf.

By then, Canadian Imperial Bank of Commerce had received its first breakdown of Olympia & York's consolidated cash flow and a list of its debts. The CIBC later disputed the accusation that it had lacked sufficient data. "A great deal of financial information was known and continuous dialogue was maintained," it said in a statement. But in December, CIBC had shifted the Olympia & York file to veteran loan negotiator Paul Farrar in the bank's special loans department and put insolvency lawyers from Blake Cassels & Graydon on retainer.

On Thursday, January 9, 1992, Morgan Stanley took Olympia & York to court over the timing of the US$240 million payment. Publicity about the British lawsuit sparked public fears about a liquidity crisis at Olympia & York.

Then, on Thursday, February 13, 1992, Dominion Bond Rating Service downgraded one of Olympia & York's two outstanding commercial paper programs. (Commercial paper consists of short-term promissory notes or bonds. It is a lower-cost form of financing generally available only to the most creditworthy corporations.) The agency chopped the rating on Olympia & York's largest $500 million program. "We never saw O&Y statements," a DBRS analyst later recalled. "We were rating single-purpose companies. We did not rate O&Y on their own cash flow." Olympia & York also had an outstanding $300 million program secured by the Exchange Tower.

Olympia & York quickly depleted a $60 million credit line from the Royal Bank of Canada, using the funds to buy back its maturing commercial paper. Holders had begun to demand payment of their commercial paper when it matured rather than renewing the note as had been their practice. Olympia & York's private crisis was about to become very public.

Chapter 13

The Emperor Had No Clothes

On February 28, 1992, in the Toronto law offices of Davies Ward & Beck, Olympia & York was set to close on the US$240 million credit facility, meant to be a lifeline for Canary Wharf. Then, at the last minute, representatives from the four banks — Canadian Imperial Bank of Commerce, Royal Bank of Canada, Bank of Nova Scotia and the National Bank of Canada — withdrew to hold an emergency meeting down the corridor. There the Royal Bank representative revealed Olympia & York Development's commercial-paper problems. The bankers returned and abruptly withdrew the loan.

Paul Reichmann sent a delegation to the four banks' head offices the following Monday, March 2, 1992, but his entreaties failed. Olympia & York was told that the US$240 million facility would not be funded. Unfortunately, some of the security for the facility, a third mortgage on First Canadian Place and a second mortgage on Scotia Plaza, had already been registered against title the previous Friday morning. It did not take long for word to spread through global markets that four Canadian banks had cancelled a major loan to Olympia & York.

Early in the morning on March 3, Paul Reichmann began receiving frantic calls from North American traders who told him that rumours were rife that Olympia & York was about to file for bankruptcy protection. To top it off, $40 million of commercial paper was maturing that day and Olympia & York hadn't yet transferred the money to redeem the notes. By late afternoon, Olympia & York had arranged the transfer, but it was clear that the company had serious liquidity problems.

On Thursday, March 5, Olympia & York announced it would close down its $500 million commercial-paper program, but intended to maintain its $300 million program financing the Exchange Tower. There was also about $100 million outstanding in another commercial-paper program that Olympia & York had been winding down. By that time, the Bank of Canada had joined the federal government's talks with Olympia & York lenders out of concern for the stability of the Canadian dollar and debt markets and the integrity of the banking and financial systems.

That same Thursday, GW Utilities accepted a proposal from a group of Bay Street underwriters for a secondary public offering of its Interprovincial shares on an instalment basis. Olympia & York made some complicated arrangements to get some of its proceeds immediately in the form of a $158 million interest-free demand loan.

The next day, Olympia & York negotiated with the four Canadian banks which had recently withdrawn their US$240 million credit facility. The banks agreed to advance $96 million if Olympia & York cross-collateralized the security (second and third mortgages on two towers and pledges of shares on the Aetna Centre and the Exchange Tower) for that facility with the pre-existing £400 million loan provided by the four banks in mid-1989, as well as a £50 million facility provided by the Bank of Nova Scotia in August 1990. Separately, Bank of Montreal advanced US$20 million after Olympia & York agreed to cross-collateralize the security on the bank's pre-existing $162 million revolving loan. Canadian Imperial Bank of Commerce also advanced $13.7 million. Olympia & York didn't have much choice about these controversial cross-collateralizations. It needed cash right away.

At noon on Sunday, March 8, Paul Reichmann met with a New York investment banker in Olympia & York's Park Avenue Atrium offices. Reichmann told the banker he was trying to raise a few hundred million dollars of additional financing for Canary Wharf by borrowing against 25 Cabot Square at Canary Wharf. The banker said he might be able to come up with something, but he expected a big fee and a premium interest rate. Reichmann said no thanks. That Monday, March 9, a London court ruled against Olympia & York on the sale-leaseback of 25 Cabot Square. Olympia & York would have to pay US$240 million to Morgan Stanley. The banker was stunned by the news. Reichmann had tried to get the banker to refinance a building that Olympia & York hadn't paid for.

The London court ruling was a devastating blow for Olympia & York. On Wednesday, March 11, its commercial paper started defaulting. The four Canadian banks had to advance another $30 million to Olympia & York from the US$240 million credit facility. (Separately, Canadian Imperial Bank of Commerce and the Royal Bank of Canada together advanced $5.4 million, after Olympia & York pledged Exchange Tower commercial paper to the two banks.)

A week later, on Wednesday, March 18, Dominion Bond Rating Service put Olympia & York's commercial paper on alert because it was illiquid. No one was picking it up. A couple of hours later, Olympia & York announced it was retiring its remaining commercial paper, including the Exchange Tower program. (That day, Canadian Imperial Bank of Commerce drip-fed another $6.5 million to Olympia & York, which pledged more Exchange Tower paper to the bank.)

Canadian Imperial Bank of Commerce then pressured the so-called Club of 11 lenders to provide an emergency loan of £52.5 million for Canary Wharf, getting an agreement for the funding on March 20. The amount was added to their pre-existing £500 million Construction Club loan. All the banks, apart from Finnish Kansallis-Osake-Pankki, participated.

At the same time, Olympia & York set up backgrounders with Paul Reichmann for reporters from the *Financial Times* of London and *The Wall Street Journal*. Olympia & York's media strategy was to feed stories about its restructuring to six newspapers in its biggest centres of operation. In the first tier were the *Financial Times* of London and *The Wall Street Journal*; in the second tier were *The Financial Post* and *The Globe and Mail* of Toronto, *The Times* and its affiliated *Sunday Times* of London, and *The New York Times*. The rest of the media, except for the Japanese, were expected to pick up information from those six papers, apart from the occasional press release and press conference by Olympia & York. It was a way for Olympia & York to control the information flow.

For example, on March 21, the *Financial Times* reported that the Olympia & York debt restructuring would have a bank advisory committee co-chaired by Canadian Imperial Bank of Commerce, Citibank NA and Hongkong & Shanghai Bank, quoting unidentified sources. Two days later, a front-page article in *The Wall Street Journal* pegged Olympia & York's total debt at US$20 billion (C$17.4 billion). "If, like some banks, a real estate company can be 'too big to fail' O&Y appears to be that company," the paper said. It also reported that Olympia & York had retained J.P. Morgan & Co. and one other financial firm to advise it, and was in serious negotiations with banker Thomas Johnson, president of Manufacturers Hanover, to take a senior role at Olympia & York.

In fact, Tom Johnson, chief financial adviser Steve Miller from Wolfensohn & Co. and financial advisers from J.P. Morgan had already flown up to Toronto from New York. Olympia & York quietly set them up in private suites in a hotel on the 28th and 29th floors of Scotia Plaza, two towers away from O&Y corporate headquarters in the Exchange Tower. The 58-suite hotel had once been the dream of Toronto entrepreneur Robert Hanson, owner of the then-popular Telfer's restaurant on King Street. But the Bank of Nova Scotia had filed a petition of bankruptcy against Telfer's Tower Club in 1990, after general delays in Campeau Corp.'s completion of Scotia Plaza had delayed the opening of the hotel by 15 months. The hotel reopened for business in 1991 as the Camberley Club Hotel, under the ownership of its biggest creditor, SPE Ltd., which managed Scotia Plaza. When Olympia & York took over Camdev in 1991, it got 100% ownership of SPE Ltd., and control of the hotel.

The Camberley Club Hotel was later judged by *Toronto Life* to be the city's best place to have an affair, presumably because it was in the middle of a busy office tower. But in the spring of 1992, most of the hotel's split-level suites were used only by Olympia & York's out-of-town advisers, to catch a few hours of sleep each night before they trudged back, soldier-like, to the Exchange Tower.

At 10:00 a.m. on Tuesday, March 24, Olympia & York executives gathered in the vast 28th-floor boardroom in the Exchange Tower, with its smoked-glass windows overlooking slate-grey Lake Ontario. Seated at the head of the table was Paul Reichmann. Beside him were Tom Johnson and Steve Miller. In short order, Johnson was named president of Olympia & York Developments, and the advisers from J.P. Morgan and Bay Street's Burns Fry Ltd. began work on a presentation to be made to the company's 20 biggest lenders that Friday. (That day, Citibank Canada advanced US$1 million to Olympia & York, adding to the US$55 million outstanding in the 1992 credit facility.) Paul Reichmann would concentrate on salvaging Canary Wharf.

The following day, Tom Johnson, accompanied by some of Olympia & York's advisers, called on Royal Bank of Canada chairman Allan Taylor. Then Johnson made the rounds of other top officials at the Canadian banks.

"O&Y not as leveraged as many thought," read the front-page headline in *The Financial Post*, on Thursday, March 26, 1992. Editor Diane Francis had been fed the same numbers that the Reichmanns had been quietly passing around in the financial community for the past three months, and splashed them across the front page as an exclusive. "The Reichmann empire is in sound financial condition despite cash flow problems, according to figures from Olympia & York Developments Ltd.'s 1991 financial statements released exclusively to The Post," Francis wrote. "These are the numbers, and the problem O&Y has is a liquidity problem," said her unidentified source. A rating alert by Dominion Bond Rating Service had caused the equivalent of a run on a sound bank, the source added. "Take a well-capitalized bank and if you get a run on the bank on demand deposits, nobody has that kind of cash on hand to pay it off," the source said.

Internally, Francis's article caused an uproar among *The Financial Post* staff. Why print figures that were 14 months out of date when what the world wanted to know was the current cash flow of the Reichmann empire? Was it even positive? And where were the debt figures? Francis didn't have enough information to deduce that the Reichmann empire was in "sound financial condition." In her op-ed column, Francis wrote, "The Reichmanns are in great shape — for the shape they're in....Skeptics will question these figures and perhaps question the [January 31, 1991] audit, but the information is bona fide. And what it tells us is that the empire appears to be pretty darn secure, suffering mostly from a combination of bad publicity and skittish bankers." As the CBC's Der Hoi-Yin later remarked to me before a Royal Bank of Canada press conference, "How could [Diane] have been so naive?" But Francis had plenty of company.

At the afternoon press conference, Royal Bank of Canada chairman Allan Taylor conceded it was "very recent that any effort was made toward having large discussions about restructuring O&Y's debt," then added, "Events began to unfold when O&Y's commercial paper wasn't rolling over." Taylor claimed the planned debt restructuring was "not a life-threatening event for the Royal Bank of Canada, not in any way." But he would not reveal the bank's exposure to Olympia & York, citing "client confidentiality." Those two words had become the mantra for all the banks. (Altogether the Canadian banks accounted for roughly $3 billion of Olympia & York's $14.3 billion of debt — Canadian Imperial Bank of Commerce was owed $860 million; Royal Bank of Canada, $780 million; Bank of Nova Scotia, $630 million; the National Bank of Canada, $473 million; and Bank of Montreal, $320 million.)

Around 11 o'clock that Thursday night, three of Olympia & York's out-of-town advisers stumbled back to the Camberley Club Hotel and sat down at a table in the dark northwest corner of its library-like lounge, unaware that I was eavesdropping on their conversation from a nearby couch. The three men ordered scotches and began to unwind, swapping stories about previous debt re-structurings they had worked on, such as Campeau Corp. and Rupert Murdoch's News Corp. One man said he was stunned by the level of animosity directed at the Reichmanns. He said the Canadian banks wanted to force the sale of the Reichmanns' private jet but couldn't because the plane seemed to belong to the family, not Olympia & York. More people trickled in, including a few female advisers. Finally they were joined by chief adviser Steve Miller and by Tom Johnson, whom they addressed as "Mr. President," and the talk got progressively looser. Johnson confessed he hadn't known much about Olympia & York until the executive recruiter called him. Then one adviser complained about the long hours they had been working and about going without sex for a week. He couldn't wait to get back to New York City the following night — "Thank God the Reichmanns are orthodox Jews," he quipped. That meant the team didn't have to return to Toronto until the Jewish Sabbath ended.

The next morning, Friday, March 27, the out-of-town advisers had an early breakfast in the same library-like lounge and trudged back to the Exchange Tower through the underground tunnel connecting Scotia Plaza with First Canadian Place, for the regular 8:00 a.m. meeting, ahead of the big 10:00 a.m. meeting with the company's 20 largest lenders. One of Olympia & York's out-of-town advisers, who had carted over his luggage from the Camberley Club Hotel so that he could go directly to the airport after the meeting, was asked to store it in some empty office space on the 27th floor. An hour before the meeting was scheduled to start, security was posted outside a bank of elevators on the tower's main floor and behind the Olympia & York reception desk on the 28th floor. Journalists were asked to leave the Olympia & York floors. Earlier, the Reichmanns had arrived by limousine in the underground parking lot and taken their private elevator directly to the 28th floor. The bank negotiators and their lawyers had to use the two public elevators. The meeting ended a few hours before sundown. Tom Johnson had reportedly told the creditor representatives, "You will soon receive every scrap of financial information you need. I am here to tell you that we want to work with you." Olympia & York issued a press release saying it was working on an interim plan to be presented on April 6 and had asked the banks to roll over their debts until then. In effect, it was asking for an informal standstill agreement.

On Thursday, April 2, in Hong Kong, billionaire Li Ka-shing told reporters that he was interested in some of Olympia & York's assets, following Ka-shing's surprise resignation from the board of Hongkong & Shanghai Bank. Several hours later on the same day, in Toronto, Olympia & York announced it would postpone its big meeting with bankers one week to Monday, April 13. Not long after, sources told journalist Gayle MacDonald of *The Financial Post* that Ka-shing planned to fly into Toronto on the evening of the big meeting to participate in talks with Olympia & York and its bankers on Tuesday, April 14. Ka-shing later cancelled those plans.

Meanwhile, on that same Thursday, April 2, in Toronto, the directors of the Canadian Imperial Bank of Commerce — a board that included Conrad Black, Galen Weston and Alf Powis — met on the 50th floor of Commerce Court West to elect a new chairman to replace retiring Donald Fullerton. Bank director Paul Reichmann had submitted his resignation by letter, and was told he would be welcome to return to the board after Olympia & York was on sound footing. In his memoirs, Black said he engaged in a "modest amount of lobbying" on Reichmann's behalf with the CIBC, as well as the Canadian and British governments, "within the bounds of indisputable arithmetic" — perhaps recalling Black's own humiliation in 1986, when the CIBC called his loan and he was hounded by CIBC junior officials. The CIBC board meeting lasted almost five hours, with heated discussion. In the end, CIBC decided to take loss provisions on almost its entire exposure to Olympia & York. And Al Flood, head of the Corporate Bank, was named successor to Fullerton.

It was said that, as the person in charge of the Olympia & York file, Al Flood had been at the office around the clock in the early days of the crisis. At that meeting, the CIBC board gave Flood "a standing ovation," he recalled four months later. "I assume my fair share of the responsibility for dealing with O&Y. I don't think I can avoid that. I was in charge of the lending portfolio for the bank," Flood said.

Asked whether banks should change their pack mentality, Flood replied: "All the bankers around the world are beginning to realize they've got to make their own decisions. Traditional lending...asset lending is becoming a much higher risk. A lot of that will be cash flow lending...[when there is] no hard collateral available. We have to do a better job at [assessing] asset quality. We can't afford the losses we are taking."

Responding to criticism that CIBC's lending standards were not up to par, Flood said, "We operated with the O&Y group within our own guidelines...as far as the board, committees...we've gone through the analysis. Did we follow the guidelines and adhere to policies? One of the basic fundamentals of banking is to diversify. This is a case where we had a large real-estate group that was diversified in various countries — our portfolio has O&Y stuff in Canada, the U.S. and the U.K. and commodities such as Gulf Canada. The bottom line is did anyone anticipate that we were going to go into a deep recession? There are [90] other banks involved. Should we have done it differently, should we change our policies? We are assessing that."

When asked if the CIBC was happy with Olympia & York's disclosure, Flood indicated that the bank had seen information about the projects. But had the CIBC seen Olympia & York's financial statements? "We had information, sure," Flood said. Then why didn't the CIBC see the problem coming? "If not for Canary Wharf, there would not be a problem," he responded. "It [was] also the problem of leasing, the death of the market." That April, the CIBC hired Peat Marwick Thorne to do an independent feasibility study of Canary Wharf.

The following week, Olympia & York president Tom Johnson flew home to New York in a huff, after losing a power struggle with Paul Reichmann. Johnson reportedly had wanted to provide the creditors with more disclosure than the secretive Reichmann was comfortable with. "Restructuring [is] a cultural shock to the Reichmanns. They're not used to others seeing their stuff," Unicorp CEO James Leech explained to me in a phone interview. "The guys underneath Paul in the corporate office know very little. It's very hard on those people."

Albert Reichmann tried to persuade his brother to go along with Johnson, but Paul Reichmann wasn't willing to cede control. "Paul is a bit of one-man show," semi-retired Burns Fry executive David Brown told me. "He's difficult to work for." Brown had worked on Olympia & York's 1985 deal to roll Abitibi-Price into newly purchased Gulf Canada Corp.

There was also a dispute over pay. Apparently Tom Johnson wanted his $3 million pay package guaranteed. Canadian Imperial Bank of Commerce had earlier agreed to provide a $3 million letter of credit but backed away when Olympia & York's other bankers refused to share the risk. Ultimately, Paul Reichmann ended up paying Johnson $2 million for less than three weeks' work. The cheque was reportedly drawn on Paul's personal account, not Olympia & York's, at his brother Albert's insistence.

Meanwhile, as Olympia & York scrambled to find a replacement for Johnson before its big meeting with creditors it set up backgrounders with Paul Reichmann and chief adviser Steve Miller for one reporter from *The Wall Street Journal* on Thursday, April 10, 1992, and two reporters from the *Financial Times* of London on Saturday night, to give them a preview of the restructuring plan. On Sunday, April 12, Margaret Philp, a reporter with *The Globe and Mail*, got a call summoning her to an interview at Paul Reichmann's house in north Toronto. When she returned to the *Globe* newsroom late that afternoon, she had only a few hours to write up her story. It was said that Olympia & York offered a similar deal to Diane Francis, editor of *The Financial Post*, but since that paper didn't publish on Mondays, she asked instead for an exclusive with Paul Reichmann further down the road.

That Sunday evening, April 12, the new Olympia & York president, Gerald Greenwald (a U.S. executive who had worked with Steve Miller on the restructuring of Chrysler Corp.), flew into Toronto, as a snowstorm blanketed the city. Later, around 11 o'clock on the eve of the big meeting, two *Financial Post* reporters, Eric

Reguly and I, tried to shift the advantage. We attempted to get into the Dominion Ballroom, hoping to find copies of Olympia & York's 270-page Information Book, but hotel security barred our access. I decided to call it a night and go home. Not Reguly. Later that night, he walked through the Sheraton's kitchen to reach the service entrance into the ballroom. The tables and screens had been set up for Olympia & York's 1:30 p.m. Monday meeting, but there were no Information Books lying around. Reguly taped one of the exit doors so that he could regain access the following morning.

At a 7:30 a.m. meeting at *The Financial Post*, assignment editors Glen Flanagan and Michael Babad paired Adrian Bradley with Reguly on the paper's A Team. At the Sheraton Centre, Reguly and Bradley sneaked into the Dominion Ballroom through the taped door and hid. Everything went according to plan for two or three hours — then the ballroom was swept for bugs. Reguly and Bradley had to get out before their hiding place was discovered. When they returned, the tape had been removed from the door. Foiled, Reguly and Bradley descended to the basement where they "borrowed" waiter's uniforms from a pile of dirty laundry. Suitably attired, they made their way to the ballroom through the hotel kichen. They were in sight of Paul Reichmann when they were apprehended. Both over six feet tall, they were given away by their too-short uniforms. Hotel security threatened to call in the police, convinced that the two journalists were hitmen. Olympia & York had to vouch for their relative harmlessness. But security still wanted to charge them — for stealing hotel property.

Meanwhile, outside the security net, the 400-odd creditor representatives had to walk through a media gauntlet to get to the Dominion Ballroom. It began at the entrance to the hotel lobby. Once they stepped off the lobby escalator and turned left, the lights of video cameras filled a long hallway lined with journalists from around the world. Some of the creditor representatives froze in the bright lights like deer in the road, as the media yelled questions at them. Others were not so easily intimidated.

Behind the security net, the creditor representatives picked up their numbered copies of the Olympia & York Information Book. Paul Reichmann spoke first, introducing the new president, Gerald Greenwald. Then Steve Miller walked the creditors through a slideshow presentation about Olympia & York. Michael Dennis spoke about Canary Wharf.

The Olympia & York executives told creditors that the downgrading of the commercial paper had precipitated a "run on the bank" requiring cash and refunding totalling $800 million almost instantly. They said Olympia & York had used part of a US$240 million loan facility from four Canadian banks to help repay the commercial-paper programs, starving Canary Wharf of funds at a critical time and requiring an emergency bridge loan to the project of £52.5 million. Then Olympia & York's "balance sheet had seized up," they said.

Although the U.S. operations were healthy, Olympia & York said it needed $75 million over the next three months to fund its Canadian operations. It suggested that the money come from a drawdown of the US$135 million remaining in the US$240 million credit facility from the four banks — Canadian Imperial Bank of Commerce, Royal Bank of Canada, Bank of Nova Scotia and National Bank of Canada. Olympia & York said it also needed £110 million for Canary Wharf and suggested that the money be provided by the Club of 11 bankers (Canadian Imperial Bank of Commerce, Royal Bank of Canada, National Bank of Canada, Citibank NA, Manufacturers Hanover and six European banks).

Olympia & York promised that during implementation of the plan, it would not provide additional collateral to any lender except in the context of the overall restructuring plan. The Information Books did not contain information about cross-collateralizations.

By the time the meeting ended, Eric Reguly and the *Financial Post* photographers had stationed themselves outside the hotel. When Paul and Albert Reichmann emerged, Paul couldn't suppress a grin at the sight of "hitman" Reguly, as photographer Jeff Wasserman snapped a rare photo of the two brothers together. When Reguly asked if

Olympia & York had managed to placate its lenders, Paul Reichmann replied, "It'll take some time; not today." About the planned debt restructuring, he said, "It's moving well."

At 10 o'clock on Monday evening, Steve Miller and Michael Dennis sat down for a late snack in the lounge at the Camberley Club Hotel, unaware that journalist Rufus Olins, from the London *Sunday Times*, was eavesdropping nearby. In a postmortem of the day's events, Miller told Dennis that some lenders were still suspicious and "overwhelmed by the mess."

That was an understatement. Bank of Nova Scotia's Peter Godsoe was outraged that Paul Reichmann was asking for more money from his bank. "They don't seem to realize that we already effectively own the company," Godsoe roared in a telephone conversation with Eric Reguly.

Paul Reichmann should have apologized to the creditors and "turned over the keys," lawyer Andrew Kent of McMillan Binch, counsel to the Royal Bank of Canada, later told a meeting of the insolvency section of the Canadian Bar Association-Ontario. The creditors were so desperate they would have given them back, he said.

"It's difficult to impossible to envisage [Paul Reichmann] having the courage to do that," Ed Lundy, senior vice-president of corporate banking for the Royal Bank of Canada said at the same meeting. But of "all the lenders in [the Dominion Ballroom], no one could be immune to having committed some sins. Everybody wanted a piece of the deal. The bigger the name, the hungrier they got, the thinner the spread, the less the analysis," Lundy said.

The next day, Tuesday, April 14, there was an uproar at a meeting of the 21 banks involved in the $2.5 billion "jumbo loan." Over lunch in the private dining room of law firm Osler Hoskin & Harcourt, representatives from the Hongkong Bank, Credit Lyonnais and other "jumbo loan" banks pored over copies of a confidential Olympia & York memorandum, detailing the recent cross-collateralization of certain loans. The Hongkong Bank and Credit Lyonnais were angriest at the four Canadian banks (later dubbed the "Gang of Four"), which seemed to have had inside information when they grabbed extra collateral to support their loans more than a month before Olympia & York publicly admitted its cash crunch.

On April 15, at a meeting in Olympia & York's boardroom, Credit Lyonnais's Charles Heidsieck told Canadian Imperial Bank of Commerce's Paul Farrar that the cross-collateralizations must be undone. Farrar argued that the four Canadian banks had insisted on the collateral transfer as an incentive to provide the new money that Olympia & York so desperately needed.

On Easter Monday, April 20, the banks met again in Olympia & York's boardroom. Because it was Jewish Passover, security guards confiscated all the snacks that the bank negotiators had carried in with them. Hongkong Bank's Richard Ross announced that his bank would not lend any more money to Olympia & York until the cross-collateralizations were cancelled and everyone agreed to a standstill. Nova Scotia's Dennis Belcher then shocked the gathering when he said his bank could not agree to a standstill because it had been already declared a default and was preparing to seize its security on a loan. There was an uproar, until Belcher eventually backed down after consultation with Peter Godsoe and other senior executives at the bank's headquarters. But the restructuring was a shambles and Olympia & York was doomed. Olympia & York had asked for $75 million for its Canadian operations at the April 13 meeting, but the banks would provide only $8 million to pay its bills and keep its operations going.

On April 22, the Gang of Four signed off on a $5 million drawdown from the US$240 million loan facility, which was then converted into a $131 million demand loan. Olympia & York wouldn't be able to draw down any more money from that facility. The other $3 million came from the Hongkong Bank, after Olympia & York pledged Exchange Tower commercial paper to the bank.

The same day, in London, Steve Miller met with the Club of 11 lenders, providing them with about 100 pages of information and asking them for the £110 million for Canary Wharf. But the Club of 11 wasn't satisfied with Olympia & York's disclosure. It hired Ernst & Young and property surveyors to do its own feasibility study of Canary

Wharf. (Canadian Imperial Bank of Commerce, the Club's lead bank, would not allow Peat Marwick to act as an auditor for the entire syndicate, and it refused to share Peat Marwick's findings with the Club.)

The following week, on Thursday, April 30, the Club of 11 advanced £5 million to Olympia & York to keep Canary Wharf going, while the Club waited for Ernst & Young's report. Hongkong & Shanghai Bank participated in the small loan, joining the original 11-member banking consortium for that one transaction, because Canadian Imperial Bank of Commerce had agreed to transfer up to £5 million of its funding commitment to the Hongkong Bank on March 20. "[Hongkong Bank] made a small investment [£50,000] but they [were] not part of the Club," CIBC's Al Flood later told me. "They did come in for a minor amount. That was the only way we could give them support. It was early days."

On Monday, May 4, there was another meeting of the Club of 11 lenders in Olympia & York's Toronto boardroom. The participants were asked to stand up and introduce themselves to ensure that no journalists had crashed the meeting. Paul Reichmann reportedly rose from his chair and announced: "Hello, my name is Paul Reichmann. And I'm with the CBC." But there was little else to joke about. When discouraged lawyers from Davies Ward & Beck returned to their offices after the meeting, one said there was a 70% chance the Reichmanns would lose Canary Wharf.

By then, Peat Marwick Thorne had given its report on Canary Wharf to the Canadian Imperial Bank of Commerce. The consultants estimated it would cost at least £600 million to complete the first phase of Canary Wharf, double Olympia & York's own estimate of £300 million. As one of the bank's insolvency lawyers told me, Canary Wharf looked beautiful, but it was sitting on "the equivalent of a financial toxic waste dump." Olympia & York had taken over so many leases and spent so much money on inducements to get tenants to commit to the project that the numbers didn't work, even in a best-case scenario with the project fully leased and the British government picking up the entire tab for the subway extension. "The thing about Canary Wharf is the more you look at the numbers, the worse the whole thing looks. You can turn the numbers upside-down, sideways, horizontal and vertical and it just doesn't look any better. There is no way, no matter how you twist it and turn it, to change that," said the lawyer, who began calling Canary Wharf "the scene of the crime."

Senior executives at the Canadian Imperial Bank of Commerce felt betrayed. They turned on Paul Reichmann with a vengeance because they felt Olympia & York had kept the bank in the dark about its true financial health.

Later that week, on the morning of May 7, Paul Reichmann met with the Club of 11 lenders in London at Olympia & York's 30th-floor offices in the Canary Wharf Tower to ask for an emergency £50 million loan. Canadian Imperial Bank of Commerce's Paul Farrar shocked the gathering when he announced that his bank wasn't putting another penny into Canary Wharf. Predictably, Reichmann and the other Club bankers were furious. Citibank N.A. negotiator Anne Lane let forth a string of expletives. Wasn't it the CIBC which had persuaded them to make a £52.5 million emergency loan on March 20? Had the CIBC misled the other banks? Why wouldn't the CIBC tell them what was in the Peat Marwick report? The other Club bankers put extreme pressure on Farrar to get CIBC to contribute to the loan.

Late that evening, Paul Farrar said CIBC might participate in smaller loan to keep Canary Wharf going, but just for the next two weeks. A few days later, CIBC contributed to a £21 million loan for Canary Wharf.

Back in Canada, the first-mortgage-bond holders of First Canadian Place were preparing to seize their security. On May 13, the Gang of Four refused to advance Olympia & York the $17 million it needed to pay the interest on the First Canadian bonds the following day. The banks told Olympia & York it was time to file for court protection in Canada.

The next morning in London, the British Court ruled against Olympia & York's appeal in the Morgan Stanley case. (Paul Reichmann and Steve Miller had flown to New York on April 27 to try to talk Morgan Stanley into putting off the US$240 million payment, but the investment banker wanted its money.) The court gave Olympia & York until May 21 to come up with the money, before Morgan Stanley could seize the building. Steve Miller called Olympia & York with the bad news.

It was 11:00 a.m. in Toronto when Paul Reichmann, Albert Reichmann and Gerald Greenwald gathered in corporate headquarters on the conference call with Steve Miller in London. After a brief discussion, the four men agreed that an out-of-court restructuring was no longer feasible for the Canadian operations. "There was no straw that broke the camel's back," Miller said later. "But finally we came to the conclusion that the voluntary method was not going to succeed because there are too many lenders involved with too diverse a set of credits and we just didn't think we were going to be able to hold everyone in line."

The four men decided it was time for Olympia & York to file for court protection in Canada, under the Companies' Creditors Arrangement Act (CCAA). Olympia & York informed Finance Minister Don Mazankowski of the plan. His department and the Bank of Canada would monitor developments on the domestic stock and currency markets the next day, Friday, May 15.

In the Toronto newsroom of *The Financial Post*, the staff made call after call, going down the list of lawyers likely to be summoned to an Olympia & York filing. No one had been contacted yet. Shortly after 6:00 p.m., one lawyer phoned back to tell me that he had heard from Olympia & York. He was to report to the Bankruptcy Court office on Queen Street at 8:00 p.m. Some of the Bay Street's insolvency lawyers had left already for the Blue Jays game at SkyDome and could not be reached. One later joked that Olympia & York should have flashed a message on the stadium's JumboTron: "All insolvency lawyers report to Bankruptcy Court on Queen Street for O&Y filing." As it was, *The Financial Post*'s Gayle MacDonald and I were among the first to arrive, while photographer Peter Redman waited outside to snap pictures of the lawyers as they streamed up from the centre of the financial district. One Olympia & York lawyer held up a binder to cover his face.

The crowded courtroom buzzed with excitement as the lawyers waited for Justice Robert Blair to enter. Some lawyers worried aloud about how they would be paid for their work, while others had visions of huge fees dancing in their heads. In fact, at least 29 law firms would ultimately pocket more than $11 million of fees from Olympia & York's court-supervised restructuring.

An hour earlier, Eric Reguly had phoned Paul Reichmann on his private line at Olympia & York. Surprised to hear a journalist's voice, Reichmann snapped, "I can't talk right now. I'm in a meeting." The Reichmanns did not show up in the courtroom that night, but Olympia & York senior vice-president Gary Goodman kept them informed of the proceedings by cellular phone.

Lawyer David Brown from Davies Ward & Beck quietly outlined the mounting problems that had led to Olympia & York's application. He asked for court protection until the end of October while Olympia & York negotiated a restructuring plan for the $8.6 billion of debt in its Canadian operations.

When Brown was finished speaking, lawyer Ronald Robertson, representing the Hongkong & Shanghai Banking Corp., stood up and said he wanted to "stop the clock from running." Hongkong Bank wanted the chance to undo the cross-collateralizations if Olympia & York's restructuring failed.

Then lawyer David Baird, representing the Bank of Nova Scotia, spoke. Scotiabank didn't want the Reichmanns to remain in control, Baird said. The bank didn't want to see any more of "its money" diverted from Olympia & York's Canadian operations to the U.S. or Britain. It also wanted the surplus value of Olympia & York's assets made available to creditors. Later Baird would make moves to force the Reichmanns to disclose their private assets and to get the family to fund the restructuring efforts of Olympia & York.

Around 9:00 p.m. Justice Blair left the courtroom to consider what he had heard. A group of lawyers immediately scrummed David Brown to negotiate changes to the draft order. Shortly after 11:00 p.m., Blair returned. The hearing had been arranged "on short notice [and it] was not possible for the court to absorb it all [but he] was satisfied that the applicants [had] met the test," Blair said. He had decided to "grant the [CCAA] order but [did] so with caution." It would provide Olympia & York "with some breathing space," he explained, but noted that the creditors' lawyers had "raised some legitimate concerns" and agreed to set aside a day the following week to address them. After Blair left, many of the lawyers milled about the courtroom until after 1:00 a.m.

In early overseas trading the Canadian dollar dropped 55 basis points to US82.58 cents, as the news of the filing flashed across the wires. Later that morning, Friday, May 15, Olympia & York called a press conference for 8:30 a.m. at the Royal York Hotel. Many journalist were summoned out of bed, stumbling into the room at various points during Gerald Greenwald's speech. Greenwald said Olympia & York's British and U.S. operations were unaffected by the Canadian filing. After the question period, Greenwald and lawyer David Brown left the hotel by the east door and walked up to Olympia & York headquarters to address the employees.

Two weeks later in London, on May 27, Ernst & Young gave its report to the Club of 11 bankers. The consultants said it would take £500 million to complete the first phase of Canary Wharf, far in excess of Olympia & York's own estimate of £300 million. Shortly after the lenders heard the report, a majority voted to put the project into administration. (The seven in favour of administration were Canadian Imperial Bank of Commerce, Royal Bank of Canada, National Bank of Canada, Lloyds Bank and Barclays Bank; the four against were Citibank NA, Credit Lyonnais, Credit Suisse and the Finnish bank.) The Club of 11 informed British Prime Minister John Major and the Bank of England of their decision.

At 9:00 a.m. on May 28, construction work stopped at Canary Wharf, and the workers were given notice. Half and hour later, Stephen Adamson, an insolvency partner from Ernst & Young, walked into the British High Court of Justice to take control of the project. After a brief hearing, the judge appointed Adamson and his three colleagues to take over management of Canary Wharf.

At 10:00 a.m. the Ernst & Young administration met with Canary Wharf's 400 employees in Cabot Hall. Said one staff member, "I don't think anyone had really expected this. We knew it was possible but we always thought the banks would support the company." A couple of days later, the Club of 11 bankers (plus Hongkong Bank this time) advanced £11 million to the administrators for Canary Wharf. Ernst & Young had three months to produce a proposal that would satisfy the creditors, or else the project would be liquidated.

"It was criminal that [Canary Wharf] wasn't successful," Royal Bank's Ed Lundy said later.

"A wonderful project, beautifully conceived," lawyer David Brown said, "but a distinct lack of tenants."

By then, Olympia & York had invested almost $3.8 billion in Canary Wharf. Paul Reichmann had to find some way of salvaging that equity. He assembled a team of Olympia & York executives and corporate finance partners from Price Waterhouse to develop a rescue proposal and assemble a posse of U.S. investors.

Reichmann personally approached U.S. media billionaire Laurence Tisch, former Salomon Brothers vice-chairman Lewis Ranieri and Primerica Corp. chairman Sandy Weil (the former head of American Express).

On July 20, 1992, the Ernst & Young administrators revealed that four out of six potential buyers of Canary Wharf were sufficiently serious to sign secrecy agreements. Two days later, I reported in *The Financial Post* that Paul Reichmann had filed a memorandum with the administrators outlining the deal to salvage Canary Wharf with unnamed U.S. investors.

The proposal involved the Reichmann-assembled U.S. group pouring £350 million into Canary Wharf (including a contribution to the building of the Jubilee subway extension) for a 50% equity stake. A condition of the offer was that the new loans would rank ahead of the £576 million of debt already provided by the Club of 11 bankers. One Club lender angrily dubbed the offer a "LIFO proposal" because the group would be the last in but the first to be paid back.

But the Club of 11 lenders did strike a committee to negotiate the offer, although representatives from Laurence Tisch, Lewis Ranieri and Sandy Weil did not attend a mid-August meeting in Canary Wharf Tower between the administrators and the Club of 11 bankers. Ranieri's camp confirmed on August 17 that it was looking at the investment on a risk-reward basis but had not completed its due diligence.

After they had completed their financial analysis, the Reichmann-assembled consortium reduced their offer to £230 million. That offer was rejected by the Club of 11 bankers on September 21, 1992. Almost a year later, the Club bankers formed a holding company called Sylvester Investments Ltd. ("the cat that swallowed the canary"), when they approved a £1.1 billion plan to take Canary Wharf out of administration.

Meanwhile, in Canada, in the spring of 1992, Olympia & York and its creditors had spent the first six weeks of court protection squabbling over who would pay for the restructuring expenses. To reach a funding agreement, the lawyers met almost nonstop for a week in late June. They negotiated in the halls and on the front steps of the courthouse until they came to a resolution late on July 2, 1992, after one lawyer suggested changing the first letter in two words in the draft agreement to lowercase from uppercase.

"There was a feeding frenzy that was allowed to go on," Royal Bank's Ed Lundy said later. "We're all part of it and the lenders have got to learn to control their professional advisers."

It was agreed that Olympia & York would fund expenses from the sale of assets it valued at $70 million. By late July, the Reichmanns had sold their Gulfstream III jet to American Barrick (part of Peter Munk's Horsham group) for net proceeds of $7.7 million and their interest in the Hungarian office tower to Andrew Sarlos.

Paul Reichmann also reached an agreement to sell a one-acre property, complete with a pond and bird sanctuary, on Hampstead Heath in north London, where he had planned to build a new home. The sale, which closed in early September, generated net proceeds of US$3.7 million.

Bit by bit, Olympia & York was paying for the restructuring expenses, but the six-week dispute over their funding meant Olympia & York had not begun serious talks with its creditor groups until early July. Angry at how little had been accomplished in court, Olympia & York attempted to take the proceedings out of the hands of the litigators and put the negotiations back in the boardrooms. Even so, there was no way Olympia & York would be able to present a complete plan to restructure $8.6 billion of debt by August 21.

Within days of Olympia & York's filing for court protection from creditors on Thursday, May 14, 1992, the market asked, Who's next? Bay Street singled out Edper Group's Bramalea as the next most likely company to fail.

Bramalea had announced a $100 million rights offering on Monday, March 2, 1992, the same day that rumours of Olympia & York's imminent collapse swept around the globe. The panic had unsettled the financial markets and public support of the issue had disappeared, as did a number of Bramalea's property sales that were nearing completion. Bramalea's parent Trizec became the sole participant in the rights offering, boosting its stake in Bramalea to 72% from 66%, at a cost of $76 million.

The March credit crunch made Bramalea's 1992 business plan unachievable. The plan, as it had been presented to Bramalea's principal lenders, was to slash overhead expenses by $35 million a year, raise $86 million of new common equity and sell enough land and income-producing properties to repay $420 million of debt. Not only were Bramalea's lenders reluctant to renew Bramalea's loans, they were demanding repayment.

Meanwhile, the Edper Group had trouble on another front. Carena learned that Olympia & York's financial difficulties had affected Battery Park Holdings' interest in the World Financial Center, after reading in *The Financial Post* on April 8, 1992, that Tower B of the World Financial Center had defaulted on its US$62 million annual interest payment on US$800 million of mortgage notes. After discussion with Olympia & York (U.S.), it became clear that the money had been diverted from the Tower B partnerships to buy back Olympia & York's commercial paper in Canada.

In April 1992, Carena's and the Reichmann family's joint ownership of Battery Park Holdings was still a secret, but some of Olympia & York's U.S. executives grew suspicious that the family had a direct stake in the World Financial Center, and to save face with lenders withheld regular operating cash-flow distributions that month to the equity owners of the U.S. buildings, including Battery Park Holdings. (Seven months later, on November 20, 1992, Battery Park Holdings sued the U.S. arm of Olympia & York to recover its cash-flow distributions. The two parties implemented a standstill arrangement three days later.)

In late April 1992, I ambushed Jack Cockwell at the Noranda annual meeting to ask him if it was true that Olympia & York had defaulted on a loan from Hees the year before, long before its liquidity crisis became public. If so, why hadn't Hees disclosed it? Cockwell declined comment. He knew it was the Reichmanns, not Olympia & York, who had defaulted on the loan. But, with a charming smile, Cockwell told me to call Gordon Arnell. The Carena CEO was the designated group spokesman for all inquiries about Olympia & York.

At the end of May 1992, Carena and several other Edper Group companies moved into their new office space in BCE Place, which had been sucking tenants out of Olympia & York's First Canadian Place.

Meanwhile, Edper's Bramalea was forced to restructure its $4 billion of debt. But it had learned some lessons from the fall of Olympia & York. It did not ask its principal lenders — Toronto-Dominion Bank, Canadian Imperial Bank of Commerce, Royal Bank of Canada, Bank of Nova Scotia and Bank of Montreal, who together were owed $1.6 billion — for much more new cash and it was quick to provide information about its operations and its plans. And Bramalea's parent, Trizec, kept pumping in the needed cash to keep its subsidiary afloat while it negotiated with its creditors.

On June 5, Dominion Bond Rating Service Ltd. slashed its rating on Bramalea debt by four grades, one of the steepest cuts ever made by the credit monitor. Trizec went back into the market and raised $250 million through the private placement of shares, using some of the money to support Bramalea.

Two weeks later, on June 18, Bramalea earned the dubious distinction of becoming the first Edper Group company to halt dividend payments to conserve cash. At the end of the month Bramalea also decided to miss a $5 million interest payment on a $100 million issue of senior debentures, and initiated discussions with those creditors.

On July 8, Bramalea managed to avoid seeking bankruptcy protection when it raised $131 million by selling malls and other assets, but parent Trizec had to help out by buying two of the properties, pumping another $40 million in cash into Bramalea.

By then, Trizec CEO Kevin Benson had quietly informed the Edper Group that he planned to leave Trizec. Insiders said that Benson was unhappy with Edper's demands that Trizec keep supporting Bramalea, even if it put Trizec at risk. Whatever the reason, the Edper Group began looking for a replacement. Six months later, they hadn't found one, so Hees president Bill L'Heureux volunteered for the job.

By July 30, 1992, Bramalea had reached a tentative deal with the Big Five banks, which held almost 40% of its debt. But negotiations with Bramalea's senior debenture holders, who were owed $500 million-plus, proved more difficult. The committee of debenture holders demanded concessions from Bramalea's secured lenders, including the big banks. The business plan was revised and rejected several times over the next five months. Finally, on December 22, Bramalea sought court protection to get an orderly ratification of its revised plan. Three months later, it emerged as a restructured company, with the debenture holders controlling the company and Trizec owning less than 10%.

Bramalea had learned a key lesson from Olympia & York, Royal Bank's Ed Lundy said later: Time might have saved the empire. Lundy argued that if Olympia & York's application for restructuring had been a year earlier, the outcome might have been different. But two years later, in March 1995, Bramalea was back under court protection and facing the liquidation of its assets.

Chapter 14

Crisis of
Confidence

In late August 1992, Edper's Carena sent a letter to Olympia & York demanding "fair treatment" in the company's negotiations to restructure its U.S. debts.

Olympia & York's U.S. executives showed the letter to some U.S. banks, and rumours started to swirl on Wall Street that an Edper Group company had invested in the World Financial Center. A source phoned *The Financial Post*'s Eric Reguly to tell him that the investment was through Battery Park Holdings, but no one, including the top O&Y executives in New York, seemed to know the details. If true, the story would be a blockbuster because it would put the Edper Group in the centre of the Reichmanns' collapse.

In Toronto, I did a preliminary corporate search, but didn't turn up anything. There was no way to tie the Edper Group to Battery Park Holdings. In mid-September, I flew to New York to visit Reguly in *The Financial Post*'s Manhattan bureau.

Another disclosure search, conducted in New York with the help of one of Reguly's contacts at private investigators Kroll & Associates, revealed that a company called Battery Park Holdings had been registered in Delaware in December 1989, the same month that Reguly's inside source suspected the World Financial Center investment was made. However, the Delaware filing did not name Battery Park Holdings' directors or owners.

Meanwhile, Reguly's and my calls to various Edper group executives in Toronto had not borne fruit. Trilon Financial's Ken Clarke claimed to know nothing about Battery Park Holdings and he recommended that I direct my enquiries to Carena CEO Gordon Arnell. Yet again, all roads led to Arnell. This time it was Reguly who made the call, around midday on September 15. According to the notes Reguly took during the conversation, Arnell said, on the record, "We have no relationship with O&Y other than the partnership with Trizec." It was the same dead end.

Reguly decided to call Trevor Eyton, who was busy arranging the funeral of his father, Jack. The loss of his beloved father had put Eyton off balance. When Reguly asked if he knew anything about Battery Park Holdings, Eyton replied, "I'm familiar with it." He said Carena had used it to buy into the World Financial Center. Eyton ended the conversation abruptly, but he had confirmed a link between Carena and Battery Park Holdings. Reguly called Hees's media adviser Tom Reid and told him what Eyton had said and that he was going with the story. Reid persuaded Reguly to hold the story for one day in exchange for detailed clarification from Arnell about the World Financial Center investment and a promise that the story would not be leaked to *The Globe and Mail*.

On Wednesday morning, September 16, Reguly got a four-paragraph fax from Gordon Arnell. It said: "Following your telephone conversation with Tom Reid last night, we felt we should restate the facts surrounding our relationship with the Reichmann family to help clarify your article." Arnell confirmed that Carena, through Battery Park Holdings, owned "an effective 17 1/2% or $138 million Canadian interest in the World Financial Center." (Carena's initial investment was US$309.4 million; it had been diluted when Carena sold half of Battery Park Holdings to the Reichmanns in October 1990, financed with a loan from Hees.) Arnell said in his letter that Carena, a publicly traded company, had never disclosed the investment because "these private interests are not material to Carena, a $14 billion company."

"Carena confirms $138M O&Y link," read the headline in *The*

Financial Post on Thursday, September 17, 1992. In fact the link was to the Reichmanns, not Olympia & York, but the *Post* exclusive sent shock waves through the Bay Street village, causing Carena stock to fall 15%. Gordon Arnell suggested that the stock price drop might have been triggered by worries about other possible skeletons in Carena's closet. "There may be people out there concerned that there may be connections with the Reichmanns that we haven't talked about yet," he said. "There aren't."

The next day, *The Wall Street Journal* provided another piece of the puzzle when it reported that, according to bankers familiar with the situation, the Reichmann family held the other half of Battery Park Holdings. Meanwhile, *The Globe and Mail*, which had been chasing the same Battery Park rumours as *The Financial Post*, had been frustrated by the Gordon Arnell dead end. "I've told 50 people in the last year that we had no relationship with O&Y outside of the Trizec connection," Arnell later explained to the *Globe*. He said he had been able to do that "without a twitch of conscience" because Carena's original investment in the World Financial Center was part of an arrangement under which the company expected to be paid back with Olympia & York's Trizec shares.

The Toronto Stock Exchange began a normal course investigation into Carena, to find out why it had not disclosed its investment in the World Financial Center to its public shareholders. John Carson, the TSE's director of market integrity, said the exchange wanted to determine whether the Edper Group's failure to disclose this investment earlier contravened any of the exchange's rules governing the distribution of significant information to shareholders. And the Ontario Securities Commission announced that it too was conducting an investigation into Carena's nondisclosure. Sixteen months later, the Commission issued a notice that "proceedings were not warranted" against the Edper group companies that had failed to disclose a $138 million investment in the World Financial Center.

But the editorial in *The Globe and Mail* on September 26, 1992, argued for public disclosure: "The news [of Carena's secret investment] brought an audible gasp even from Bay Street's most cynical analysts, a this-time-they've-gone-too-far reaction in a community where Edper's penchant for sailing rather too close to the regulatory wind is well known."

All the important players from the Edper Group, including Trevor Eyton and Jack Cockwell, arrived at Olympia & York's offices that week to negotiate with the Reichmanns. Ultimately the parties struck a deal. The Reichmanns would sell their 50% stake in Battery Park Holdings to Dick Shiff, a director of Trizec and Bramalea. Shiff would assume the US$120 million loan that Hees had originally provided to the Reichmanns to buy their Battery Park Holdings stake.

On Wednesday, September 30, 1992, Olympia & York (USA) presented a restructuring proposal to 75 creditors at a meeting at One Liberty Plaza in New York.

(It took more than two years of intercreditor manoeuvring before the U.S. managers of Olympia & York (USA) were able to present their preliminary restructuring plan for the unit. In mid-December 1994, they proposed rolling together the company's 10 prime office buildings, including three of the four towers that made up Manhattan's World Finance Center (owned 65% by Olympia & York (USA)), into a new company, with the tentative name of O&Y America. Carena and partner Dick Shiff were invited to roll Battery Park Holdings' 35% interest in three of the four towers of the World Financial Center into the new subsidiary, in exchange for one-third ownership. Bank creditors of the U.S. operations, including Canadian Imperial Bank of Commerce and Citibank NA, were invited to swap their debt for one-third ownership. And Leon Black's Apollo Real Estate Investments, a vulture real-estate fund that picked up US$120 billion (face value) of Olympia & York (USA)'s secured debt in the spring of 1994 was invited to swap its debt for one-third ownership. But the preliminary plan met counter-offers, negotiations and other potential owners. For example, the court-appointed administrator of the parent company, Olympia & York Developments, warned the unsecured creditors of the Canadian operations on Friday, January 6, 1995, that they would be left out of the reconstituted U.S. operations unless they participated in the debt-for-equity swap. That meant coming up with several hundred million dollars to buy a significant chunk of Olympia & York (USA)'s secured and unsecured debt. Meanwhile, Battery Park Holdings considered forming an alliance with Canadian Imperial Bank of Commerce and interests controlled by Hong Kong billionaire Li Ka-shing in an attempt to end up with the controlling stake in O&Y America, at the expense of Leon Black. To complicate matters, there was also the problem of falling valuations.)

Almost a month later, in Toronto, on Tuesday, October 27, 1992, Olympia & York (Canada) proposed a complicated settlement with its creditors in its plan of compromise and arrangement.

Olympia & York asked the Gang of Four to become its partner in the four downtown towers — First Canadian Place, Scotia Plaza, the Aetna Centre and the Exchange Tower. But the bondholders, who had first claim on First Canadian Place, wanted to seize their security.

"I made one mistake," Paul Reichmann told Olympia & York lieutenant William Kennedy at a particularly fractious meeting with creditors. There was a long, dramatic pause. Then, with the timing of a stand-up comedian, Reichmann continued, "I got out of bed today."

At secret late-night meetings in Toronto on November 11 and 12, the Gang of Four negotiators warned Olympia & York representatives that the existing plan would be voted down by creditors. They proposed amendments allowing the creditors to walk away from the proceedings. "Everything is up in the air," one creditor representative told me for *The Financial Post* on Friday, November 13. "We don't know how it will shake out." But after the Jewish Sabbath, Olympia & York responded with a letter saying it would revamp the plan if the banks agreed to delay the November 25–30 voting dates until January. It was time to call representatives from the other creditor groups and secure their agreement to the changes.

Early Tuesday night, November 16, Olympia & York started phoning representatives from the bond syndicates to invite them to that evening's meeting with the Gang of Four negotiators at the law offices of Davies Ward & Beck in First Canadian Place. After almost five hours of negotiations, the mortgage-bond holders of

First Canadian Place and several other buildings came on side. Lawyer Rick Orzy, known as "the terrorist" or "Carlos" for consistently sabotaging the Gang of Four's deals, was on a flight from Toronto to New York City, and had to negotiate from his seat, using one of the plane's phones. The bond holders had opposed any delay because they hoped to vote against the plan at the earliest opportunity so that they could seize their security. But Olympia & York promised not to use a U.S. court to stop them. "The company promised there would be no more delays, so we adjourned our motion," Orzy recalled. In Toronto, the Reichmann brothers signed the term sheet shortly after midnight.

The next morning, Olympia & York began circulating the term sheet to its creditors, but not all the creditors signed on. For example, Citibank demanded that the Reichmanns retain the equity of Olympia & York, because a change of legal control would mean giving up hundreds of millions of dollars of tax credits in the U.S., and Citibank held a US$250 million note payable by one of O&Y's U.S. subsidiaries. Because the equity "wasn't worth anything" — Olympia & York owed more than it was worth — the other creditors agreed. But they insisted that the unsecured creditors be on the board of directors and that the Canadian court appoint an administrator, so that creditors could control the operations and cash flow of Olympia & York, without owning the company.

Within days of signing the term sheet, Paul Reichmann phoned his brother Albert's friend Andrew Sarlos and asked him to drop by his office in the Exchange Tower. Reichmann wanted Sarlos to help him raise $250 million of financial backing so that he could start over. Reichmann didn't think he would survive the trauma of overseeing the slow liquidation of an empire he had assembled over 35 years. This time Reichmann planned to develop properties outside of the industrialized nations, in the developing economies of Mexico, Eastern Europe, Russia and China. A potential source of financing was Sarlos's former partner, George Soros. "I [had] approached Paul [Reichmann] when his first cash shortage arose," Soros later told Eric Reguly for *The Financial Post*. "Then it was too early. Reichmann still thought he could salvage Canary Wharf." But by the autumn of 1992, Reichmann had left most of his family fortune, as well as his pride, buried in the docklands. "He wants to stage a comeback," Soros told Reguly. "I'm very happy to be able to provide the financial means for him to do it."

In January 1993, Paul Reichmann met George Soros in Soros's Manhattan offices and they signed an agreement to form a new real-estate company called Reichmann International L.P. of New York and Toronto, which would be jointly owned by the Reichmanns and Soros. Their first project would be commercial office construction in Mexico City. At the same time, Soros appointed Reichmann International L.P. as the adviser of his new fund, the Quantum real-estate fund, already capitalized at US$600 million. Soros and Reichmann committed to buy a US$75 million stake in the fund, which would invest in ailing and bankrupt properties in Canada and the U.S. (It was a vulture fund similar to Sam Zell's new fund.)

Meanwhile, Olympia & York's creditors were voting on the new plan of arrangement, which would allow them to seize their security. Olympia & York emerged from court protection on Friday, February 8, 1993. A few days later, Soros and Reichmann announced their new partnership.

On Thursday, September 3, 1992, Royal Trustco announced that Michael Cornelissen was stepping down as CEO.

Almost two months earlier, on July 27, 1992, Royal Trustco had reported a second-quarter loss. It had also cut its dividend in half and made a decision to sell its U.S. thrift, Pacific First. Jack Cockwell was quietly appointed to Royal Trustco's board and its nine-man executive committee.

The executive committee started looking for a replacement for Cornelissen. Chairman Hartland MacDougall later told shareholders at the 1993 special meeting that Cornelissen and the board had "recognized that confidence in the institution could not be restored under [Cornelissen's] leadership. It was agreed he would step down."

MacDougall also told shareholders that the failures of Olympia
& York, the Romans' Standard Trust, the Belzbergs' First City
Trust and Reuben Cohen and Leonard Ellen's Central Guaranty
Trust "created an atmosphere of great uncertainty in the minds"
of Royal Trust clients.

Royal Trustco's executive committee soon abandoned its pursuit of high-profile possibilities such as former Canadian Imperial
Bank of Commerce executive Paul Cantor.

"Rightly or wrongly, they decided Royal Trustco already had talented executives who understood the financial services business,"
a source close to the board told me. "The committee decided it
would be best to find someone, for a shorter period of time, who
would work with these executives and build succession."

Courtney Pratt suggested James Miller, the former national
managing partner of Touche Ross, a man renowned for his leadership skills. "The legends around Jim are very real," said Tom Cryer,
one of Miller's recruits to Touche Ross in the mid-1960s, who became the national managing partner of the merged Deloitte &
Touche. "He's a good coach and a good leader."

James Miller, 61, a strong family man who had been married for
almost 40 years to the same woman, Mary, would also be an anti-
dote to Michael Cornelissen, who had had to apologize to the board
of the Royal Canadian Yacht Club that summer for streaking naked
through the club.

After a background check, Royal Trustco approached James
Miller in late August. Royal chairman Hartland MacDougall, who
met with Miller in Vancouver in early September, described him as
a cross between a teddy bear and a grizzly. It was a perceptive
comment. Miller had been called "the Big Bear" at Touche Ross,
for both his size and his provocative management style.

On Friday, October 9, 1992, Royal Trustco announced that
James Miller would be the new CEO, replacing Michael Cornelissen,
who was planning to move to Vancouver as Royal Trustco's vice-
chairman. "We're a bit dazzled by [Miller's] selection," Trevor

Eyton said. "He's a different sort of choice." Eyton characterized Miller as "highly competitive...wonderful at motivating teams of people...with enormous personal energy."

By then, James Miller was on vacation with his wife in Hawaii, where he played 22 games of golf in 21 days and plowed through a waist-high stack of material on Royal Trustco. His son Laird, a manager with Deloitte & Touche in Vancouver, faxed him copies of the daily newspaper reports detailing Royal Trustco's latest crisis: negative reaction to a two-part deal to dispose of Pacific First, announced on October 27, and the subsequent writedowns of the U.S. and British loan portfolios, which resulted in a $243 million third-quarter loss and a second common-share dividend cut, reported on November 2.

By the time the Millers returned to Vancouver, Royal Trustco's shares had plummeted from about $5 1/2 to $3 on the Toronto Stock Exchange — a 43% drop.

Washington Mutual Savings Bank, the buyer of Pacific First, had insisted that Royal Trustco take back $853 million of loans, of which $317 million were classified as nonperforming. At a Hallowe'en party for the Royal Trustco employees, Michael Cornelissen appeared with a pair of foam breasts strapped to his chest, in reference to a recent *Canadian Business* cover story titled "Royal Bust." The liquor-loosened Cornelissen also reportedly referred to Pacific First as "a piece of shit." Chairman Hartland MacDougall later disputed the press account, arguing that he would have heard about the remark. Within weeks of that party, Cornelissen tried to pull a condom over his head while he was out on the town in Vancouver, calling himself "the dickhead." Cornelissen was not showing grace under pressure.

On November 2, Royal Trustco reported the $243 million third-quarter loss. It had set up a further $150 million as a general loan-loss provision for Canada and Britain. It also announced its intention to raise capital with a $200 million share issue.

Two days later, analysts met with Royal Trustco executives to discuss the sale of Pacific First and the quarterly loss. They emerged from the meeting convinced that there were inadequate loss provisions against the southern California rump of the U.S. thrift. They estimated that losses on these loans could approach $300 million.

On November 6, a wave of Edper Group selling slammed the Toronto stock market and the Canadian dollar. A group spokesman said he was baffled by rumours in the U.S. and Canada that Canadian Imperial Bank of Commerce, the group's lead banker, was withdrawing its financial support for the group, which could force one or more group companies to file for court protection from creditors. The rumours had no basis of fact. Bay Street characterized the development as a crisis of confidence in the group, sparked in part by the announcement of Royal Trustco's huge third-quarter loss.

Four days later, James Miller arrived at Royal Trustco's head office in Toronto, a day ahead of his scheduled November 11 appearance at Royal Trustco's budget and planning sessions for 1993. Miller wanted to ask questions about the deal which had precipitated the latest drop in Royal Trustco's stock.

"I would have been a fool not to ask questions after the market had flown such a big flag," he told me. Critics of Royal Trustco's deal to Pacific First said it did not rescue the company from the troubled U.S. market because it had to take back Pacific First's California loans, one-third of which were classified as nonperforming.

On November 10, Miller asked Merrill Lynch Inc., advisers on the deal, to walk him through the transaction. Royal Trustco had said it wanted to sell California loans as quickly as possible, and Miller wanted details about the time frame and the plans for disposal.

Miller said the talk dispelled some of his nervousness about the loans, but he did not expect to change analysts' perceptions until there were concrete recoveries.

"I'm an outsider," he explained. "I come with a certain healthy skepticism. You have to prove [things to me]. When I have proof, I will tell people the straight goods."

At the planning sessions, Miller asked Laurent Joly why Royal Trustco could not get it right with its British loss provisions on nonperforming loans. Joly was able to show on a chart that almost

all the sour loans had been made over a two-year period from 1988
to early 1990. Joly, who had led a new management team to London
in mid-1990 to clean up the mess, said early estimates of anticipated losses were based on forecasts for the British economy by
the Organization for Economic Co-operation & Development.

As the OECD downgraded its forecasts, Joly had set aside additional reserves for possible failed loans. What was a one-time
writeoff of about $200 million in 1990 ballooned to almost $600
million in provisions by third-quarter 1992.

On Wednesday, November 12, I interviewed James Miller in a
tiny conference room he planned to convert into his office. With
characteristic frankness, he refuted rumours that Royal Trustco
was about to sell Royal Trust. It was a "good franchise," and the
company had no reason to sell, he said.

On December 1, James Miller replaced Michael Cornelissen
at the helm of Royal Trustco, a month ahead of schedule, at an
annual salary of $200,000, plus stock options. Cornelissen, who
would not be staying on as vice-chairman, had had "five good
years" with Royal Trustco, Miller said. But he left with "no reputation, no money and no family." Royal Trustco chairman Hartland
MacDougall told shareholders at the 1993 special meeting that the
board had asked Cornelissen to step down early. "It had become
apparent that the continued presence of Mr. Cornelissen until the
anticipated January 1, 1993 date was damaging the company. He
had become synonymous with the company's problems. He was a
lightning rod," MacDougall told shareholders. "I can only tell you,
as time has proven, we were a little late."

An internal survey of Royal Trustco employees had revealed that
there was a company-wide distrust of head office, Miller later recalled.
"The executive offices were hated by the other managers," he said.

On December 3, James Miller and the Royal Trustco board received a personal visit from Michael Mackenzie, Superintendent
of Financial Institutions, who warned them to watch out for Toronto
real estate, because prices were in a freefall. Miller immediately

hired credit consultants to review the Canadian loan portfolio. And on December 10, Royal Trustco retained S.G. Warburg to review strategic alternatives for Royal Trustco.

During this period, Miller was shocked to find Royal Trustco executives sobbing in his office about their financial ruin under the management share-purchase plans. One man had not been able to tell his wife that they were technically bankrupt.

Trevor Eyton said later that the Royal Trustco management share-purchase plan was the "most extreme example within the group in terms of erosion of value." But there were others. Late in 1992, several group companies adopted life-insurance schemes for their managers to help them avoid personal bankruptcy.

Over the holidays, Jack Cockwell took time out, with his wife Wendy Cecil-Cockwell, to attend Conrad Black's annual Christmas party at his Georgian-style manor on Park Lane Circle. This was Barbara Amiel's debut as the party's hostess. Later, the still-honeymooning Black and Amiel travelled to Palm Beach, where Amiel attended her first Eyton-Bitove boat party.

Meanwhile, Royal Trustco's James Miller had worked inhuman hours throughout the month of December, spending less than two days at home in Vancouver with his family over Christmas. "Within 25 to 30 days [of taking the helm at Royal Trustco], it was crisis management," Miller later recalled. In late December, the Department of Finance began to scrutinize the Edper Group, specifically Royal Trust. Following the spectacular collapse of Olympia and York the previous year, Ottawa was concerned about maintaining the international value of the dollar, as well as Canada's image with foreign investors.

"I regret not being able to do the job I was hired to do. That would have been fun," James Miller said later. "But I was stubborn enough not to leave...and if I had left, it would have sent such a signal...it would have been over for Royal Trust." He said his lifeline during the months of crisis was Jack Cockwell. Every Sunday evening Miller would go to see Cockwell for "an hour or so" at his 44th-floor office in BCE Place. It was a time when Cockwell "was in a mood to talk and respond," said Miller, adding that the Edper strategist was also "solidly into doing the right thing for the country and the financial system."

Royal Trustco was one of the many things on Jack Cockwell's mind. In early 1993, Dominion Bond Rating Service did a survey of institutional investors, asking them why the capital markets were shut to the Edper Group. Institutional investors gave two reasons. First, the structure was so complex that outside investors didn't trust it. Second, outside investors had lost confidence in the integrity of the group because of the constant stream of negative news. For example, since early 1989 the group had battled publicly with Michael Blair over Enfield, fought with Christopher Ondaatje over Pagurian, scrapped with David Hennigar over Canadian Express, been forced to pull out of Unicorp without the coveted gas utility and failed to disclose a secret investment in the World Financial Center. And there were serious financial problems at several of the group's principal operating companies, including Bramalea, Royal Trustco and Trizec. The Edper Group was "frozen," DBRS said.

Early in January 1993, James Miller identified his priorities at Royal Trustco. The first priority was the depositors, who had entrusted upwards of $140 billion into Royal Trust's care. (Over the course of 1992, deposits had already shrunk an astounding 13%, as investors lost confidence.) Second was the Canadian financial system as a whole. Third were the debt holders. Fourth were the employees, without whom Royal Trustco would have nothing to sell. Somewhere further down were the common shareholders, including parent Trilon Financial Corp.

That same month, Royal Trustco's financial adviser, S.G. Warburg, set up initial meetings with five Canadian chartered banks, two trust companies, two insurance companies, four foreign banks and another large domestic financial institution. They later provided a confidential memorandum, which contained information about Royal Trustco's operations, as well as an outline of the form of investment that was sought, to a smaller group of parties who had indicated an interest in investing in Royal Trustco.

On Tuesday, January 19, 1993, James Miller told Royal Trustco's board of directors that it was too late to try to restore confidence in the financial institution. The review of the loan portfolios had identified more deterioration that would result in year-end loan-loss provisions in addition to those that had already been taken. (Ultimately, Royal Trustco took further loss provisions of $140 million on the Canadian and British loans, resulting in a cumulative loss of $852 million for 1992.) Miller said Royal Trustco had to find a stable, outside partner, preferably one of the big banks, before there was a run on the trust's deposits, causing untold damage to Canada's financial system.

"I had to deliver some tough messages," Miller later recalled. He also believed that under the security rules he was required to disclose Royal Trustco's new strategy.

On January 20, James Miller announced that Royal Trustco was trying to link up with a major financial institution, and Royal Bank of Canada chairman Allan Taylor confirmed that the bank was "one of apparently a number of financial institutions" approached by Royal Trustco's financial adviser S.G. Warburg. The Bank of Nova Scotia was also interested in Royal Trustco, but did not make a public statement. Dominion Bond Rating Service said the addition of another major shareholder had "the potential to be a positive development" but "timing, terms and completion of such a deal [were] still uncertain." So the Toronto rating agency put all debt ratings of Royal Trustco and its Canadian units on alert with negative implications, also citing concern about the uncertain outlook for Royal Trustco's proposed $200 million equity issue. Trilon Financial said it still planned to buy half the issue.

Later that evening, back at his Toronto hotel suite, James Miller conceded in a telephone interview that Trilon Financial was not the "best sponsor for Royal Trust in the future. The Edper Group can weather bad news but a financial institution like Royal Trust requires a high degree of confidence. I'm doing what I think is right for the trust company." Miller's published remarks annoyed the new Trilon Financial CEO, George Myhal. "I don't bow and scrape. And

I was not very well liked at the Edper Group," recalled Miller, who thought that some of the young Edper managers, like Myhal, had "too much influence" over Jack Cockwell. "Some of his associates said stupid things," Miller recalled. Why did Cockwell listen to them?

In the final weeks of January 1993, short sellers swarmed the Edper Group, anticipating its collapse. It "was fairly widespread" because "the market smelled blood after the fall of Olympia & York," said short seller Pierre Panet-Raymond. Shares of the group's 32 publicly traded companies lost 10% of their collective value on the Toronto Stock Exchange during the month of January, and short selling on 15 group stocks almost doubled to 11.4 million shares in the final two weeks of the month. The short position of Royal Trustco A shares tripled to 2.77 million on January 31 from 873,600 on January 15; and Hees almost tripled to 1 million from 338,900 in the same period.

"Edper stocks lose $320 million" read the headline on the front page of the *Globe*'s Report on Business section on Monday, February 1, 1993. "Pressure is on at Hees-Edper" read *The Financial Post*'s page one headline on February 2.

Meanwhile, four Burns Fry corporate finance specialists — David Bird, Brent Fullard, Jonathon Mishkin and Carl Renzoni — brainstormed. There had to be some way to alleviate the pressure on the Edper Group. What about a major asset sale? Burns Fry was familiar with MacMillan Bloedel, having searched for a buyer for Noranda Forest's 49% stake four years earlier. As Noranda CEO David Kerr later recalled, "The MacMillan Bloedel sale was one we [had] been talking about for…years, but basically left on the back burner because there really wasn't a market for [a] block the size that we owned in MacMillan Bloedel." Since it was difficult to find a single buyer for the control block, the Burns Fry team decided to propose instead that Noranda Forest sell its entire MacMillan Bloedel stake to Burns Fry in a bought deal, priced at the stock's 4:00 p.m. close on the Toronto Stock Exchange the day before the announcement of the deal. An underwriting syndicate would then resell the 55.5 million MacMillan Bloedel shares as instalment receipts to institutional and retail clients. Because of the huge size of the deal

— it could be as high as $1 billion depending on the stock's close —
Burns Fry decided to break up the deal into three instalments. On
February 3, Burns Fry had preliminary talks with Noranda Forest.

The next day, the Burns Fry team tabled their intial offer.
Senior Edper Group managers were called in to make a decision, and
within an hour and a half the Burns Fry team had a green light.
"The fact that Burns Fry came in was strictly speculation on their
part, but it was pretty good speculation," Noranda CEO David Kerr
later recalled. Even after "Burns Fry walked into our offices and
suggested [the MacMillan Bloedel control block] could be sold, we
didn't think there was a market. In fact, after they'd left, we kept asking ourselves, is this for real? We can't believe they can sell a whole
block." Over the next three days, Burns Fry, Noranda Forest and
their respective law firms hammered out the details, fearful that
news of the deal would leak out before it was announced.

On Monday morning, February 8, 1993, the board of Noranda
Forest met and approved the MacMillan Bloedel transaction. By
4:00 p.m. the $971 million deal was in place and Burns Fry had
called a syndicate meeting that night so that other investment dealers could participate. The MacMillan Bloedel shares would be resold
as instalment receipts for $17.50 each. Ultimately, what was then
the biggest bought deal in Canadian history was co-led by Burns
Fry and RBC Dominion Securities. Of the major dealers, only Wood
Gundy and Nesbitt Thomson declined to participate in the 10-
member syndicate. The following morning, February 9, at about
7:30, the investment dealers began calling clients about the shares.

"Should we [have been] able to get a control premium?" David
Kerr later responded. "Not in the way we sold it. You'd have to find
a single buyer if you wanted to get a control premium. And I think
that the odds on us in the next few years finding a single buyer
who would want to buy a control position in MacMillan Bloedel
were rather slim. Most of the forest companies which would be the
potential buyers [had] been under a significant amount of financial pressure over the last few years....[Even] MacMillan Bloedel
was not carrying itself. The balance sheet improvement that went

along with [the sale of the MacMillan Bloedel stake] was important to us as well." Although MacMillan Bloedel was sold roughly at book value, it was a good value for Noranda because it reduced corporate debt, Kerr said. "The MacMillan Bloedel part of our balance sheet has been the part where the debt was growing. Without MacMillan Bloedel our debt was actually shrinking, but that wasn't getting shown to the shareholders because we consolidate MacMillan Bloedel. Without MacMillan Bloedel our debt no longer would have been growing. It would have been coming down."

On the same day that Edper sold the MacMillan Bloedel control block, Michael McKenzie, federal Superintendent of Financial Institutions, issued a request that all banks, trust companies and insurance companies under his jurisdiction submit detailed reports of their loan exposure to the Edper Group, as well as any investment in the companies' numerous public equity and debt issues. The reports were due four days later, on Friday, February 12.

Wood Gundy, which had moved its head offices to BCE Place from the Royal Trust Tower, proposed to Brascan that it undertake the same exercise with its 37% controlling stake in John Labatt.

"The Labatt sale came to us Thursday afternoon and it was fully priced [at $28.25 a share, that day's 4:00 p.m. close on the Toronto Stock Exchange]," Brascan chairman Trevor Eyton later recalled. "We thought it fully valued Labatt for our purposes." Brascan had a couple of hours to respond to Wood Gundy's offer. Once Wood Gundy got the green light, the same process began and moved even faster because "people had been put through a dress rehearsal a few days prior."

"Theoretically, you [could] get a control premium [on the Labatt sale]," Trevor Eyton said later. "You'd have to find someone that wants to buy the whole company…[and] if you wanted to exceed the [Ontario Securities Commission's] 15% guideline, you've got to buy it all at that same price, and that's a lot of money and there [are] potentially three or four [buyers] in the world that [are] prepared to make that size investment.…[Then there's] the uncertainty [of] a process where you negotiate with someone and

undoubtedly, you'd need regulatory approvals, and be subject to
this and that condition. And that uncertainty...made the cash offer
a better deal for us...[because] we thought we got full value and
we got it in the form of cash or near cash right away." The sale of
a second prized asset brought to almost $2 billion the money the
Edper Group raised that week.

Peter Bronfman said the public rumours and negative speculation had wounded him personally. "People are looking for blood,
I guess," Bronfman told Brenda Dalglish for *Maclean's*. "It's like
[talk show host] Joan Rivers. When things started to go wrong,
they all joined in to beat up on her."

That Friday night, most of the investment dealers and lawyers
involved in the two Edper bought deals danced it up at Toronto's
annual Brazilian Ball in the Metro Toronto Convention Centre. It
was customary for the top executives of Brascan to make an appearance at the ball, renowned for its scantily clad Brazilian
dancers. Trevor Eyton usually attended, but the 1993 ball was not
Brascan's night. The biggest partiers were the investment dealers
who had made $78.6 million that week from their 4% commission
on the back-to-back deals.

On February 16, *The Financial Post* published a caricature
of a bespectacled Peter Bronfman, stripped down to an undershirt
and boxer shorts, walking away from four smirking, fully dressed
investment dealers named Wood Gundy Inc., Gordon Capital
Corp., Burns Fry Ltd. and RBC Dominion Securities, who yelled
after him, "If you've got anything else, don't be shy....[We're] glad
we could help." The Edper Group bought one of the five limited-
edition prints for its suite of offices in BCE Place, where the caricature was displayed along with other earlier drawings, Bronfman's
Group of Seven artworks and Inuit carvings, Blue Jays World Series
memorabilia and miniature Stanley Cups

Later, Hees president-in-waiting Robert Harding tried to correct
some of the myths about "the week that was" in an op-ed column
he planned to publish in *The Financial Post*: "Our interests in
MacMillan Bloedel and John Labatt were sold virtually back-to-back

on February 9 and February 12. At the same time, the Superintendent of Financial Institutions requested information from Canada's chartered banks about exposures to the Edper Group. His action received wide media publicity. And it fueled speculation that these matters were connected. They were not. The offers to purchase these assets flowed from opportunities created by a surge in demand and a new depth found within the Canadian equity markets. Not by external pressures on the group to sell them. Perspective on these events has now begun to emerge. For example...it became clear that none of the chartered banks had exceeded federal guidelines in their lending to Edper companies. 'Edper loans are fine with MacKenzie,' one Toronto newspaper headlined. Earlier, the Investment Dealers' Association said its request for information about broker exposure to the Edper Group — which also triggered a lot of conjecture in the media — produced nothing out of the ordinary."

Yet, at the height of the crisis, Jack Cockwell had secretly telephoned Peter Munk suggesting Horsham come in as an equity investor in Pagurian at the top of the Edper empire. Separately, Cockwell had also approached Henry Slack, CEO of Minorco Ltd., the international investment arm of the giant South African conglomerate Anglo American. Cockwell wanted either Horsham or Minorco or both together to invest in Pagurian, but not to the point where Cockwell & Co. lost operating control. Pagurian was a good investment, Cockwell told the two men, because fundamental values underlying the Edper holdings were not being recognized by the market. For an investment of $500 million or less, Horsham or Minorco would get a 25% interest in an empire with a capital base of $20 billion.

Meanwhile, James Miller was trying to save a trust company. In late January 1993, Royal Trustco had given interested parties an opportunity to carry out due diligence, including on-site loan file and legal document reviews, management presentations and meetings and access to informations on operations. Each party had signed a confidentiality agreement. But it quickly became apparent that the banks weren't interested in making an equity infusion into Royal

Trustco, so that option was dropped. By early February, Royal Trustco had received proposals from Royal Bank of Canada, Bank of Nova Scotia, Canadian Imperial Bank of Commerce, Canada Trust and one foreign bank, believed to have been the Hongkong Bank. Miller said the proposals from the Royal Bank of Canada and Scotiabank were the most attractive, since they had expressed the broadest interest in Royal Trustco; the others wanted to cherry-pick Royal Trustco's best assets. Royal Trustco would go as a unit, he said.

Miller formed a three-man negotiating team comprising himself, Laurent Joly and Royal Trustco chief financial officer Tony Flynn. Conspicuously absent from the team was Bill Inwood, the president of the Canadian trust operations.

By that point, Miller's office furniture and a stereo had been shipped out from Vancouver for his tiny office. There was no artwork, apart from his collection of cheap porcelain figures, including a tortoise and a hare which Miller said represented the bureaucratic Royal bank and the entrepreneurial Royal Trustco. "The bank didn't think it was funny," he later recalled. A group of Japanese debenture holders who had met with Miller's team left a porcelain figure symbolizing good luck. But they also told Tony Flynn that in their country the chief financial officer of Royal Trustco would have committed *sekkapu*, ritual suicide.

At the same time, Royal Trustco was getting trashed in the news, as a spate of negative stories questioned whether it would ever find a new sponsor. "The press really destroyed confidence in this company," Miller said later. "The press were irresponsible. They hit and questioned our disclosure, but I was bound by confidentiality agreements. We always had liquidity, but certain things can happen and we were walking a very fine line."

On February 19, Royal Trustco and the Royal Bank entered into an exclusivity agreement: Royal Trustco agreed to negotiate exclusively with the bank, but that agreement would terminate if the bank had not signed a letter of intent by March 5. The deadline was later extended to March 17. "We signed the preliminary deal at 7:15 a.m. [on March 18]," Miller later recalled. He had been awake for 48 hours.

Later that morning, Royal Trustco and Royal Bank announced that they had reached a two-part preliminary agreement. Royal Bank would buy Royal Trustco's Canadian and international operations for $1.65 billion, but, in a separate agreement reminiscent of the Pacific First deal, Royal Trustco would have to take back $3.6 billion of loans. And it would have to raise almost $900 million to close the deal. There was also a potential deal-breaker. A condition of the acquisition agreement was that Royal Trustco find a solution for the management share-purchase plans. The bank didn't want its future employees encumbered with stock-loans that they couldn't pay for. Ultimately arrangements were made with a life insurer for the Royal Trustco managers to purchase whole-life insurance coverage in an amount equal to the principal amount of their management share-purchase plan loans. The policies would be held as additional security for MSPP loans, and any excess proceeds payable on the manager's death would be paid to his or her estate. Royal Trustco, later renamed Gentra Inc., had to fund the insurance scheme, paying $20 million to get 151 managers off the hook.

Miller said that the Bank of Nova Scotia was around until the agreement in principle. He said he deliberately left material from that bank on his desk whenever the negotiating team from Royal Bank was coming over. Scotiabank "were excellent to deal with," Miller later recalled. "They couldn't commit the resources and manpower, but they drove the hell out of the Royal Bank."

"I think Royal Bank did a good deal," Trevor Eyton later said. "On completion of the transaction, [the Royal Bank] will be pre-eminent in almost every category of financial services except one. And they've done it really at a very modest cost. And it's not something they could have done themselves in ten years."

Meanwhile, the Edper Group was embroiled in another press mess. Hees president-in-waiting Robert Harding had dropped in to see Toronto Sun CEO Paul Godfrey. The Edper Group wanted to find a way to tell its "side of the story" in the press. The group managers didn't think their story had been told "with the right kind of balance." They proposed an op-ed columan as a "kind of shorthand for putting some points together," followed by some kind of editorial board meeting. Godfrey called Doug Knight, publisher of *The Financial Post*, inviting him up to Godfrey's office to meet Harding. The three men discussed the idea, eventually settling on a two-pronged plan: *The Financial Post* would print an op-ed column written by Harding, and there would be an on-the-record round-table discussion between the *Financial Post* editors and Edper Group senior executives. When news of the arrangement spread through the newsroom, the *Post* staff expressed concern.

On the morning of March 18, executive editor David Bailey called a rare staff meeting to discuss the issue. Forty angry writers and editors crammed into a small boardroom to challenge the paper's decision to run the op-ed column by the Edper Group. They requested a meeting with Paul Godfrey. When Godfrey began to address the staff at 2:30 p.m., he was assailed by reporters concerned about the credibility of the *Post*. "The Hees-Edper people are bullies," said one. "It would look like the *Post* was caving in to them." Other staff members disagreed. What was the problem with an op-ed column? There were precedents for such things. As long as the column wasn't on the news pages, shouldn't the Edper Group be allowed their say? Another debate about journalistic ethics ensued. Then other concerns were raised, specifically about the organizational politics of Godfrey making such a decision for *The Financial Post*. There were accusations of cronyism. Was this a backroom deal between two SkyDome buddies — Godfrey and Trevor Eyton? The debate was full, frank and heated.

Meanwhile, in the *Globe and Mail* newsroom, Kimberley Noble had received a call from a *Post* staff member who had been present at the morning fracas. Noble logged on to the *Globe*'s in-house computer system to send a memo to Report on Business editor Margaret Wente. In the memo, entitled "Postcave," Noble reported the events at the rival newspaper, arguing that it was "along the lines of what the Hees Edper people have been trying for years with the [Canadian] media."

Within hours, someone from *The Globe and Mail* had printed out a copy of the memo and faxed it to the *Post* newsroom. Managing editor Fred Lebolt was enraged when he saw it. This was supposed to be an internal matter. Who had leaked the story to a competitor? He started pulling staff phone records to determine who had called Noble that morning. Lebolt summoned four suspects to his office on March 19, to interrogate them individually. Their reasons for the phone calls were varied. One had called a friend at *The Globe and Mail* to set up a squash game, another to set up a lunch. By that point the newsroom was in open revolt over management's "witch hunt." At noon, Lebolt began to circulate among the staff to explain his actions and to apologize for overreacting. He said he had "viewed the phone call [to Noble] as a betrayal." But it was too late for damage control.

"Journalists question credibility of paper," read the front-page headline in *The Globe and Mail* on Saturday, March 20, 1993. Kirk Makin's two-page cover story detailed recent events at *The Financial Post* and dredged up scandals, such as *Post* editor Diane Francis's front-page defence of Olympia & York the year before, as evidence of the *Post*'s lack of credibility. In the illustration accompanying the article, *The Globe and Mail* had superimposed the faces of senior Edper Group managers Trevor Eyton and Jack Cockwell, *Toronto Sun* CEO Paul Godfrey and *Financial Post* editor Diane Francis on the windows of four *Financial Post* newspaper boxes. In contrast to their cosy relationship with the "pro-business" *Post*, Kirk Makin reported, Edper executives were frequently incensed about Report on Business coverage. Indeed, Eyton had once told senior *Globe* figures at a party to fix the *Globe* or sell it to him so he could fix it for them. Makin had interviewed his editor, William Thorsell, and Kimberley Noble for the cover story. Noble told Makin how the Edper Group tried to wear down its opponents. "Anybody who has said anything negative about them would be shut out fast." After a story, Noble said she could expect a multipage letter featuring her article annotated with complaints like "This is libellous" or "This shows a vendetta."

Hees's media adviser, Tom Reid, who was finishing his contract with Hees that summer, told Makin that it didn't surprise him in the least to hear that journalists and investment analysts considered the group abnormally hostile. "Their style is they are always ready to do battle," Reid said. "They are vey impetuous in the way they react to information." Money manager Ira Gluskin told Makin that he thought the press had been far too easy on the Edper Group. "The reality is much worse than has been reported. I can read their annual reports. All of their annual reports and speeches have turned out to not even be garbage. The press won't find even one mediocre, pedestrian toadie analyst on Bay Street to say nice things about them."

Ira Gluskin's comment was hyperbolic. Although the sentiment had turned against the Edper Group, the group companies had never been challenged successfully on their accounting practices, and many still had supporters. But Gluskin's published quote shocked Bay Street. It was the first time one of their own had gone on the record with negative comments about the Edper Group. There had been the odd rogue analyst quoted by name in the press, but never someone whom the Street considered a player. Gluskin later told me in an interview that Trevor Eyton had called him to ask if Gluskin had meant what he said in *The Globe and Mail*. Had Gluskin been misquoted? The answer was no. That autumn Gluskin gave a speech publicly mocking the Edper Group at the annual dinner of the Toronto Society of Financial Analysts. Edper bashing was in season. Ironically, within months of the speech, Gluskin Sheff had decided it would move its offices from the Cadillac Fairview building into BCE Place — the same tower as the Edper Group — in the summer of 1995. Gluskin said he wasn't looking forward to it: "I don't want to ride up and down the same elevators as those guys."

Meanwhile, on Tuesday, March 23, Robert Harding sent over several copies of a 50-page Edper Group Information Book, specially-prepared for *The Financial Post*, which contained information extracted from confidential documents, such as the Supplementary Financial Information Books prepared for lenders and credit rating agencies by the group's principal operating companies. It also contained information prepared to update the group's boards of directors. "It's the first time we have prepared something like this for the media specifically. It is an on-the-record document, and we hope it helps in your understanding of our group," he said.

Harding also sent over his op-ed column, which began, "It is understandable that comparisons have been drawn between the demise of Olympia & York and the status of the Edper Group....The comparison is invalid. The two groups are fundamentally different. As different as public companies are to private. As different as long-term financing is to short-term debt. As different as equity is to debt. Equity not debt — more than any other corporate axiom — characterizes the way in which the Edper Group was built through the 1980s and into the 1990s. And it is the spinal [cord] for a three-to-five year program devised by the group in 1990 to cope with the financial shocks erupting in the capital markets." But the *Post*'s executive editor David Bailey decided not to run the column. "Basically, we thought it didn't really add much to the mix, and it was a recapping. Not a bad recap, but it didn't really take you much further," Bailey told Harding. "Well I understood editing took out a few words and changed things, I didn't know it took them all out though," Harding later quipped. "I now know what a writer feels like when they're rejected."

Despite the rejection, the Edper Group decided to go ahead with the round-table discussion the following day, March 24. It was held in the *Toronto Sun* boardroom on the 6th floor of the Toronto Sun Building. On one side of the table were Senator Trevor Eyton, Gordon Arnell, Robert Harding, George Myhal and David Kerr. On the other were David Bailey, Fred Lebolt, Philip Mathias, Bob Catherwood and me. After Toronto Sun CEO Paul Godfrey had briefly recounted the events that had led up to the meeting, he welcomed all the participants. "Senator, you and I have to see each other quite often at Dome meetings and other meetings," Godfrey said.

"Much more than I'd like," Eyton quipped.

"I'll remember that," Godfrey vowed.

Then it was Eyton's turn. "Let me start by saying we're all pleased to be here at what I know to be a secret meeting," Eyton joked. He referred to the previous week's "difficulty and embarrassment" at *The Financial Post*, which Eyton said he had read about in the *Globe*. "I thought *The Globe and Mail* on their coverage was just plain silly," he continued. Eyton then paused to point out the obvious — Jack Cockwell was not there. "Jack Cockwell, the mysterious Jack Cockell," Eyton said. "He's not all that mysterious....Many of you know him and know him to be approachable and amusing and good company, but his absence...represents a...division of labour, a division of skills, that we agreed to probably 20 years ago, maybe more." With respect to the round-table discussion, Eyton said, "This process...is a first for us...It's part of an attempt on our part to be more candid and as frank as we can about events and developments within the group."

It was now time for me to ask the first question: "Given the meltdown in [group] shares, I was wondering if those of you who are personally bankrupt could please raise your hands?" Trevor Eyton was caught off guard. Gordon Arnell glared. No one raised a hand.

The aim of the question was to shake the group's composure, so that they would not be able to control the session with scripted answers. What I wanted was confirmation of the private measures, such as the insurance schemes, that had been taken within the group to deal with the fallout from the management share-purchase plans. I had heard that Eyton, in particular, had been in serious financial trouble. But the information was not forthcoming. I then asked why, given the financial state of the Edper Group, there had been no management changes at the senior level.

"The shortfall, I don't think has been at the senior level. I believe our financing has been well and intelligently done," Eyton said. "Our disappointment has been a significant recession in Canada...that impacted on, in a really unexpected way, many of our operations at the same time." He added, "Let me say that in the mid-1960s when the exercise began, Peter and Edward [Bronfman] and their family were probably worth something like $15 to $20 million. There's no question that we suffered significant erosion in recent years, but in terms of the overall exercise from the time we began, there's been significant reward and significant gains."

Later in the discussion, Gordon Arnell interjected, "The fact is that we have had a very, very tough recession. The toughest recession that...I can ever remember. It has impacted very negatively on Canadian industry as a whole, in all of its segments. We are not an island. We operate in the Canadian economy and are subject to the same economic forces that operate on all of the other companies that are listed on the Toronto Stock Exchange, as well as our own. And I think when you stack up our organization and our group of companies against that perspective, I think we've done quite well in very difficult times."

Meanwhile the preferred-share base in the group was shrinking, George Myhal said. "A lot of preferreds issued in the '80s have sunset features, or they have redemption or retraction features." As a result, the total "number of preferreds which we, as a group hold...[will] decline significantly."

Although Edper Group companies continued to issue perpetual preferred shares, Myhal continued, they didn't hold them. "Of the Edper group preferreds that we do own, very few are perpetual. People quite rightly go to the paper, and they see a lot of the preferred shares that we've issued trading at pennies on the dollar. And then, when they pick up a Labatt annual report and it's disclosed that there are Edper preferreds there, they wonder how on earth can those not be worth pennies on the dollar? I think the key to that is that we, as a group, have...not been heavy purchasers of perpetual preferred shares....[M]ost of the preferred shares that we do own within the group...are, in fact, retractable preferred shares which largely...have retained their value [because] the holder has the right to force the company to redeem the shares."

Post managing editor Fred Lebolt went through the 103-page transcript of the round-table discussion, condensing it into a question-and-answer format, which was published on Saturday, March 27,

1993, with the headline "Hees-Edper on the Record: 'There is no wholesale program with list of assets for sale.'" But Edper's effort to be more candid about events and developments within the group did not assuage critic Ira Gluskin, who told me, "They would have given you the same answers if you'd run into them on the streetcar."

Meanwhile, James Miller was working frantically to close the Royal Bank deal. Royal Trustco directors had formed an independent committee headed by Fraser Fell, which subsequently met 10 times. On April 13, 1992, the directors approved what was called the Trilon Undertaking: Trilon Financial would provide Royal Trustco with $100 million of financial assistance to help close its deal in exchange for the termination of a controversial $1 billion investor standby facility dated December 31, 1989.

"The investor standby facility was...signed by Trilon and Great Lakes in order to provide Royal Trust with assured access to the capital markets," Trilon Financial CEO George Myhal later recalled. "Under the terms of that agreement, what it calls for is, if Royal Trust ever do go into the public equity markets to raise funds, that we would be there to support them. In October when Royal Trust announced that they were going to raise $200 million of equity, Trilon fulfilled its obligation under that standby agreement. That's all the agreement calls for. The agreement says we will participate in any equity issues. It doesn't say we will be the only buyer. And I think that's a very key understanding here....The essential ingredient is, there has to be public participation as well."

Royal Trustco deputy chairman Trevor Eyton pointed out that Royal Trustco's business-conduct-review committees were made up of independent directors and "one of the things they...approved was this standby facility."

On the eve of Royal Trustco's special annual meeting on Friday, June 18, 1993, the board of directors met to consider the Royal Bank-Royal Trustco Acquisition Agreement and Excluded assets Agreement.

James Miller provided an update for the Royal Trustco board, and Tony Flynn and Laurent Joly described the major steps taken since the signing of the agreement in principle on March 18. Financial advisers S.G. Warburg recommended that the directors authorize the execution of the new agreements. They did, and the senior management of Royal Bank and Royal Trustco signed both agreements that Friday morning.

"From the agreement in principle through to annual meeting, I was terrified at what would happen [if we didn't get a deal]," Miller later recalled. "There was no way Royal Trust would survive."

The Royal marriage was announced in a joint press release, as 2,000 shareholders made their way to the basement of the Metro Toronto Convention Centre for that Friday's special meeting. For obvious reasons, there was tight security; everyone had to pass through a metal detector. During the four-and-a-half-hour meeting, Royal Trustco chairman Hartland MacDougall and CEO James Miller both addressed the angry shareholders and then answered questions.

At one point, chairman Hartland MacDougall said that management had saved the company. There was a round of stunned laughter, and two yahoos in the back of the room yelled "Sit down, ya bum" at MacDougall. Others found it more difficult to lash out at the patrician chairman. "You remind me of my father, sir," one shareholder said. "But we do not classify 35 cents a share as having saved the company."

Another shareholder said there should be no parachutes for anyone unless there were parachutes for the common shareholders who paid for their stock. "You're morally bankrupt, all of you," he yelled. (Indeed, the top five Royal Trustco executives earned $3.2 million for seven months' work in 1993, including a raft of special bonuses and consulting fees. Three former executives, Bill Inwood, Laurent Joly and Tony Flynn, received bonuses of $100,000, $200,000 and $150,000 respectively when the Royal Bank deal closed. Inwood and Flynn were also paid $200,000 apiece for consulting services provided after the deal closed.)

"The transaction with Royal Bank must be stopped right now," another shareholder yelled before she lost control, raving into the microphone until it was cut off.

In reference to Royal Trustco's parent, Trilon Financial Corp., one shareholder said he could hear a "great sucking sound, the sound of money being sucked out of the company."

"I didn't like to take the abuse, James Miller said later. "But I took it from the small shareholders. I didn't take it from the debtholders."

Miller departed from his script to thank Jack Cockwell for his support, telling the shareholders that Cockwell had always been there for him during the months of crisis.

The shareholders reluctantly approved the name change to Gentra Inc., and Miller began meeting with the creditor groups. "The legal community were like pigs at the trough," he later recalled. "I really question whether they [were] giving the best counsel. They were busy ambulance-chasing for more fees, but you don't play around with a financial institution."

Miller decided that Derrick Tay, lawyer for the senior debenture holders, was the best of a bad lot. Tay later recalled how he and Miller frequently spoke on the phone after creditor meetings to discuss ways of getting the deal done. Other lawyers had expressed moral outrage over the bailout of Royal Trustco's managers and the Trilon undertaking. But Tay felt that the relatively small dollar amount involved in the golden parachutes made them an irrelevant issue. Like Miller, Tay believed the Royal Bank-Gentra deal was the only solution. In their alliance, the two men became friends of a sort. Miller told Tay that he and Mary planned to renew their wedding vows in Hawaii, to celebrate their 40th anniversary. Lawyers representing the other creditor groups nicknamed Tay "Casper, the friendly lawyer."

By early September, the Royal Bank-Gentra deal had closed, Miller's team had met all their deadlines, and Royal Trust had been saved. "It's a bloody miracle," Miller concluded.

A week later, James Miller had begun to pack for his return home to West Vancouver. When I arrived for a parting interview, Miller's office was stacked with going-away presents from the staff. He confessed that he had become somewhat of a folk hero at Royal

Trust. At the end of the two-hour interview, Miller lumbered off down the wide hallway. "I'm so tired," he sighed.

Seven months later, James Miller died suddenly, at home with his family in West Vancouver on Easter Sunday, April 3, 1994. It was a tragic end to a tragic story.

In the summer of 1993, the Edper Group embarked on another reorganization. This time the objective was to simplify the structure by eliminating the private holding companies and consolidating the senior holding companies into one entity. Peter Bronfman agreed to hand over legal control of the group to the senior Edper managers, who held their stake in the empire through Pagurian. (By then, Jack Cockwell's discussions with Horsham and Minorco had ended. After several phone calls, conversations and meetings, Peter Munk had decided the proposed investment was antithetical to Horsham's principles. Horsham was not interested in passive investments. The discussions had been broad, and Horsham was never close to a deal. Munk had not even presented the proposal to the Horsham board. And of course there was no due diligence. Shortly after Munk walked away, Minorco followed.)

Two years later, in February 1995, Peter Bronfman purchased his three children's interests in family-owned Edper Investments Ltd. and announced he would be giving up control of the empire he had co-founded with his brother Edward. Ultimately, Pagurian would be renamed The Edper Group Ltd. Peter Bronfman said that he wanted to see the Edper Group continue, anchored by Noranda Inc., and that he would own and manage the business along with the senior managers.

Chapter 15

The New Establishment

Edgar Bronfman Jr. took his place among the acquisitors of the Information Age in February 1993, when he persuaded the Seagram board to approve the secret purchase of up to 4.9% of entertainment-information giant Time Warner Inc. For over a year, the New York-based Seagram heir had been searching for a new strategic investment for the family-controlled liquor empire.

Since becoming president of Seagram in 1989, Edgar Bronfman Jr. had moved Seagram into the juice business, spending US$1.2 billion to acquire Tropicana Products Ltd. in 1991. He had also refocused Seagram's House of Spirits on premium brands: picking up Martell cognac in 1988 and the distribution rights for Absolut vodka in 1993; keeping Crown Royal whisky, Chivas Regal, Glenlivet Scotch, Meyers rum and Mumm champagne; and selling off 23 nonpremium brands in 1992. But Bronfman Jr. still didn't know what to do with Seagram's excess cash from its Du Pont dividends.

In the summer of 1992, Michael Ovitz, chairman of Creative Management Consultants (CAA), reportedly made an informal presentation about the communications-media-entertainment industry to the Seagram board at Edgar Bronfman Sr.'s house in Sun Valley, Idaho. (Edgar Bronfman Sr. had taken a run at movie studio Metro-Goldwyn-Mayer in the 1960s.) After further discussion with investment adviser Herbert Allen Jr. of Allen & Company Inc. and two other professionals familiar with the sector, Edgar Bronfman Jr. targeted Time Warner as a takeover candidate. Ovitz approached Time Warner CEO Steve Ross on Seagram's behalf, but Ross was dying of prostate cancer, and nothing materialized from that meeting. By the time Ross died on Sunday, December 20, 1992, Bronfman Jr. had decided to go for a dominant minority position in Time Warner, instead of a takeover.

When Seagram crossed the 5% threshold in Time Warner in May 1993, Edgar Bronfman Jr. informed the new Time Warner CEO, Gerald Levin, of Seagram's investment. He also told Levin that Seagram planned to raise its stake in Time Warner to 15%.

Montreal's Power Corp. already owned 1% of Time Warner, a US$150 million investment. Power had bought its Time Warner shares before Seagram, and the two companies claimed not to be working together, although Paul Desmarais was a member of the Seagram board. Apparently André Desmarais, who oversaw Power's media interests, had wanted to make a big investment in Time Warner, but his father had reined him in. André had to settle for a toe-hold.

Thus it was a surprise to the business community when, in March 1993, Paul Desmarais agreed to come in as a white knight to save Canadian media group Southam Inc. from the clutches of Conrad Black. Desmarais phoned Black on March 10, reaching Black in his car on the way to a London airport. According to Black's memoirs, Desmarais told Black that he had been approached to make an investment in Southam and was planning to do so. Desmarais emphasized that he wasn't motivated by any unfriendliness towards Hollinger. Black retorted that Desmarais might not be unfriendly towards Hollinger, but some of the Southam directors certainly were. When Black arrived at the Toronto airport seven hours later, he was handed the notice of the Southam directors' meeting the following day.

Conrad Black immediately picked up his car phone and started rallying resistance to the Power Corp. offer. Black continued to work the phone from his Park Lane Circle mansion until after 2:00 a.m. At the Southam board meeting the next morning, the Power Corp. offer was narrowly rejected. Paul Desmarais phoned

Black that afternoon and they agreed to meet in Palm Beach over the weekend. There, Desmarais, his son André and Black met three times at their respective winter houses, where they hashed out a deal to become equal shareholders and between them own 38% in Southam. On Monday, March 15, 1993, Hollinger and Power exchanged faxed agreements.

Meanwhile, Paul Desmarais and Peter Munk were discussing possible joint-venture projects in China. Brian Mulroney would play a key role in their future ventures. In late spring 1993, Munk flew to Ottawa for lunch at 24 Sussex Drive. It was the day before the Mulroney family finally moved out of the Prime Minister's residence, and Munk was Mulroney's last lunch guest. Behind closed doors, the two men sat at a small table in the bay window of the dining room and talked about Mulroney's future. For the next few weeks, the Mulroneys would be at Harrington Lake, the prime minister's summer residence. Then the family would embark on a European vacation, before returning to Canada to settle into their new upper Westmount home on Forden Crescent in Montreal. Mulroney had decided to rejoin his former law firm, Ogilvie Renault, as a senior partner.

In late September, Brian and Mila Mulroney flew to Toronto to have dinner at Peter Munk's house in Rosedale, to celebrate Mulroney's appointment to the Horsham and American Barrick boards. On hand was Mulroney-appointed senator Trevor Eyton, a Barrick director since 1990. Mulroney, who found it necessary to wear a bullet-proof vest in public, was reportedly accompanied to Munk's house by four RCMP and two Metro Toronto police officers.

That autumn Horsham footed the bill for the annual gala of the Writers Union of Canada at the Four Seasons Hotel in Yorkville, and Peter Munk hosted a gala book launch for his friend Andrew Sarlos. Trevor Eyton was at the party for Sarlos and was also one of the 1,850 celebrities and VIPs who packed the gala opening of the musical *Showboat* on October 17.

Eight days later, interim Prime Minister Kim Campbell and the rest of the Conservative party were wiped out in the federal election, winning only two seats in the House of Commons. André Desmarais's father-in-law, Jean Chrétien, was elected Prime Minister in a Liberal landslide. Brian Mulroney's old friend Lucien Bouchard, who had broken with the Tory party over the failure of the Meech Lake Accord to found the separatist Bloc Québécois, was the leader of the opposition. At least Trevor Eyton's favourite sports team, the Toronto Blue Jays, had won their second consecutive World Series that weekend — this time in the SkyDome.

Within days of the Tory wipeout, Conrad Black's memoirs, *A Life in Progress*, were officially launched in Toronto with a book-signing at Edwards Books & Art in the Park Plaza Hotel. The sun-tanned, suddenly silver-haired media mogul graciously posed for pictures at Edwards with a few middle-aged female fans, who expressed disappointment that "Barbara" wasn't there. When I asked for his prognosis on the Edper Group, Black replied, "I have great faith in Jack Cockwell, but it is worrisome." That evening, a dour Trevor Eyton attended Black's book party, hosted by publisher Anna Porter, wife of Eyton's long-time friend Julian Porter.

The following week, on November 1, Trevor Eyton was seated to the right of Conrad Black at the head table of the Canadian and Empire Clubs when Black gave a rousing postelection speech — slamming Brian Mulroney — to thunderous applause from a partisan Bay Street crowd. Seated on Black's left was his chic wife, Barbara Amiel Black. And in the audience, beside an attractive blonde, was the deposed head of Royal Trustco, Michael Cornelissen, who by then was living in Vancouver and refusing all interviews with the media.

Meanwhile, Brian Mulroney was up and running in his post-prime ministerial life. On November 8, his board appointments were announced and he was granted options on 250,000 shares of American Barrick, exercisable at $34.87 a share, and on 250,000 shares of Horsham, exercisable at $18 a share.

In January 1994, Brian Mulroney helped bring about an alliance between Peter Munk and Paul Desmarais to develop existing gold mines in China with a Chinese partner. Horsham's Barrick, which would own 75% of the joint venture, had the technology while Paul Desmarais's Power Corp., which would own 25%, had the Chinese contacts. But Munk credited Mulroney as the key to the deal. "He [Mulroney], in person, took our proposals to the right people I could never get them to," Munk said.

Back in North America, Time Warner popped a poison pill on January 20 to block Seagram's advances, as Seagram raised its stake from 10.4% to 11.7%. It was a blow, but Edgar Bronfman Jr. took it in stride. He was about to marry his second wife, Clarissa, in the garden of her grandmother's estate in Caracas, Venezuela. Bronfman Jr. had written a song for Clarissa that was sung at the wedding.

On February 2, 1994, in another media deal, Ted Rogers's Rogers Communications launched a $3.1 million unsolicited bid for Canada's largest media group, Maclean Hunter. Rogers argued that Canada needed a Ted Turner, and it might as well be him.

Back in the 1970s, the Edper Bronfmans had played a key role in the evolution of Canada's biggest media mogul. Ted Rogers had won control of his first takeover target, Canadian Cablesystems, in 1978 when he triggered a buy-sell agreement with Edper Investments. Rogers Communications, which already owned 26% of Canadian Cablesystems, bought out Edper's 25% stake in the cable company in what Canadian Cablesystems later complained was a backdoor takeover.

Edper's sale of its minority investment in Canadian Cablesystems took the group out of the communications-media-entertainment industry, apart from a small investment in Astral Bellevuc-Pathé, a private conglomerate controlled by Montreal's Greenberg family. That same year, 1978, Edward Bronfman's eldest son, Paul, joined Astral Bellevue-Pathé's sound and production studio subsidiary, working his way up through the ranks over the next decade to become a vice-president of development at the parent company, before striking out on his own. In 1988, Paul Bronfman borrowed money against his shares in Edper to set up Comweb, a private management company with about $50 million worth of investments in the film industry. Among other things, Comweb owned almost half of Vancouver's North Shore Studios, Canada's largest motion picture and television production complex; half of William F. White, Canada's largest supplier of lighting and grip equipment; and a stake in Montreal's Covitec Group, a multipurpose film studio. Like his relative Edgar Bronfman Jr., who was named chief executive of Seagram at the company's annual meeting on June 1, 1994, Paul Bronfman had a passion for producing. But compared to Seagram and its 15% investment in Time Warner, Comweb was a minnow. On an even smaller scale, Peter Bronfman's only son, Bruce, a former substance abuser, Trizec executive and Hees partner, had a toehold in the booming information sector through his National Hav-Info Communications Inc., a private venture set up in partnership with Steven Reichmann.

Conrad Black was already one of the world's information monarchs. On June 9, 1994, Black, Barbara Amiel Black and Peter Munk walked down to Toronto's King Edward Hotel together, laughing in the bright sunshine. They were on their way from Hollinger headquarters to the company's annual meeting, where Amiel Black and Munk were introduced to the shareholders as new directors of Hollinger. Although Black was loyal to his friends, the Hollinger board was a lagging indicator of corporate influence: Robert Campeau was long gone, and Paul Reichmann and Peter Bronfman had left the previous autumn.

A week and a half later, on June 21, Barbara Amiel Black co-hosted a party at London's Ritz Hotel in honour of Sir James Goldsmith, who had won a seat in the June elections to the European Parliament. Celebrity guests included Princess Diana and actor Michael Caine. At the dinner, Peter Munk, whose American Barrick had attempted to merge with Goldsmith's Newmont Mining Corp. in 1986, was seated next to Pamela Harriman. Harriman's son, British MP Winston Churchill, was a neighbour of Munk's in Klosters, Switzerland. But when Harriman turned to Munk and said, "I believe you know my son," British-bred Melanie Munk had to kick her husband under the table. From Munk's blank look, it was obvious that he didn't know who Harriman was. Pamela Digby Churchill Hayward Harriman, the U.S. ambassador to France and a *femme fatale* at 60-something, was the political godmother of U.S. president Bill Clinton, widow of Democratic legend Averell Harriman, former daughter-in-law of Sir Winston Churchill, and one-time lover of many prominent men. "Conrad [Black] and Jamie Goldsmith were chasing after her at the party," Munk later recalled. But Harriman was not Munk's "kind of woman."

The next day, June 22, Conrad Black slashed *The Daily Telegraph*'s cover price, in a British newspaper price war with Rupert Murdoch, who had cut the cover price of *The Times* six months earlier. Black and Murdoch later claimed that their personal relations continued to be "excellent" despite the price war and Murdoch's unwelcome designs on the John Fairfax newspaper group of Australia, 25% owned by the Telegraph Group.

A few weeks later, on Thursday, July 14, Rupert Murdoch, dubbed the borderless tycoon, touched down in Idaho. It was the eve of Allen & Company Inc.'s annual conference of 150 corporate leaders at the Sun Valley Lodge, a resort built 60 years earlier by Averell Harriman.

Edgar Bronfman Jr. was making his debut at this private party for the so-called New Establishment. Seagram's US$25 million Gulfstream IV was one of the more than 20 Gulfstream jets at the local airport, belonging to such other moguls as Microsoft's Bill Gates, Tele-Communications' John Malone, Viacom's Sumner Redstone, Time Warner's Gerald Levin, CAA's Michael Ovitz, Disney's Michael Eisner and the soon-to-be "DreamWorks" entertainment triumvirate of Steven Spielberg, Jeffrey Katzenberg and David Geffen (DreamWorks SKG would form a joint venture with Microsoft in March 1995). On the Friday night at the conference, Bronfman Jr. reportedly presented Levin with an inflatable raft in the shape of a Seagram's bottle, and kissed the Time Warner CEO on both cheeks, mafia-style. Back in New York, Levin still refused to put Bronfman Jr. on the Time Warner board, but the two men were meeting regularly for lunch at The Four Seasons restaurant in the Seagram building.

In Toronto, the coming out for the new power elite was Gluskin Sheff's $1.25 million-plus opening-night gala in honour of the Barnes Exhibit at the Art Gallery of Ontario, on September 12.

Gluskin Sheff also donated $1 million to help fund the art show, for a total outlay of more than $2.25 million. But Horsham and American Barrick director Joe Rotman, the president of the Art Gallery, was considered the driving force behind the Barnes Exhibit. The night before the Gluskin Sheff gala, Rotman held an elite dinner party for 150 in the formal garden of his Forest Hill home. Peter and Melanie Munk were there.

At the Gluskin Sheff gala, media moguls Conrad and Barbara Amiel Black, Ted and Loretta Rogers, and Ken and Marilyn Thomson were among the 3,000 invitees who drank Pol Roger champagne and grazed on South African gooseberries hand-dipped in Belgian chocolate, oysters and racks of lamb under a 14,000-square-foot canvas tent. Edward Bronfman, whose family members were clients of Gluskin Sheff, attended. But Bay Street's dealmakers of the 1980s — Peter Bronfman, Trevor Eyton, Jack Cockwell and the Reichmann brothers — were not there.

The Reichmanns were busy elsewhere. In June 1993, Reichmann International LP, the joint venture between the Reichmanns and George Soros, had embarked on US$1.5 billion of commercial projects in Mexico City, including an office building, a historic preservation project and the mammoth Santa Fe development in a wealthy suburb — it would be another office city, consisting of 10 office buildings plus shops and housing.

Reichmann International was also looking at developments in Eastern Europe, Russia and China, and had hired many old Olympia & York stalwarts, such as Ken Leung and Ron Soskolne. Reichmann International also hired Don McCutchan, the former Canadian director of the European Bank for Reconstruction and Development, who was recalled to Canada in mid-1993 by Brian Mulroney after he blew the whistle on Mulroney's friend, the EBRD president Jacques Attali (dubbed "Jacques Antoinette" by the British press for his extravagant spending).

But by late 1993, there was a cooling in the Reichmann-Soros partnership. Paul Reichmann was no longer involved in the day-to-day management of Quantum Realty, which was performing poorly. There had been three different fund managers in as many months, and Reichmann had been bumped up to nonexecutive chairman of the fund. George Soros pushed Reichmann to hire someone to run operations at Reichmann International.

Paul Reichmann decided on South African-born Vernon Schwartz, a Reichmann protégé, then president and CEO of Catellus Development Corp. (the former Santa Fe Pacific Realty Corp). Schwartz's links with the Reichmanns went back to 1978, when, at 28, he was the Bank of Montreal's vice-president of real estate. In 1981 Schwartz moved to Trizec, as executive vice-president of Trizec's U.S. shopping-centre division, the Hahn Co.

On May 14, 1994, Reichmann International was one of the six corporate sponsors for a Royal Ontario Museum exhibition called Human Body, Human Spirit: A Portrait of Ancient Mexico. Ten days later, Vernon Schwartz was named president and CEO of Reichmann International Mexico and president and deputy CEO of Reichmann International Development Corp. Three months later, I interviewed the tall, tanned Schwartz at the Studio Café in Yorkville. Schwartz was concerned about press reports that Reichmann International was bidding on Cadillac Fairview, which had buckled under a $3 billion debt load. (In fact, Peter Munk's Horsham was one of the interested bidders, and a team had spent weeks analyzing Cadillac Fairview before Munk decided to go after Trizec instead.) "The Reichmanns [have] enough on their plates," Schwartz said.

About the Mexican projects, Schwartz accurately predicted that the valuation of the Mexican peso would be his biggest concern. While in Toronto, Schwartz spent some time househunting for his family in the Forest Hill area, expecting to split his time between Toronto and Mexico City. But the plan changed. Schwartz was told to report to New York City, where George Soros was based, in September.

By late 1994, George Soros, who was known as "the man who broke the Bank of England" since his Quantum funds had made more than US$1 billion in a September 1992 assault on the British pound, was on the receiving end of a financial crisis in Mexico.

During the mid-January 1995 World Economic Forum in Davos, Switzerland, Soros attended Peter Munk's annual dinner party at the family's ski chalet in next-door Klosters. Among the guests were Horsham director and former Bundesbank chief Karl Otto Pohl, Horsham director Andrew Sarlos, Ontario Hydro chairman Maurice Strong and NDP Ontario Premier Bob Rae.

On January 31, U.S. president Bill Clinton ordered a bailout for Mexico — a US$47.5 billion package of money from the U.S. exchange stabilization fund, the International Monetary Fund and the Bank for International Settlements. There was also a US$3 billion commercial bank standby credit facility led by Citibank NA and J.P. Morgan, with Bank of Nova Scotia kicking in $200,000 of the total.

The next day, February 1, Reichmann International announced that it might delay two of its Mexico City construction projects, valued at more than US$850 million, in the wake of the country's financial crisis. "There will probably be some delay, perhaps a number of months, before construction begins," Ron Soskolne said. A few weeks later, Reichmann International announced that it would delay all three of its Mexico City construction projects indefinitely.

Meanwhile, Trizec, once the building block of the interlocking Edper Bronfman and Reichmann empires, was toppling.

On August 3, 1993, Trizec co-chief executives Kevin Benson and Bill L'Heureux held a press conference to announce their Crisis Avoidance Plan. Trizec proposed a debt-for-equity swap which would give senior debenture holders 49% of the company, junior debenture holders 16%, preferred shareholders 12% and existing common shareholders 23%. Under the plan, Carena's equity stake in Trizec would fall from more than 50% to about 12%.

What had happened to this bluest of blue-chip investments? Peter Munk, whose Horsham Corp. took control of Trizec a year later, blamed Trizec's fall on Jack Cockwell's efforts to save Bramalea.

"The empire-building Jack Cockwell was threatened. He could not have a chink in [the Edper Group's] armour. [Bramalea] was the first," Peter Munk told me. Cockwell "had to defend the individual pieces, so he forced Trizec to put $150 million into Bramalea. Then it had to pump in more. That endangered Trizec."

In fiscal 1992, Trizec took a $669 million writedown ($457 million after tax) against its investment in Bramalea at its October 31 year-end, resulting in a net loss of $544.1 million.

In January 1993, Dominion Bond Rating Service slashed Trizec's credit rating. A DBRS analyst, looking ahead, told me that Trizec's "problem really lies in 1995. They've got good bank lines. They have a good shot at making it....Their problem is that nobody wants to touch them as a credit." The banks and insurance companies didn't want any more exposure to real estate.

Said Carena's Gordon Arnell, "I don't think there are a lot of operational difficulties [at Trizec]...and I think [the group's real-estate companies] are well managed and the businesses will run along fairly well. It's no secret, though, that there's a liquidity problem. There aren't the lenders available to the [real-estate] industry that there used to be. Not just our companies, but the industry as a whole. Therefore we have a period of time...[when] we are going to [have to] beaver away on ensuring that the obligations of these companies are met when due. The big challenge is to deal with liquidity, and the way everybody in the industry thinks it's going to happen is by... the de-leveraging of the business...the introduction of equity capital into the various companies to replace debt capital."

In a February 22, 1993, letter to the Edper Group's principal bankers, Trevor Eyton wrote that the group would "consider investing approximately $400 million in equity in the real estate sector...and would expect this to be at least matched by other investors." It was a good plan, but what if the Edper Group couldn't regain access to the capital markets?

In May 1993, Trizec quietly hired RBC Dominion Securities to act as a financial adviser on a possible financial restructuring.

In mid-June 1993, Trizec announced that it did not expect to be able to pay interest and principal on $1.1 billion in outstanding debentures. A restructuring plan was in the works, it said. On June 17, Dominion Bond Rating Service downgraded Trizec debt below investment grade.

In an affidavit, Trizec director Vernon Schwartz said, "The restructuring process initiated [on August 3, 1993] had been intended to anticipate a requirement to restructure and re-capitalize Trizec as a result of cash-flow deficiencies forecasted to occur in 1995 and 1996. Given the then current state of the capital markets, a consensual restructuring appeared to be the best possible means of meeting these maturities. Furthermore it was decided that recognizing these problems and addressing them head-on was preferable to waiting for the maturities to occur without any realistic plan for refinancing in place."

The day after the Crisis Avoidance Plan was announced, Trizec common shares fell 35 cents to $1.03 on the Toronto Stock Exchange. The following week, Trizec's Kevin Benson and chief financial officer Henry Roy spent the week in New York, Toronto and Montreal pitching the plan directly to debenture holders at information meetings.

"Trizec did the honourable thing. They told creditors they were going to restructure," recalled lawyer Derrick Tay, the spokesman for the senior debenture holders' committee.

Meanwhile, U.S. vulture funds were snapping up Trizec's junior debt at 65 cents on the dollar, as Trizec's Kevin Benson and Henry Roy flew to Zurich, London and other financial centres to hold additional information meetings.

On August 19, Carena suspended its common-share dividend. Five days later, Trizec held a two-hour information meeting in Toronto with common and preferred shareholders.

Two months later, on October 14, Trizec applied for and obtained an interim order from the Court of Alberta with respect to a proposed plan of arrangement under the Canada Business Corporations Act. Trizec hoped to complete its recapitalization plan by the end of 1993.

But some of the senior debenture holders raised concerns that Trizec's scheduled principal repayment of bonds would lead to an unequal treatment of debenture holders. On October 18, Trizec announced that it would suspend interest and principal payments on its debt until early December, despite the fact that Trizec had the money to make the payments.

On October 21, Trizec defaulted on $100 million of debenture redemptions. Lawyer Derrick Tay said that default put the senior debenture holders in the driver's seat. "They could seize their security, the common shares, ahead of everyone." All the senior debenture holders had to do was hold together until Trizec "shot all its bullets." As Tay put it, "We were playing chicken."

In his affidavit, Vernon Schwartz said, "In connection with the restructuring negotiations, Trizec declared a moratorium on principal and interest payments on its funded debt in October 1993....[A]s a result of that fact, events of default occurred under the Trust deed. The Senior Debenture Holders Committee had made it clear on numerous occasions that, if they did not receive an offer they considered adequate in the Plan of Arrangement they would rely upon the existing events of default under the Trust Deed to cause a liquidation to take place."

On October 31, Trizec was de-consolidated from Carena's balance sheet and Brookfield Developments, owner of BCE Place, was consolidated. (Brookfield had almost the same square footage of office space as Trizec.)

During the final months of 1993, deadlines were postponed and the senior debenture holders' committee began conducting its due diligence of Trizec. By then, the only viable alternative for Trizec was to seek an outside investor willing to provide an infusion of capital.

"There were some highly emotional board meetings," Trizec director Vernon Schwartz recalled. "But Peter Bronfman, to his credit, was willing to make the tough decisions."

That December, Trizec adviser Tony Fell of RBC Dominion Securities approached Peter Munk with a proposal. He told Munk that Trizec's financial restructuring was a strategic business opportunity for Horsham.

Toronto Life had just declared Peter Munk, "the man with the golden stocks," the biggest winner on Bay Street in 1993. "Prices for his gold-mining concerns — American Barrick, Horsham Corp. — are up more than 50% over last year." By contrast, the magazine had declared Jack Cockwell the biggest loser on Bay Street. "Labatt was sold. Royal Trust was sold. Trizec Corp. had to default. All in all, a bummer of a year for the titan of the 80s."

A few months earlier, on September 23, 1993, Horsham had formed a corporate development team with a broad mandate to focus on using its core holding in American Barrick to diversify. Gregory Wilkins, the former executive vice-president and chief financial officer of American Barrick, joined the Horsham board of directors and was appointed executive director in Horsham's office of the chairman to work closely with Peter Munk on strategic planning.

To raise cash for Horsham's new ventures, the company had done an innovative exchangeable debenture financing on November 18, 1993, underwritten by RBC Dominion Securities. By giving bond holders the right to swap their debt for shares in American Barrick, Horsham had wangled an annual interest rate of just 3.25%, less than half the current prime rate of 7.25%. The financing was completed on December 10, raising US$600 million, the largest bought deal in Canada without installment receipts. Horsham was now extremely liquid, with US$1 billion in its war chest.

On January 11, 1994, Tony Fell made a presentation about the Trizec opportunity to the Horsham board. "Trizec fit our [investment] criteria," Peter Munk later recalled. "We would be buying a major company, buying it out of bankruptcy, at the bottom of the cycle." A few days after meeting with Fell, Munk retreated to Switzerland for his annual skiing holiday. "It's a time to be on my own," Munk said. "My mind works better."

Back in Toronto, on January 25, the steering committee of Trizec's senior debenture holders had rejected the company's proposed recapitalization plan. "Our valuation differed significantly from Trizec's," said lawyer Derrick Tay. Two weeks later, Trizec and the senior debenture holders signed a standstill agreement, extendable a week at a time, and Trizec formed an independent committee of directors, with Vernon Schwartz as its chairman.

On February 17, Horsham retained Merrill Lynch as its investment adviser, and by March 9, Horsham had made a preliminary offer to Trizec, indicating that it was willing to invest $600 million in the company through a combination of existing debentures and shares. Trizec management informed the senior debenture holders' committee of the rescue package, but did not name the potential investor. The senior creditors said the offer was inadequate, and asked to be represented at the negotiating table. Trizec management said no, and the senior creditors threatened to have the company declared insolvent.

Meanwhile, Peter Munk was pacing back and forth at his ski chalet in Switzerland. Munk had been calling Horsham's Greg Wilkins each day at 4:00 p.m. (midnight in Switzerland) in Aspen, Colorado, where Wilkins was skiing during the March break. Back in Canada, Trizec management was forced to go to the Alberta court on March 19 to keep the senior debenture holders at bay. Trizec had to ask the court to grant a stay of any enforcement proceedings until March 31, so that it could complete its negotiations with Horsham.

Then, on Sunday, March 27, Horsham entered into a preliminary agreement to infuse $600 million into Trizec for a 43% stake: $500 million to be used for repayment or conversion of all corporate debt into new shares and $100 million to exercise 50% of a $200 million rights offering dedicated to strengthening the capital structure. "We managed to get the first signed agreement on Sunday," Greg Wilkins later recalled, "but there was a seven-day period of due diligence before we could finalize it." Until April 4, Trizec was also free to shop around for better offers. After that date, Horsham would reportedly get certain rights of first refusal and $15 million if management accepted a higher bid.

Three days later on March 30, Trizec's senior debenture holders, owed $1.2 billion plus about $70 million in interest, asked the

Alberta court to declare Trizec insolvent. But the judge decided to extend the stay from March 31 to April 25.

That same day, Trizec approached New York real-estate developer and fund manager Jerry O'Connor of the O'Connor Group. When Trizec received an offer from the O'Connor Group the first weekend in April, it agreed to pay $5 million to keep O'Connor at the negotiating table.

By Easter Monday, April 4, Horsham had completed its due diligence and sweetened its offer. It entered into a final agreement to infuse $600 million into Trizec for a reduced 40% stake, but with $117 million of liquidity for an additional 8% interest, taking its stake up to 48%. "It was a consensual arrangement," Greg Wilkins later recalled. "It made us one with Kevin [Benson] and Bill [L'Heureux]."

Trizec's senior debenture holders said the offer wasn't much different from the preliminary proposal. "We want a deal that gets all of our principal and interest out before other stakeholders," said Derrick Tay, the Toronto lawyer representing the committee of senior creditors. Greg Wilkins, who was named president of Horsham at the annual meeting in Montreal on April 27, had to fly down to New York to talk to the senior debenture holders at the Union Bank of Switzerland's Park Avenue offices.

On Sunday, May 1, the senior debenture holders served a notice of motion to have Trizec declared insolvent so that they could seize their security, but the next day they agreed to defer court proceedings one week to determine whether a deal could be reached. Late Monday, Trizec's Kevin Benson and Bill L'Heureux met with Jack Cockwell and some other Edper senior strategists at BCE Place in Toronto to work out their negotiating position. Trizec's discussions with the senior creditors began that Tuesday in Toronto and ended late Wednesday night with mutually agreed-upon revisions to the plan of arrangement.

At a late afternoon Trizec board meeting on May 6, Dick Schiff was the only Trizec director to vote against approval of the revised plan of arrangement. The junior debenture holders — mostly distressed-debt "vulture" investors who had bought much of the $320 million owing for between one-quarter and one-half of its original value — were also opposed. They wanted to reduce by $25 million the amount that would go to Trizec's common shareholders. But on May 10, the Alberta court rejected the junior creditors' motion to amend the plan.

Meanwhile, Horsham and the Argo Partnership had been holding secret talks about a possible joint venture in Trizec. "Peter [Munk] had met [Jerry] O'Connor and Tom Quinn [of J.P. Morgan] and felt we could work with them," Greg Wilkins later recalled. "Jerry is a micro-manager and Peter is a strategist…and more money would be helpful. We came to terms."

On June 10, Horsham struck a deal with the Argo Partnership. O'Connor brought more operational expertise to Trizec and a second liquidity offer of $300 million. Horsham's and Argo's total investment in Trizec would be slightly over $1 billion, split 65%/35% with Horsham contributing $661 million and Argo $356 million.

Almost a month later, on July 5, the senior debenture holders voted 99% in favour of the plan of arrangement. The next day, the preferred shareholders voted 93% and the ordinary shareholders 84% in favour of the plan. But only 33% of the junior debenture holders voted yes.

Greg Wilkins had lunch with Jack Cockwell that week in Toronto, where Cockwell told Wilkins what a good company Trizec was. The following week, on July 13, I arrived at Horsham's Yorkville headquarters, a three-story converted townhouse with external security cameras, to interview Wilkins. There was a blank space on his office wall where a framed drawing of vultures had once hung. Horsham was not a vulture investor, Wilkins argued, despite its teaming up with Sam Zell in the late 1980s. It avoided hostile deals. For example, Wilkins said he had spoken to Trizec's co-chief executives, Kevin Benson and Bill L'Heureux, at least once a day since their preliminary agreement in late March.

Indeed, Bill L'Heureux would be staying on as Trizec's chief executive under Horsham's control. (When L'Heureux had left Hees for Trizec in Calgary, he got an interest-free bridge loan of almost half a million dollars to facilitate relocation, which he paid off in January

1994. If L'Heureux's employment had been terminated, he was entitled to receive payment of two years' annual compensation and a
proportionate share of the current year's bonus, plus relocation expenses, including reimbursement for any loss on the sale of his home.)

Meanwhile, Horsham was on to its next acquisition. Peter
Munk, who usually retreated to his island in Georgian Bay for the
summer months, had decided that American Barrick would join the
bidding war for gold producer Lac Minerals. On July 25, following Barrick's surprise announcement that morning of its matching
$2.1 billion bid for Lac Minerals, Munk returned to his desk at
one end of an otherwise unfurnished corner office at Barrick headquarters in the Royal Bank tower, took a phone call from Barrick
director Brian Mulroney, who was in Russia, and briefed him on the
progress of the bid. At the same time, Horsham had just closed
its deal to take control of Trizec with a $1 billion-plus cheque
from Horsham Acquisition Corp., signed by Munk. Munk had meant
to take his acquisition team out for a celebratory lunch, but there
was no time.

That afternoon the Horsham chairman and CEO went directly
from the Barrick offices to a Trizec directors' meeting, where he
was named chairman of the board, and later that evening to a
Barrick directors' meeting, where he met up with his long-time
friend Senator Trevor Eyton of the Edper Group.

The next day, July 26, Peter Munk's teenage daughter Cheyne
padded around the Barrick offices, helping out her father's executive secretary. Cheyne was the calmest person on the floor. The
morning and early afternoon had been one long strategy session,
with brief respites to return other phone calls. Horsham's vice-
president of investor relations, Vince Borg, had returned from lunch
to find the desk missing from his new office at Barrick, and phone-
message slips from journalists around the world scattered on the
floor. When he tracked down the desk, he found it set up at a right
angle to Munk's in the corner office. Horsham president Greg Wilkins
had claimed it. Borg would have to make other arrangements.

In the midst of the hubbub, I arrived to interview Peter Munk. When I was ushered into the corner office, Munk apologized; he had to take a call. The caller was Lawrence Bloomberg, whose securities firm, First Marathon Inc., had played a key role in building Barrick, with an early financing. First Marathon was already involved in the Lac deal, having arranged the $100 million financing for Royal Oak Mines following its bid. Bloomberg wanted to know if there was anything the firm could do for Munk. Ever gracious, Munk explained to Bloomberg that Barrick had plenty of cash on hand and that his Barrick team was already in place, throwing in an affectionate "my friend" or two before he ended the call.

Then the aristocratic Munk turned back to me, responding to my questions with rapid-fire speech and a slight Hungarian accent. He called in director William Burchill to clarify reports of an early transaction with Hees. Munk expressed embarrassment about his spartan office space at Barrick. It was in sharp contrast to his luxurious office at Horsham. But despite the inauspicious backdrop, Munk was clearly enjoying every minute of his dealmaking.

Over the next month, Barrick waited for Royal Oak Mines's latest bid to play out, and for Lac Minerals to come to Barrick if it wanted to do a deal.

Just after 4:00 p.m. on August 23, RBC Dominion Securities chairman Tony Fell called Barrick and asked to speak to Peter Munk, but Munk was on his way back from New York City, where he had been meeting with Lac's institutional shareholders for the past day and a half. Two and a half hours later, Munk and Barrick president Robert Smith were back at Barrick headquarters in the Royal Bank Plaza's south tower, in a meeting with other Barrick officials. Just before eight o'clock, Fell telephoned again and Munk stepped out to take the call.

Fell and Munk agreed to meet to discuss cutting a deal. Within 15 minutes, Fell and his associate Gary Sugar were at Barrick headquarters. Fell reportedly wanted to know whether Barrick would be prepared to put more cash on the table if it meant the Lac board would recommend Barrick's offer to shareholders. Munk and Horsham president Greg Wilkins said they would. After Fell and Sugar left, the Barrick meeting reconvened, this time with Barrick's financial advisers, including one on the phone from Holland.

They knew from meeting with institutional investors that sweetening the offer by $1.00 to $1.50 a share would clinch the deal. At nine o'clock the Barrick meeting broke up. Meanwhile, at the Lac offices in the Royal Bank Plaza's north tower, a meeting of the Lac board's special committee, including RBC Dominion Securities' James Pitblado, convened and continued late into the night, as the midnight deadline approached for the $2.4 billion Royal Oak bid.

The next day, August 24, the Lac board met at 8:00 a.m. Half an hour later, Fell and Sugar arrived at Barrick's offices accompanied by lawyers. There was not much debate on price. The two sides talked for a couple of hours and ended up agreeing on an improved $2.2 billion package that was roughly equal to $1.46 more a share.

By September, Barrick Gold (the renamed American Barrick) was the world's biggest gold producer outside of South Africa. And Peter Munk had surpassed even Ted Rogers, who had spent $3.1 billion to buy Maclean Hunter, as Canada's biggest dealmaker in 1994. In less than two months, companies in the Horsham group had spent more than $3.35 billion on back-to-back deals. At the end of 1994, Munk brought in new management depth, including his son Anthony, as Horsham's senior vice-president, business development.

In the winter of 1995, Trizec moved its headquarters to Toronto from Calgary. Ironically, Trizec's new offices are on the 39th floor of BCE Place — five floors below Trevor Eyton and Jack Cockwell of the Edper Group. Peter Munk's Horsham would join its subsidiary in the new space, as the next corporate empire to rise on Bay Street. Would it last?

SOURCE NOTES

All quotations in the text are from interviews conducted by the author unless otherwise noted.

PROLOGUE

pages 1–3 The account of the Edper-Olympia & York collision is reconstructed from interviews, newspaper reports; Roderick McQueen, "Joining the towers that be," *Maclean's*, March 26, 1979; Diane Francis, *Controlling Interest: Who Owns Canada?* Macmillan, 1986; and Peter Foster, *Towers of Debt: The Rise and Fall of the Reichmanns*, Key Porter, 1993.

page 2 The quotation is from Peter C. Newman, *The Canadian Establishment. Volume Two: The Acquisitors*, McClelland & Stewart, 1981.

PART ONE: THE RISE

Chapter 1: A Beautiful Friendship

pages 7–9 The history of the Bronfman family is detailed in Michael Marrus, *Mr. Sam: The Life and Times of Samuel Bronfman*, Viking, 1991.

page 9 "You look forward..." quote first reported in Susan Gittins, "Goodman the dealmaker," *The Financial Post*, October 7, 1991.

pages 9–10 Trevor Eyton's life and career is discussed in Rod McQueen, "Keeper of the Keys," *Toronto Life*, May, 1986.

page 11 Eyton's quote from a roundtable discussion with *The Financial Post*, March 24, 1993. Transcribed by Atchison & Denman Court Reporting Services Ltd.

pages 11–13 Jack Cockwell's life and career is detailed in and quotations are from Harvey Enchin, "The empire's all right, by Jack," *The Globe and Mail*, October 9, 1990.

pages 13–15 Early history of Edper is detailed in Francis, *Controlling Interest*; and Patricia Best and Ann Shortell, *The Brass Ring: Power, Influence and the Brascan Empire*, Random House, 1988.

pages 13–14 Profile of Paul Desmarais in Peter C. Newman, *The Canadian Establishment*, McClelland & Stewart, 1979; and Francis, *Controlling Interest*.

pages 14–18 Account of Trizec restructuring detailed in and quotations from Best and Shortell, *The Brass Ring*.

page 15 "It should have..." quote from Peter C. Newman, *Bronfman Dynasty: The Rothschilds of the New World*, McClelland & Stewart, 1978.

pages 16–17 Jack Cockwell's formula detailed in Brian Baxter, "The Hees team's formula for curing sick companies," *The Financial Post*, May 7, 1990.

pages 18–20 Early history of the Reichmanns detailed in Newman, *The Acquisitors*; Francis, *Controlling Interest*; and Anthony Bianco, "Magnificent Obsession," *Vanity Fair*, October 1992.

page 19 "a quiet little..." quote from Foster, *Towers of Debt*.

pages 22–24 Quotations from Kimberley Noble, "The Edper Puzzle: Change of Control. A Hees deal leaves its mark," *The Globe and Mail*, February 9, 1991; and Kimberley Noble and Margaret Philp, "How Bramalea's dream became a nightmare," *The Globe and Mail*, November 7, 1992.

page 23 Quotation from Gayle MacDonald, "Shakeup woes hit Bramalea as Marshall takes over," *The Financial Post*, August 20, 1990.

Chapter 2: Deals, Deals, Deals

pages 25–31 A detailed account of the Brascan and Noranda takeover battles in Newman, *The Acquisitors*.

page 27 Quotation from Andrew Sarlos, *Fireworks: The Investment of a Lifetime*, Key Porter, 1993.

page 28 Quotation from Newman, *The Acquisitors*.

pages 32–34 Lt. Col. Ken White quotations are from Robert Campeau's testimony during the Ontario Securities Commission hearing into the Royal Trustco takeover and were first reported in Rod McQueen, *The Moneyspinners: An Intimate Portrait of the Men Who Run Canada's Banks*, Macmillan, 1983. Another detailed account of the takeover in Patricia Best and Ann Shortell, *A Matter of Trust: Power and Privilege in Canada's Trust Companies*, Viking, 1985.

pages 34–36 Quotations are from Susan Gittins, "Retirement no life of leisure for ex-CEOs," *The Financial Post*, February 13, 1989; Gordon Pitts, "The man on Royal Trustco's hot seat," *The Financial Post*, November 25, 1991; and Kimberley Noble, "Col. Mike: He did it his way," *The Globe & Mail*, September 15, 1992.

Chapter 3: Bright Lights, Big City

pages 38-40 Construction of the World Financial Center detailed in Olympia & York Developments Ltd., Information Book, April 13, 1992 and Foster, *Towers of Debt*. Reichmann life in Toronto detailed in Newman, *The Acquisitors*; and Francis, *Controlling Interest*.

page 41–43 The Gulf and Hiram Walker takeovers are detailed in Olympia & York Developments Ltd., Information Circular, November 9, 1992; David Olive, "What's Gone Wrong with the Reichmanns?" *Report on Business Magazine*, December, 1986; and Foster, *Towers of Debt*.

page 45 Quotations from Marrus, *Mr. Sam*.

pages 44–49 The lives and careers of Edgar and Charles Bronfman are discussed in Francis, *Controlling Interest*; and Marrus, *Mr Sam*. Details about Cadillac Fairview in Alanna Mitchell, "The rise and fall of Cadillac Fairview," *The Financial Post*, February, 6, 1989. History of Edgar Bronfman Jr. in Colin Leinster, "The Second Son is Heir at Seagram," *Fortune*, March 17, 1986; Bertrand Marotte, "Guiding Spirits," *Financial Times of Canada*, May 21, 1990; Eric Reguly, "The coming of age of Edgar Bronfman Jr.," *The Financial Post*, January 30, 1993; Ken Auletta, "Rising Son," *The New Yorker*, June 6, 1994; and Mark Stevenson, "Indomitable Showman," *Canadian Business*, October 1994.

page 46 Quotation about Seagram building from Robert A.M. Stern, *Pride of Place: Building the American Dream*, New York: Houghton Mifflin Company, 1986.

Chapter 4: The Bay Street Village

pages 50–53 Quotations from and the battle for Union Enterprises is detailed in Best and Shortell, *The Brass Ring*.

pages 54–60 Life and career of Conrad Black detailed in and quotations from Nicholas Coleridge, *Paper Tigers*, London: William Heinemann Ltd., 1993; Conrad Black, *A Life in Progress*, Key Porter, 1993; and James FitzGerald, *Old Boys*, Macfarlane Walter & Ross, 1994.

pages 58–59 Life and early career of Brian Mulroney detailed in John Sawatsy, *Mulroney: The Politics of Ambition*, McClelland & Stewart, 1991.

page 61 Quotations from McQueen, "Keeper of the Keys" and Best and Shortell, *The Brass Ring*.

pages 61–65 The account of House of Commons' Finance Committee Hearings detailed in Best and Shortell, *The Brass Ring*.

page 63 Quotation from Francis, *Controlling Interest*.

page 64 Barry Critchley, "Financial reforms: Edper fighting back," *The Financial Post*, July 26, 1986.

page 65 Account of Stevens' Hearings detailed in Rod McQueen, *Blind Trust*, Macmillan and quotation from Best and Shortell, *The Brass Ring*.

Chapter 5: Financial Architecure

pages 67–69 Edper Group business principles listed in its Corporate Information Book, 1991.

page 70 George Myhal's quote from a roundtable discussion with *The Financial Post*, March 24, 1993.

pages 72–73 Account of Allied takeover detailed in and quotation from John Rothchild, *Going for Broke: How Robert Campeau Bankrupted the Retail Industry, Jolted the Junk Bond Market and Brought the Booming Eighties to a Crashing Halt*, New York: Simon & Schuster, 1991.

pages 73–74 The account of Toronto-Dominion Bank's campaign against Scotia Plaza is detailed in Francis, *Controlling Interest*.

pages 75–77 Olympia & York's financing practices also detailed in John Milligan, "Blind Faith," *Institutional Investor*, September, 1992; and Foster, *Towers of Debt*.

page 77 Profile of Lewis Ranieri and account of the sale of Olympia & York bonds detailed in Michael Lewis, *Liar's Poker*, New York: Norton, 1989.

PART TWO: THE ALARM BELL

Chapter 6: Blood in the Street

page 82 Personal history of Edward and Peter Bronfman detailed in Best and Shortell, *The Brass Ring*.

page 83 Account of the death of Delores Ann Sherkin from Tim Harper, "Death of billionaire's girlfriend stuns posh Yorkville," *The Toronto Star*, May 25, 1983.

page 85 "handle [the] liability..." quote taken from Best and Shortell, *The Brass Ring*.

page 85 Goldman Sachs quote taken from Lewis, *Liar's Poker*.

pages 88–91 Account of the Federated takeover detailed in Rothchild, *Going for Broke*.

pages 89–90 Quotation from Barry Critchley and Eric Reguly, "Off the Record: Reichmanns' interest in Campeau passive," *The Financial Post*, April 6, 1988.

page 90 Quotation from Sarlos, *Fireworks*.

page 91 Quotation from Richard Siklos, "Campeau keeps his champagne on ice," *Financial Times of Canada*, March 7, 1988.

pages 93–94 Profile of Sam Zell in Hilary Rosenberg, *The Vulture Investors*, New York: Harper Business, 1992.

page 94 Eric Reguly, "Reichmanns return to property roots, *The Financial Post*, September 22, 1990; and Foster, *Towers of Debt*.

Chapter 7: Workout Wizards

page 95 Quotation first reported in Kimberley Noble, "Edper Hees' disastrous prayer," *The Globe and Mail*, February 12, 1993.

page 98 List of investors in arbitrage fund and quotation from Sarlos, *Fireworks*.

page 99 "We had no..." quote from Susan Gittins, "Corporate doctors specialize in right Rx for LBO sufferers," *The Financial Post*, March 26, 1990.

page 100 Quotation from Baxter, "The Hees team's formula for curing sick companies."

page 100 "I often feel..." quote from Gittins, "Corporate doctors specialize in right Rx for LBO sufferers."

page 102 Quotation from Leslie Holstrom and Ann Dugan, "The House That Jack Built," *Euromoney*, August, 1990.

page 102 "furnished to resemble" quote from Newman, *The Acquisitors*.

page 103 Quotation from Holstrom and Dugan, "The House That Jack Built."

page 105 Quotation from Brian Baxter, "Super-achiever takes helm of fundraising for diabetes," *The Financial Post*, March 18, 1988.

page 106 Detailed description of Jack Cockwell's temper tantrum in Best and Shortell, *The Brass Ring*.

pages 107–108 Details of ownership of Townsview Investments and of Westcliff Management in Kimberley Noble, "The Edper Puzzle: In-house deals. Bronfmans prefer preferreds," *The Globe and Mail*, December 3, 1990; and Noble, "The Edper Puzzle: Change of Control. A Hees deal leaves its mark"; Dan Westall and Kimberley Noble, "George Mann now a six," *The Globe and Mail*, February, 9, 1991; and Barry Critchly and Susan Gittins, "Off the Record: Unicorp muddle," *The Financial Post*, April 26, 1991.

pages 109–110 Andrew Coyne and Bill Watson, "Free Trade: Everything you want to know about free trade, but no one's telling you," *The Financial Post*, November 17, 1988.

pages 110–111 History of Toronto Sun Publishing detailed in Jean Sonmor, *The Little Paper That Grew: Inside the Toronto Sun Publishing Corporation*, Toronto Sun Publishing, 1993.

Chapter 8: The Edper Puzzle

page 112 Quotation from Best and Shortell, *The Brass Ring*.

pages 113–116 Life and career of Christopher Ondaatje detailed in Alexander Ross, *The Traders: Inside Canada's Stock Markets*, Collins, 1984; John Stackhouse, "A man of many parts," *Financial Times of Canada*, January 2, 1989; Christopher Ondaatje, *The Man-Eater of Punanai: A journey of discovery to the jungle of old Ceylon*, HarperCollins, 1992; and John Stackhouse, "Return of the Native," *Report on Business Magazine*, September 1994.

pages 114–115 Quotation from Ira Gluskin, "Smart Money: Christopher Ondaatje's art of the shuffle," *Financial Times of Canada*, November 13, 1989.

page 115 "If we were…" quote first reported in Susan Gittins, "Pagurian's declining share price draws fighting words at meeting," *The Financial Post*, May 19, 1988.

pages 116–117 Profile of Bill L'Heureux and quotation from Vivian Smith, "Banjo-player picked for his people skills," *The Globe and Mail*, January 30, 1989

page 117 Profile of Manfred Walt in Deirdre McMurdy, "Edper assignment puts spotlight on Walt," *The Financial Post*, May, 22, 1989.

page 118 Quotation from Phil Mathias, "Hees-Edper: Empire Under Pressure. Lost in the Pagurian shuffle," *The Financial Post*, February 14, 1991.

page 118–122 Detailed account of Enfield takeover battle in Patricia Best, "Manfred vs The Red Baron: For Michael Blair, the party's over," *Financial Times of Canada*, April 17, 1989.

pages 119–120 Profile of Michael Blair in Deirdre McMurdy, "Renegade role suits Blair at Enfield," *The Financial Post*, March 13, 1989 and in Vivian Smith, "Former fighter pilot Blair gets in dogfight with Hees," *The Globe and Mail*, March 14, 1989.

page 122 "overzealous junior" quotation from Richard Siklos, "Can Mike Blair beat the mighty Hees boys?" *Financial Times of Canada*, March 13, 1989.

pages 122–123 Quotations from Jacquie McNish, "Enfield, Canadian Express make peace," *The Globe and Mail*, April 19, 1989.

page 123 Peter Bronfman quotation first reported in Patricia Best, "Taking the Ed out of Edper, an empire changes the guard," *Financial Times of Canada*, May 22, 1989.

page 123 Quotation from Philip Mathias, "Hees-Edper: Empire Under Pressure. Mystery men manoeuvre in Pagurian deal," *The Financial Post*, February 13, 1991.

page 123 Report of Bill L'Heureux's response to Osler Hoskin Harcourt opinion in Kimberley Noble, "The Edper Puzzle: Legal Loopholes. Edper's arm's length family," *The Globe and Mail*, April 15, 1991.

page 124 Ownership of Partners Holdings from prospectus for Edper Enterprises Ltd., Rights offering, October 23, 1991.

pages 127–128 Profile of Ross Johnson in Bryan Burrough and John Helyar, *Barbarians at the Gate: The Fall of RJR Nabisco*, New York: Harper & Row, 1990.

page 129 Henry Knowle's quote from Francis, *Controlling Interest*.

pages 129–130 Detailed account of Enfield shareholders' meeting in Deirdre McMurdy, "Hees-Enfield uproar," *The Financial Post*, July 21, 1989.

page 130 "Well, there's things..." quote first reported in Patricia Best, "The TKO of Michael Blair," *The Financial Times of Canada*, October 2, 1989; and later in the affidavit of Manfred Walt, *Algonquin Mercantile v. Enfield*, Supreme Court of Ontario, June 18, 1990.

page 130 Account of the battle for Enfield detailed in and quotation from Deirdre McMurdy, "Enfield gives Hees's nose a tweak," *The Financial Post*, August 12, 1989.

page 132 Testimony of Patricia Maclean from *Ontario Pension Commission v. Michael Blair, Carol Penhale, Ben Webster and Jacques Lavergne*, Old City Hall, Toronto, 1991. Profile of Garrett Herman in Deirdre McMurdy, "A pushy powerhouse at Merrill Lynch," *The Financial Post*, March 8, 1989; and Anne Kingston, "Trading up," *Financial Times of Canada*, February 26, 1990.

page 133–134 Christopher Ondaatje quotation from Kimberley Noble, "The Edper Puzzle: Secret Deals. 'The answer to a maiden's prayers'," *The Globe and Mail*, February 12, 1991.

page 134 Justice John Holland (Endorsement), *Canadian Express v. Michael Blair, Enfield Corp. and Montreal Trust Co.*, Supreme Court of Ontario, September 26, 1989.

page 135 Account of Edper-Merrill Lynch Canada spat detailed in and quotations from Deirdre McMurdy, "Bronfmans vent ire on old ally Merrill," *The Financial Post*, October 21, 1989; and Patricia Best, "When opinions are unwelcome at Edper," *Financial Times of Canada*, October 30, 1989.

page 136 Quotations from McMurdy, "Enfield gives Hees's nose a tweak"; and Best, "The TKO of Michael Blair."

pages 136–137 Quotations from Charles Davies, "Men at Work", *Canadian Business*, March 1990.

pages 137–138 Quotation from Deirdre McMurdy, "Edper firms cultivate a more human face," *The Globe and Mail*, February, 5, 1990.

Chapter 9: Big Boys' Games

pages 139–140 For more about partying at America's Cup see Eric Reguly, "Cup Capers," *Canadian Sailing*, February 1989. The author's sister also watched the 27th Challenge Match.

pages 141–142 Press coverage of the U.S. savings and loans scandal is detailed in Suzanne Garment, *Scandal: The Culture of Mistrust in American Politics*, New York: Times Books, Random House, 1991; and Howard Kurtz, *Media Circus: The Trouble with America's Newspapers*, New York: Times Books, Random House, 1993.

pages 144–148 Noranda's early pursuit of Kidd Creek Mines detailed in Best and Shortell, *The Brass Ring*; and quotations from Patricia Best and

Jennifer Wells, "High noon at Noranda," *Financial Times of Canada*, November 28, 1988.

pages 148–149 Account of the battle for Falconbridge detailed in and quotations from Barry Critchley and Brian Baxter, "Off the Record: Hold the Mayo," *The Financial Post*, August 30, 1989; "Off the Record: The ins and outs of Falconbridge bid/Deli deals," September 5, 1989; "Off the Record: Falconbridge tales," September 19, 1989.

page 151 Detailed account of Paul Reichmann's call to Kenny Field in Walter Stewart, *Too Big to Fail. Olympia & York: The Story Behind the Headlines*, McClelland & Stewart, 1993.

page 152 "it was Ben's..." quote from Noble and Philp, "How Bramalea's dream became a nightmare."

page 152 Swirsky quotations first reported in Susan Gittins, "Bramalea's $2-billion game plan," *The Financial Post*, August 10, 1988.

page 153 Description of the Opera Ball in Rosemary Sexton, *The Glitter Girls. Charity & Vanity: Chronicles of an Era of Excess*, Macmillan, 1993.

Chapter 10: Playing Monopoly

pages 154–155 Profile of Jack Poole in Newman, *The Acquisitors*; Alanna Mitchell, "Poole's one-man show closes at BCED," *The Financial Post*, May 8, 1989; and Ann Shortell, "The fall of the house that Jack built," *Financial Times of Canada*, August 28, 1989.

pages 156–169 Detailed accounts of meetings between Paul Reichmann and Robert Campeau in Rothchild, *Going for Broke*.

pages 158–163 Account of the battle for BCE Development detailed in and quotations from John Stackhouse, "The Mighty Crash of BCED," *Report on Business Magazine*, June, 1990.

page 164 Chuck Young quotation from Ross Fisher, "Digging in at Canary Wharf," *Canadian Business*, February, 1990.

pages 164–168 Alanna Mitchell, "Campeau, The Inside Story: Crumbling of an Empire," *The Financial Post*, October 30, 1989.

pages 170–171 Quotations first reported in Gittins, "Corporate doctors specialize in right Rx for LBO sufferers." Further details of restructuring from prepared remarks by Lawrence Herbert to securityholders' meetings of BF Realty Holdings Ltd. in October 1992.

page 172 Discussed in Statement of Pleadings, *Battery Park Holdings Inc. v. Olympia & York*, Supreme Court of the State of New York, November 22, 1992.

PART THREE: THE FALL

Chapter 11: The "R" Word

page 174 Eric Reguly and Alanna Mitchell, "Campeau: Chapter 11 closes the book in U.S.," *The Financial Post*, January 13, 1990.

pages 176–177 Quotation from Black, *A Life In Progress*.

page 177 Money manager quotation from Claire Makin, "Short-changed?" *Institutional Investor*, January 1993; Feshbach quotation from Julie Rohrer,

"A walk on the short side," *Institutional Investor*, April 1989; Jacquie McNish, "Short story long on profit," *The Globe and Mail*, March 3, 1993.

page 180 From a speech entitled "Your Annual Report" by Royal Trustco Managing Partner Public Affairs Sheila Robb to a Financial Post Conference, Royal York Hotel, September 18, 1990. Details about Sheila Robb's share purchases from Douglas Bell, "Golden Handcuffs," *Canadian Business*, April 1991.

pages 181–184 Barry Critchley and Susan Gittins, "Off the Record: Joly's good show moves to London," *The Financial Post*, August 29, 1990; Barry Critchley and Susan Gittins, "Off the Record: Canadians figure in stock trials abroad," *The Financial Post*, November 15, 1990; Barry Critchley and Susan Gittins, "Off the Record: Edper-style pay for Pacific First People," *The Financial Post*, October 18, 1990; and Barry Critchley and Susan Gittins, "Off the Record: Royal Trustco mum after earnings drop," *The Financial Post*, August 23, 1990.

page 185 Barry Critchley and Susan Gittins, "Off the Record: Will black hole in U.S. kill Unicorp's plans?" *The Financial Post*, September 6, 1990.

page 186 Jacquie McNish, "Unhappy Ondaatje gives up posts with Pagurian, Hees," *The Globe and Mail*, May 2, 1990.

pages 186–187 Patricia Best, "Hees' dealings come under an uncomfortable spotlight," *Financial Times of Canada*, May 14, 1990; and Patricia Best, "David and Goliath," *Financial Times of Canada*, November 12, 1990.

page 187 Canadian Express Ltd. Directors' Press Release, October 15, 1990.

pages 187–188 Affidavit of Manfred Walt, *Algonquin Mercantile v. Enfield*, Supreme Court of Ontario, June 18, 1990.

pages 189–190 George Myhal quotation from roundtable discussion with *The Financial Post*, March 24, 1993.

page 190 Deirdre McMurdy, "The Bottom Line: The long road back," *Maclean's*, May 16, 1994.

pages 190–191 Further details of restructuring from prepared remarks by Lawrence Herber to securityholders' meetings of BF Realty Holdings Ltd. in October 1992.

page 191 Barry Critchley and Susan Gittins, "Off the Record: BCED's Brookfield lining up lenders," *The Financial Post*, August 24, 1990.

pages 191–192 Barry Critchley and Susan Gittins, "Off the Record: Ode to an OSC policy," *The Financial Post*, October 16, 1990.

page 192 Barry Critchley and Susan Gittins, "Off the Record: Dealers find a fairy godmother in OSC," *The Financial Post*, August 15, 1990.

pages 192–193 Story of the Central European Development Corp. detailed in Susan Gittins, "Bay Street dealmaker takes a European View," *The Financial Post*, February, 9, 1990; and Sarlos, *Fireworks*.

pages 192–193 George Soros' early history detailed in Eric Reguly, "Soros: the selfish saint," *The Financial Post*, May 6, 1993; Gary Weiss, "The Man Who Moves Markets," *Business Week*, August 23, 1993; and Connie Bruck, "The World According to Soros," *The New Yorker*, January 23, 1995.

pages 193–196 Sources for Peter Munk profile include Jennifer Wells, "The second coming of Peter Munk," *Financial Times of Canada*, July 4, 1988; Arthur Johnson, "Who's Laughing Now?" *Report on Business Magazine*, September 1988; Eric Reguly, "The Man with the Midas Touch," *The Financial Post*, October 23, 1993; Brenda Dalglish, "A man of property," *Maclean's*, April 11, 1994; and Kimberley Noble, "Can Munk make it last?" *The Globe and Mail*, September 19, 1994.

page 197 Erick Ipsen, "Call it Albatross Wharf," *Institutional Investor*, November 1990.

page 197 Michael Caine, *What's it All About?* Century, 1992.

page 198 Discussed in Statement of Pleadings, *Battery Park Holdings Inc. v. Olympia & York*, Supreme Court of the State of New York, November 22, 1992.

pages 198–199 Susan Gittins, "Hees lashes out at short sellers," *The Financial Post*, September 14, 1990.

pages 198–199 The Hees' fight with *The Globe and Mail*'s *Report on Business* is discussed in Timothy Pritchard, "Risky Business," *150 Years in Canada, A Globe and Mail Magazine*, 1994.

pages 200–201 Susan Gittins, "Edper executives hit road to rescue freefalling shares," *The Financial Post*, September 22, 1990.

Chapter 12: Cracking Under Pressure

pages 205–213 Details of the capital recovery program from Edper Group Supplementary Financial Information Book (Extracts), February 22, 1993.

page 205 Barry Critchley and Susan Gittins, "Off the Record: Edper revamps pay philosophy," *The Financial Post*, January 24, 1991; and Barry Critchley and Susan Gittins, "Off the Record: Trilon joins crowd with options plan," *The Financial Post*, April 12, 1991.

page 206 Barry Critchley and Susan Gittins, "Off the Record: Fistful of Hees," *The Financial Post*, October 26, 1990.

pages 206–207 Quotations from Kimberley Noble, "The Edper Puzzle: Crisis of Confidence. Bronfmans keep investors in the dark," *The Globe and Mail*, November 28, 1990.

page 208 Bud Jorgensen, "Street Talk: Hees' PR adviser is used to tough challenges," *The Globe and Mail*, December 17, 1990; and Jennifer Wells, "The Week: A lone gun duels with the press hordes," *Financial Times of Canada*, February 4, 1991.

page 208 From Pritchard, "Risky Business."

page 209 Quotations first reported in Susan Gittins, "Four Hees 'workout' firms lose over 80% of stock value in year," *The Financial Post*, December 19, 1990.

page 210 Susan Gittins, "Royal Trustco loses $251M in quarter," *The Financial Post*, February 1, 1991; and Susan Gittins, "Big loss shocks Street," *The Financial Post*, February 2, 1991.

pages 211–212 Audit of The Financial Post Coverage prepared by Thomas E. Reid, Reid Management Ltd. February 26, 1991.

pages 213–214 Janet McFarland, "A Loss of Trust: The push and pull at Pacific First," *The Financial Post*, September 3, 1994.

pages 214–215 Sexton, *The Glitter Girls*.

page 215 The wedding tour is detailed in Patricia Best, "Love Story," *Toronto Life*, January 1993.

pages 216–219 Olympia & York Developments Ltd. Information Circular, November 9, 1992.

page 216 Diane Francis, "Reichmanns holding on tight to their big guns" and "The Insiders: 'We're used to financial risks' — Paul Reichmann," *The Financial Post*, June 1, 1991.

page 218 Eric Reguly and Gayle MacDonald, "O&Y may sell stake in prized properties," *The Financial Post*, December 21, 1991; and Eric Reguly and Gayle MacDonald (with Susan Gittins), "Reichmanns Under Pressure: What went wrong?" *The Financial Post*, March 27, 1992.

Chapter 13: The Emperor Had No Clothes

pages 221–241 Susan Gittins, "O&Y, lenders making deals," *The Financial Post*, August 8, 1992; and Jacquie McNish, "How banks flubbed O&Y," *The Globe and Mail*, December 4, 1992.

pages 221–241 Details about cross-collateralizations from Olympia & York, Information Circular, November 9, 1992.

pages 221–222 Paul Reichmann's meeting with the Wall Street investment banker is detailed in Bianco, "Magnificent Obsession."

page 223 Neil Barsky, "Olympia & York Plans a Huge Restructuring Involving Many Banks," *The Wall Street Journal*, March 23, 1992.

page 224 Rufus Olins and Margaret Parks (with Susan Gittins, Gayle MacDonald and Geordie Greig), "Rescuing the Reichmanns," *The Sunday Times*, March 29, 1992.

pages 224–225 Diane Francis, "O&Y not as leveraged as many thought," *The Financial Post*, March 26, 1992.

pages 227–228 Al Flood quotations from Financial Post Editorial Board meeting on August 12, 1992.

page 231 Olympia & York Information Book, April 13, 1992.

page 232 Rufus Olins, "Under Seige: Olympia & York fights off the banks," *The Sunday Times*, April 19, 1992.

page 232 Ed Lundy and Andrew Kent quotations are from a mid-1994 meeting of the insolvency law section of the Canadian Bar Association-Ontario, first reported in "Lessons learned from the fall of the O&Y empire," *Law Times*, June 27-July 3, 1994.

pages 236–238 Susan Gittins, Gayle MacDonald and Eric Reguly, "Reichmanns file for protection," *The Financial Post*, May 15, 1992.

pages 236–238 Rufus Olins, "Reichmann's Last Stand," *The Sunday Times*, May 17, 1992.

pages 238–239 Rufus Olins, Matthew Lynn and David Smith, "Disaster in Docklands," *The Sunday Times*, May 31, 1992.

page 239 Susan Gittins, "Canary Wharf bid on table," *The Financial Post*, July 22, 1992.

pages 239–241 Susan Gittins, "Scramble for Canary Wharf," *The Financial Post*, August 17, 1992; Susan Gittins, "Making a Deal for Canary Wharf," *New York Newsday*, August 22, 1992; and Jacquie McNish, "The Day the Banks said No," *The Globe and Mail*, December 5, 1992.

pages 241–243 Bramalea Ltd. Information Circular and Proxy Statement, October 1, 1992.

page 241 Susan Gittins, "Reichmann troubles cast shadow over Hees-Edper," *The Financial Post*, August 3, 1992.

Chapter 14: Crisis of Confidence

page 244 Discussed in Statement of Pleadings, *Battery Park Holdings Inc. v. Olympia & York*, Supreme Court of the State of New York, November 22, 1992.

pages 245–246 Eric Reguly (with Susan Gittins), "Carena confirms $138M O&Y link," *The Financial Post*, September 17, 1992.

pages 246–247 Editorial, "What's $300-million between friends?" *The Globe and Mail*, September 26, 1992.

pages 247–248 Janet McFarland, "Bronfman family may take stake in O&Y's U.S. unit," *The Financial Post*, January 7, 1995; and Brian Milner and Susan Bourette, "O&Y seeking cash infusion," *The Globe and Mail*, January 18, 1995.

pages 248–249 Susan Gittins, "O&Y to offer towers," *The Financial Post*, November 19, 1992.

pages 249–250 Sarlos, *Fireworks*; Reguly, "Soros: the Selfish Saint"; and Weiss, "The Man Who Moves Markets."

pages 249–250 Eric Reguly and Susan Gittins, "Paul Reichmann picks up shattered empire's pieces," *The Financial Post*, December 26, 1992.

pages 249–250 Susan Gittins, "New O&Y shadow of its former self," *The Financial* Post, January 27, 1993.

pages 250–254 Susan Gittins, "Big Bear faces a big challenge," *The Financial Post*, December, 5, 1992.

page 252 Patricia Best, "Royal Bust," *Canadian Business*, November, 1992.

page 252 Brenda Dalglish, "Behind the Hees-Edper Struggle: Weak Links in a Chain," *Maclean's*, November 23, 1992.

page 253 Gittins, "Big Bear faces a big challenge."

page 255 Sexton, *The Glitter Girls*.

page 258 Susan Gittins, "Pressure is on at Hees-Edper," *The Financial Post*, February 2, 1993.

pages 258–259 Barry Critchley, "Inside Finance: How Hees-Edper made the move on MacBlo," *The Financial Post*, February 13, 1993.

pages 259–260 David Kerr quotations from round-table discussion with *The Financial Post*, March 24, 1993.

page 260 Susan Gittins, "Regulators check exposure to Hees," *The Financial Post*, February 11, 1993.

page 261 Peter Bronfman quotation from Brenda Dalglish, "Bronfmans under fire," *Maclean's*, February 22, 1993.

page 262 Interviews with sources; Sarlos, *Fireworks*; Kimberley Noble, "Edper, South Africans in talks," *The Globe and Mail*, March 4, 1994; Janet McFarland, "Alliance rumors lift Hees-Edper," *The Financial Post*, March 5, 1994; and Janet McFarland, "Anglo American shuns Hees-Edper," *The Financial Post*, March 12, 1994.

pages 263–273 Gentra Inc. Management Proxy Circular/Plan of Arrangement, July 13, 1993.

pages 266–267 Kirk Makin, "Journalists question credibility of paper," *The Globe and Mail*, March 20, 1993.

pages 268–270 Quotations from round-table discussion with *The Financial Post*, March 24, 1993.

page 271 Philip Mathias and Susan Gittins, "Hees-Edper On the Record: 'There is no wholesale program with list of assets for sale'," *The Financial Post*, March 27, 1993.

Chapter 15: The New Establishment

pages 275–279 Auletta, "Rising Son"; and Connie Bruck, *Master of the Game*, New York: Simon & Schuster, 1994.

pages 276–277 The Black-Desmarais alliance is detailed in Black, *A Life In Progress*.

page 277 Munk-Mulroney lunch in Ottawa and Munk-Mulroney dinner in Toronto first reported in Stevie Cameron, *On the Take: Crime, Corruption and Greed in the Mulroney Years*, MacFarlane Walter & Ross, 1994.

page 279 Ian McGugan, "Such Good Friends," *Canadian Business*, April 1994.

pages 279–280 James Fleming, *Circles of Power*, Doubleday, 1991.

page 281 Ellie O'Shaughnessy, "The New Establishment," *Vanity Fair*, October 1994.

pages 281–282 "The scoop on the Barnes party," *Toronto Life*, November 1994.

page 285 Affidavit of Peter Buzzi, Court of Queen's Bench of Alberta, Plan of Arrangement proposed by Trizec Corp. and Horsham Acquisition Corp., July 11, 1994.

pages 286–287 Affidavit of Vernon Schwartz, Court of Queen's Bench of Alberta, Plan of Arrangement proposed by Trizec Corp. and Horsham Acquisition Corp., July 13, 1994.

page 288 "The Best and Worst of the City," *Toronto Life*, December 1993.

pages 288–294 William Symonds, "A New Empire Rises North of the Border," *Business Week*, July 11, 1994; and Kimberley Noble, "1994 could be Munk's year," *The Globe and Mail*, July 26, 1994; and Noble, "Can Munk make it last?"

pages 293–294 "How the deal came together," *The Globe and Mail*, August.

INDEX